BOOK SERIES:

Rethinking Research and Professional Practices in Terms of Relationality, Subjectivity and Power

BOOK SERIES EDITOR:

Bronwyn Davies

University of Melbourne

Poststructuralism at Work with Marginalised Children

Authored By

Cath Laws

Australian Catholic University

CONTENTS

FOREWORD

I find this work very moving. It is a critique of the present approach to special education informed by a poststructuralist framework, utilising extracts from the diary of the principal of a special school. Cath Laws reflects not only on existing discourses in relation to positions of 'bad, mad, and sad' within special education but also, critically, on her own practice, and therefore makes an important intervention into the practices of special education.

This work does not use Foucault in the traditional way, but more as a point of departure toward understanding the positioning of the subjects within the special school. It is this different approach which makes the work so moving and provides insights about subjectivity quite different from those in standard Foucauldian work.

The quality of this work lies in its thoughtful engagement with the discourses and practices of special education, and its use of a narrative approach, which in itself challenges the 'education as truth' doctrine found in the fields Laws critiques. It is a highly significant presentation of crucial issues for practice, set out in a clear, accessible way, and beautifully written. This work forms a much-needed critique of present practices of subjectification within special education. For that reason alone, it deserves to be taken very seriously indeed.

Valerie Walkerdine
Cardiff University

PREFACE

This confronting and challenging book by Cath Laws, *Poststructuralism at work with marginalised children*, is the second volume in this e-book series. It is based on a long term study in which the author worked both with students categorised as 'emotionally/behaviourally disordered', and with their teachers, in the context of the special education school in which she was principal. This unique work develops radically new understandings of what it means to be positioned in the world as emotionally/behaviourally disordered. Working with these understandings this book offers strategies for working with students and with staff to enable them to become people with agency. Agency for teachers, in this context, is a capacity to read the multiple and contradictory discourses shaping both teachers and students, and shaping the social world(s) they inhabit. Agency for students, similarly, involves learning to read the discourses that play on them and through them; and it involves learning how to refuse some discourses and to mobilise others. This book enables teachers and students, together, to begin dismantling the marginal positionings that these students inhabit.

Each book in this series develops an approach to research and practice that takes up the radical potential of philosophers such as Foucault, Deleuze, Butler and Nancy. Each book provides a radical model for re-thinking research and professional practices in light of poststructuralist reflections on subjectivity, relationality, ethics, spatiality and power. This series has an ongoing focus on the relations between individual subjects and the social, discursive and spatial relations within which they are produced, and produce themselves, as subjects.

Poststructuralist theory made a significant break with Hegel's structuralism, with its "model of history's unbroken intelligibility" (Foucault, 2000, p. 248). In poststructuralist theory the familiar, repetitive, and habituated practices through which the creation of individual selves is done are interesting insofar as they reveal the changing practices that produce, over time, different kinds of subjects. Seeing history as discontinuous opens up the possibility that modernity's subject, and its habitual practices, can change. Rather than being locked into present crises and patterns, such as neoliberalism with its devastating production of global economic crises, and its relentless individualising and pathologising and judgementalism, poststructuralist theory seeks the ways in which we might break loose from the already known, habitual practices through which the familiar world is produced. It opens up the ethical possibility that we might produce difference in ourselves rather than sameness, and that we might open ourselves up to new knowledges and practices.

In the modern world we have placed the sovereign individual of humanism, the agent creating and in command of his/her own life, on centre stage. Poststructuralist theory decentres that individual, examining instead the repeated citations through which 'individuals' are produced. It thus cuts loose from phenomenology and existentialism with their maintenance of "the primacy of the subject and its fundamental value" (Foucault, 2000, p. 248). This is not to deny the existence of the subject, or its value, but to open up questions about its origin, its beginning point. From a poststructuralist perspective our individual agency is an *effect* of the ways in which we are constituted; it was not through our own agency that we were made what we are, but through our location within particular histories, relations and cultural practices. We are generally unaware of the way discourse works through us to create us in predictable, historically specific ways. Poststructuralist theory suggests that it is the very conceptualisation of the individual as primary, and as originary, that blocks this awareness.

What Foucault rejects in phenomenology is the way it makes the individual subject its foundation, and sets out to "recapture the meaning of everyday experience in order to rediscover the sense in which the subject that I am is indeed responsible, in its transcendental functions, for founding that experience together with its meanings" (Foucault, 2000, p. 241). Foucault sees his own work, in marked contrast, as using experience to wrench "the subject from itself", to find ways to make the subject "no longer itself" (2000, p. 241). He wants to annihilate the subject of phenomenology, the subject that endlessly repeats itself, that understands itself as its own origin, to dissolve it, through what he calls a "project of desubjectification" (2000, p. 241; see also Davies, 2010).

Writing against the grain of the already-known is central to Foucault's radical project of opening up the not-yet-known. The already-known for Foucault, in his early years in particular, was the subject capable of permitting Nazism, or the bourgeois intellectual choosing between Truman's America or Stalin's USSR. Whereas other post-war scholars sought to realise an ethical and responsible subject no longer capable of mindless obedience, Foucault's project was more radical. He wanted to write his way into new understandings of how we become, in one historical period or another, subjects. His books are, he says, "experiences aimed at pulling myself free of myself, at preventing me from being the same" (2000, p. 242). It is the possibility of this kind of difference, of radical social change, that is the driving force of his work. He seeks to open up an experience of modernity that generates a transformative effect.

The work that has grown out of Foucault's program of writing, and the writing of other poststructuralist scholars, has also had a second and more recent driving force. That is the advent of the intensified individualism of neoliberal governmentality. Capitalism, according to Deleuze and Guattari (1987), is schizophrenic. It needs to control its labour force in order to extract maximum productivity from it, while at the same time enhancing the production of new and creative ideas. It convinces individuals they are free at the same time as it shapes them to be whatever capital thinks it wants. This madness of the modern capitalist state has had devastating effects on individuals and on the professions. The program of desubjectification is thus also aimed at the hyper-individualism of modern capitalism, that produces sameness and repetition under the banner of freedom.

Foucault also had an abiding interest in madness. He worked to re-think the ways in which madness is produced. Talking in an interview about his writing on madness, Foucault said that his aim was "that at the end of a book we would establish new relationships with the subject at issue: I, who wrote the book and those who have read it would have a different relationship with madness, with its contemporary status, and its history in the modern world" (2000, p. 242). Such thought does not discover subjects but changes them in relation to others. Poststructuralist researchers are not interested in representing a pre-existing order of things, but in changing how they are thought and thus how they are produced. Foucault's book *Madness and Civilization*, is, he says,

> a book that functions as an experience, for its writer and reader alike, much more than as the establishment of a historical truth...For one to be able to have that experience through the book, what it says and does need to be true in terms of academic, historically verifiable truth. It can't exactly be a novel. Yet the essential thing...[lies] in the experience that the book makes possible...[This] book makes use of true documents, but in such a way that through them it is possible not only to arrive at an establishment of truth but also to experience something that permits a change, a transformation of the relationship we have with ourselves and with the world...in short, a transformation of the relationship we have with knowledge...[That transformation] is not just mine but can have a certain value, a certain accessibility for others, so that the experience is available for others to have. (Foucault, 2000, pp. 243-244)

Through coming to know differently, as writer and as reader, Foucault shows how we might detach ourselves from the habitual repetitions of thought and practice through which we previously accomplished ourselves as predictable maintainers of the status quo. The individual is thus, for Foucault, not the *end-point* of a process of subjectification, but the potential sticking point, the place where thought gets stuck. Writing is the medium through which both thought and the writer/reader can be changed.

Foucault was delighted when correctional officers and social workers said of *Madness and Civilization:* "The book is paralysing. It may contain some correct observations, but even so it has clear limits, because it impedes us; it prevents us from going on with our activity" (2000, p. 245). He said in response:

> My reply is that this very reaction proves that the work was successful, that it functioned just as I intended. It shows that people read it as an experience that changed them, that prevented them from always being the same or from having the same relations with things, with others, that they had before reading it. This shows that an experience is expressed in the book that is wider than mine alone. The readers have simply found themselves involved in a process that was underway—we could say, in the transformation of contemporary man with respect to the idea that he has of himself. And the book worked toward that transformation. To a small degree, it was even an agent in it. This is what I mean by an experience book, as opposed to a truth book or a demonstration book. (Foucault, 2000, p. 246)

This book by Cath Laws, *Poststructuralism at work with marginalised children*, is just such an experience book. Laws draws on her own experiences as principal of a special school to write a transformative book, a book through which she transforms both thought and herself and, potentially, her readers. She has engaged in an experience/experiment in writing that taps into a change already underway, taking it further, participating, in doing so, in a transformation of the field that she writes about. She does not set out to produce the 'truth' about the work of teachers in schools for children diagnosed with emotional and behavioural disorders, as if the children were objects capable of being studied. Rather she shows how truths function within the discourses informing the work of special education teachers to produce the students, and the work that the teachers do with them. This book develops a new and significantly different approach to working with 'emotionally/behaviourally disordered' students. It demonstrates how those working with such children can develop and apply a poststructuralist analytic approach to their work. This approach is in marked contrast to the developmental, special education and psycho-pathologising discourses that are dominant in this field. Laws also shows in careful detail how teachers are necessarily immersed in and working out of those dominant discourses, at the same time as some of those teachers are critiquing these discourses and opening them up for change.

This is a book that makes one terribly sad, as the struggles of the students at the special school are made visible in poignant and painful detail. It is uplifting at the same time, and deeply moving, when there is a break-through, when teachers find ways to recognise these marginalised students and to offer them possibilities of agency that are not self-defeating, and that do not deprive them of viable lives. It is an inspiring book, showing the way that insights gleaned from Foucault, from Butler, and from Deleuze, among others, can make visible the complex terrain teachers are working in this field, and the possible moments when different, deeply ethical practices are made possible. We are living in a time when the necessity of re-thinking ethics is an urgent task (Wyatt and Davies, 2011). This book makes a significant contribution to that task.

Foucault (2000) makes an important distinction between two kinds of knowledge: *savoir* and *connaissance*. *Savoir* involves doing work in order to know differently and, in the process, being modified through what one comes to know. *Connaissance* makes possible the knowledge of objects, that is, it makes those objects intelligible, while leaving the subject, the determinate knower, untouched. Laws' book generates *savoir*—a knowledge of working with marginalised students and the discourses that inform teachers' practices, not as knowledge that leaves the writer and reader untouched, but as knowledge that, in the process of its thinking and writing, has implicated the writer in changing herself and will invite the reader to be similarly changed.

Cath Laws has worked in education at regular and special schools and as a policy advisor to government in the area of special education. As principal she has led teams at a number of special schools and has worked in out-of-school contexts in state child protection policy and as the state-wide Manager, Behaviour Programs. Laws has always been interested in examining the ways children living at the margins are positioned. She looked at the discourses operating for, on and with these children and young people for her PhD thesis 'Poststructuralism at work with marginalised children'. Laws is involved in community organisations and is currently New South Wales president of Protective Behaviours—a community-based child protection program. In 2006 Laws received the NSW Department of Education and Training (DET) Director-General's Award for service to public education. She continues to trouble the dominant discourses constituting those at the margins through her lecturing work at the Australian Catholic University and her research and writing work. She reads her life's work as exploring ways in which those at the margins can come to act with agency and be read and read themselves differently.

Bronwyn Davies

University of Melbourne

Book series editor

Rethinking research and professional practices in terms of relationality, subjectivity and power

REFERENCES

Davies, B. (2010). The struggle between the individualised subject of phenomenology and the multiplicities of the poststructuralist subject: the problem of agency. *Reconceptualizing Educational Research Methodology, 1*(1), 54-68.

Deleuze, G., & Guattari, F. (1987). *A thousand plateaus: Capitalism and schizophrenia.* London: Athlone Press.

Foucault, M. (2000). An interview with Michel Foucault. In J. Faubion (Ed.), *Essential works of Foucault 1954–1984, Volume 3, Michel Foucault: Power* (pp. 239-297). London: Penguin Books. Original interview conducted 1980.

Wyatt, J., & Davies, B. (2011). Ethics. In J. Wyatt, K. Gale, S. Gannon & B. Davies, *Deleuze and collaborative writing: An immanent plane of composition.* New York: Peter Lang.

ACKNOWLEDGEMENT

I sincerely thank the students and staff at the special school described in this book. Their humour, friendship and conversations provided great sustenance throughout the research. In particular, I am indebted to all the students with whom I have ever worked. I hope I can remember to learn from all they taught me about themselves and about myself.

There are many people to whom I am intellectually indebted—people whose work I have read, people with whom I have talked and people with whom I have engaged in many critical discussions. In particular, I thank the students of Professor Bronwyn Davies who share amazing insights; I am privileged to be a member of such a talented group of writers and thinkers.

Special thanks to Professor Bronwyn Davies, my editor and mentor, for her guidance and support.

I appreciate the support of the Australian Catholic University, particularly Professor Marea Nicholson for her insights and support.

I wish to thank all my friends, particularly Lee, Alicia, Susan and Julie. Their patience, advice and humour provided great support throughout this journey.

To my sisters, Madeline and Patricia, I offer this work as a tribute to our lives.

To Ian, I offer my gratitude and my love—your support and partnership sustain me in so many ways.

CHAPTER 1

Researching Special Schools: A Poststructuralist Approach

Abstract: This work involves developing the capacity to apply poststructuralism in a place where other discourses are dominant. I examine the educational practices used in a special school for those students who are read as unmanageable and too violent to be maintained in mainstream/regular schooling. In this chapter, I examine ways of collecting data in a poststructural frame, and ways of making the discursive practices of the special school more visible. I discuss the difficulties of working in a poststructuralist way and examine issues of anonymity for the students who were part of my study. I then discuss the theoretical framework, which is particularly informed by the work of Foucault. During the period of my study, I was the principal of the school in which the study was undertaken.

Keywords: education, disability, Foucault, special schools, poststructuralist research, deconstruction, emotional and behavioural disorders, binary/binaries.

We went up to the Hunter Valley on a Sunday at the end of the school holidays. We were going to visit a program near there for the school professional learning day. I drove the Coaster bus as I had the right license. I drove the teachers and support personnel around the wineries. At one of the first wineries, I bought a bottle of wine. The young man serving was about thirty years old and spoke to me.

Bill: *Are you a teacher?*

Cath: *Yes I am.*

Bill: *Did you used to teach at Park School?*

Cath: *Good Heavens! Yes I did!*

Bill: *Do you remember me?*

Cath: *I'm sorry, no I don't.*

[I really didn't—it was at least twenty years ago.]

Bill: *I'm Bill (he gave his last name).*

Cath: *Bill!*

[I gave the signs of remembering him but I couldn't dredge him up.]

Bill: *I'll never forget what you used to do for me.*

Cath: *God, Bill! That must be twenty years ago now!*

Bill: *Yeah, but I always remember the way you used to hide my dog for me when it followed me to school. Every time the deputy came looking for my dog, you'd let me hide him in the storeroom. He was a bastard for calling the pound—we could never have afforded to get him out but he never got my dog. I'll never forget that. I tell people about that whenever they are putting shit on teachers!*

We talked about what he was doing now. He said he was pleased that I was a principal. On the way out, Steve (a teacher at the special school) asked me if I had 'set it up' to teach the other teachers about how they can make a difference.

Cath: *I wish I had! But I really don't remember hiding his dog. It sounds like something I would have done but I don't remember him. I can't even picture the dog!*

Cath's Notes

Cath Laws

A BEGINNING

This work involves developing the capacity to apply poststructuralism in a place where other discourses are dominant. It focuses on working both with students categorised as 'emotionally/behaviourally disordered', and with their teachers, in the context of a special education unit/school. The scene above begins my story of my work at the special school. I was on an outing with the teachers and support personnel—our school team—from my then current special school, when a glimpse of a past teaching life visited my life as principal of the special school. Bill's memories of me, as a beginning teacher protecting his dog, and the impact he says this had on him, seemed real for me. I remember myself as someone who takes the side of those who are positioned as having less power than others: this is how it came to be that I was the principal of a school full of children living at the edge, even within the margins.

The positioning of 'principal' as one who leads, manages, teaches and encourages—one who is responsible—is a position that I cannot escape. I do not desire to escape even though I have now retired from that job. It remains part of my being. Yet, the positioning of 'principal' as one who disciplines, demands, surveills—one who wields power—is a position that I have always desired to escape. This binary of desiring myself to be 'other' than the deputy in Bill's (my) story catches me out all the time. Yet to be a 'principal' at the special school I was positioned, and positioned myself, as both one with power and one who desired to hide this power. I cannot escape, and do not desire to escape, the fact that this book is about my work at the special school, and is as much about me as it is about the students or the teachers at the school. I begin with this idea that I cannot escape being subjected, both as one desiring to 'get it right' as principal and, at the same time, as one who plays at rejecting authority. The ironic play of myself in the story of my work I will discuss in detail later. I raise it here to be clearer with myself, not to clear myself, as I am deeply implicated in the story of Bill and in the stories in this book.

Steve proposed, perhaps ironically, that I had 'set up' the encounter with Bill to 'teach' the teachers something about what it is to be a teacher, and the impact that one can have on the lives of children—an impact that can follow children throughout their lives. I did not have that sort of power or forethought. Yet I was pleased to have been read as someone who would have considered this as something important for all teachers to learn. I am emotionally implicated in the work that I do—the work that I see myself as having always done. Yet, in reading this story, I take on some sense of guilt that I do not have specific memories of the story that Bill tells. I did, and still do, have memories of the deputy and what I saw as an injustice: that he should have the pets of children impounded. I am still not able to 'let him off the hook', even now that I have more understanding about the responsibilities of keeping children safe from possible animal attacks. In saying this I open myself up to being read as taking the position of the child —even as being childish. And in re-telling this story I tried to protect myself from what I saw as this negative reading by using irony; instead, I opened myself up to being read as 'callous' because I gave the impression to Steve that I would have expected myself, at least, to have remembered the dog. Irony again.

I make this first beginning as a way of storying what I see as "the radical, indeterminate ambiguity or openness that lies at the heart" (Scheurich, 1997, p. 74) of this book about my work. While Scheurich, here, spoke of the interview process, his words have resonance for me in the whole framework of research. It is radical for me because I find writing in this way difficult—I have been so accustomed to hiding the 'me' in my work. I have been accustomed to taking up my position of 'expert' in the field of behaviour change in a way that is serious, impersonal, non-emotional and, most of all, objective. I am accustomed to seeing any 'me' in formal writing as self-indulgent. It is also radical because the very exploration of finding different ways of making sense of the behaviour of the students in a special school goes against the grain of the dominant special educational discourses. There is ambiguity at the heart of this work, including my ambiguous position as both principal and researcher and the ambiguity in the readings that I bring to the notes/data collected. In writing of this ambiguity, I cannot avoid being read as a researcher who "imposes names, categories, constructions, conceptual schemes, theories upon the unknowable" (Scheurich, 1997, p. 74). Yet I believe that I have tried to avoid being a researcher who "believes that the indeterminate is now located, constructed, known" (Scheurich, 1997, p. 74). While I can present the story of my work as having involved different ways of knowing the children in special schools, this knowing cannot ever become 'the known'.

TO BEGIN AGAIN

This work involves developing the capacity to apply poststructuralism in the context of a particular special education unit/school. To enable readers to bring to life for themselves that special school, I offer the following description.

The school

When I first saw the advertisement for the position as principal at the school I thought it would be a school that I would like to be at. For a start, it looked like a normal school—not a school attached to a medical facility. It also was set up so that the students stayed to lunch and were then supported by the teachers at their regular schools. The idea of helping children work their way back to regular school straight away really appealed—I had seen so many programs struggle to convince regular schools to integrate the students. To have it set up this way from the start seemed like a great idea.

Cath's Notes

The site of this work is a state school for specific purposes, a 'special school', in Australia, specifically in the New South Wales (NSW) state education system. The school's specific purpose is to educate those students, from Kindergarten to Year 10, (from five to sixteen years old), who are categorised as having an 'emotional disturbance'. This categorisation is given by psychiatrists or clinical psychologists. If such a label is unable to be obtained, most often because of parents' difficulty in getting to or engaging with psychiatric/psychological services, then a label can be designated by education department personnel. Students are identified as needing specialist services, provided by separate teaching and school counselling personnel in mainstream/regular schools. When the persistent, inappropriate behaviour of some students cannot be contained in regular schools, those students are referred to special schools. Part of this referral process includes obtaining a label of a disorder under the Diagnostic and Statistical Manual of Mental Disorders (DSM-IV) (American Psychiatric Association, 1994). There are a handful of schools like this in NSW as well as a few schools where educational personnel work side by side with personnel from the Department of Health. There are also schools for students in Years 5 to 8 who present violent behaviours but do not require a label indicating a disorder. Their behaviour is considered a sufficient reason for transferal to a special school without the requirement of a specific diagnosis.

The special school in this work is situated in a suburb of Sydney, NSW. The suburb is not identified as poor, but it edges onto those suburbs in Sydney that are identified as poor and have very high levels of public housing. It is in those suburbs that most of our students lived. The school site is very small when compared to the space able to be accessed by students in regular schools. The school looks like any regular small weatherboard school, built at the turn of the nineteenth century. The school catered for thirty six students, organised into six class groups, who worked in five learning spaces. One classroom was vacant and used as a spare classroom for assembly/play/time-out, and two classes (about twelve students) worked together in one classroom with two teachers.

Students arrived at the school from about 8:30a.m. each morning. As the students lived in a range of Sydney suburbs, some of which were at least thirty kilometres from the school, they were picked up from their homes and delivered to the school in special transport: small vans that hold about eight people. Each of the vans had a driver and an adult escort in case there were difficulties with and between the students. The NSW Department of Education and Training (DET) met the cost of the transport for those families who had a child with a disability but could not get their child to the special school. All our children's families met this criterion.

Most students attended the school until about 1:00p.m., when they were transported home or to their regular schools. Teachers and/or support personnel then travelled out to the students' regular schools or homes to support the students. The school had a major focus on facilitating students' return to the regular school setting. The program did not operate on a model that takes students away from the mainstream, 'fixes' them, and then returns them to the regular school. This brings to mind a medical model of students going into 'intensive care' at a specialist placement and then needing some 'home nursing' at the end of their illness. Rather, our school program attempted to maintain students' contact with regular schools by having them attend their regular schools for some of the time. This was designed to facilitate students' acquisition of the academic and social skills they needed to perform in regular schools, and then, for the remaining two hours of the school day, to allow them to practise those skills in that setting. Much of the special school's culture operated around students' returning to their local/regular schools, and behaving appropriately once there. Students began by attending regular school one afternoon each week, then two afternoons and so on. They then attended a full day, then two full days and so on. This process usually took about eighteen months. Students often returned to the special school to visit, or teachers visited students after they had returned full-time to the regular school, to provide follow-up.

Some students, about six at any one time, did not have a regular school that they could attend, usually because they had been taken into out-of-home care and could not continue to access their previous regular or special school, often because of distance. For these students the school provided a full-day program while they awaited a long-term residential placement. We then organised a new regular or special school close to their new home, and used the additional teacher position allocated to the school to provide the full-day program for these students.

Evaluation of the effectiveness of the program was carried out through pre- and post-attendance assessments of students' performances in mathematics, spelling, reading and writing. We also did pre- and post-attendance assessments of behaviour areas, such as doing quality work, getting along with others, not hurting others, looking after the school and the things in it, and cooperating with school teachers and support personnel. Evaluations were completed by students, parent/caregivers, and regular school personnel when the students left the school.

The students

Peter and his mum must have had a bad start to the day. He was walking in front of her and she was walking behind him. She was shouting: "That's the special school; that's the normal school over there. You go to the special school because no normal school will take you!"

Cath's Notes

Students were referred for placement at the special school if they displayed extremely problematic behaviour over long periods of time. While it was rare that a child in Kindergarten came to our school, this sometimes happened. Over the seven years during which my study took place, the great majority of the almost two hundred students who enrolled and then moved on from the school were boys in Years 5 and 6 (ten and eleven years of age). Almost a third of our students came from urban Indigenous backgrounds. Students from non-English speaking backgrounds were rarely referred to us. Before students were referred to the school, they attended a regular school for varying lengths of time where they might have learned how to 'get it right' in becoming students (Davies *et al.*, 2001). But they were read, and probably read themselves, as having failed in this task. When students enrolled in our school, they knew that they had been sent to the special school because their behaviour was read as too bad/too abnormal for their regular/normal school. Most students appeared ambivalent about coming to our school; they often presented anger at being made to leave their friends, resented their regular schools for 'getting rid of them' and, at the same time, expressed relief at not having to go all the time to their regular schools. They also expressed fear/concern at coming to a place where there were 'too many tough kids'. The small number of students at the school, the mixed age ranges in the classrooms, the shorter days and the individual academic work programs were but a few of the signs that students could read to indicate that the school was different to a regular/normal school. It was a special school.

It is difficult to talk of the students outside 'categories'—male, ten to twelve years old, Anglo-Saxon, Aboriginal, wards of the state, special, behaviour problems, poor, marginalised, from single-parent families.

All of these categories were used to describe most of the students in our special school, yet none of these categories can give any reliable sense of who they were. I knew them as Sam, Anne, Robert, Chrissie, Peter…each one capable of becoming someone other than the one who had been identified as belonging in a certifiable category and needing to be sent to a special school. At the same time, they had been positioned within and had actively taken up these category positions as descriptors of who they were. I would prefer to describe them as I found them. They were demanding, they were challenging and they were violent. And they were considerate, they were fun, and they stood up for themselves.

THE SCHOOL TEAM

The special school team comprised a principal, six classroom teachers two of whom were also assistant principals, a school counsellor for two days each week, three teachers' aide/support personnel positions for five days each week, a school administrator for five days each week, a clerical assistant for one day each week, and a general assistant/handyperson for two days each week. I was the principal of this school for over ten years, though the focus of this work is the first seven years of my time as principal. While there were some changes in personnel over this time, for the last six of those ten years there were very few changes.

All full-time teachers had undertaken postgraduate studies in special education and had come to this special school through specific application. They had not been 'placed' at the school through some random personnel process. They came to work at the school because they wanted to. They were very supportive of my research into our work. I could not, and would not have wanted to, do the research work without their support and consideration. Those who appear in this book include Lee, Louise, Steve, Adam, Beti, Allison and Jacqui. Lee was the assistant principal; much discussion about the research took place with her and with all the school team members. Almost all of the teachers were under thirty years of age. I see this is as significant. Just as they were 'feeling' their way in teaching, I too had been feeling my way in poststructuralism. In this sense we were beginning together.

At the beginning

I read Walkerdine's 'The Mastery of Reason' this weekend. There was a part that just had me immobilised. It was about whether the children of the working class really had conceptual deficits as they did not know that 'more' was the opposite to 'less' as did the children of the middle class. She writes that children of the working class do have this conceptual ability, but for them 'less' is not the opposite of 'more'—the opposite of 'more' is 'no more'. Walkerdine suggests that working class mothers have to regulate their children's consumption—their children can ask for more but there comes a time when they cannot have more—they get no more. Working class children cannot say 'less please'—it is the mother's task to ensure that not too much of an expensive item is consumed, yet children of the working class must be consumers. The middle class has more control over consumption and can ask for 'more' and even 'less'. This astounded me—the idea that language and class defines what can be spoken and by whom.

Cath's Notes

In the early days of my research work, I found Walkerdine's ideas about consumption (1988, p. 27) and her ideas about class to be key for me—stopping me in my tracks. I had never seen articulated so clearly how language structures, not only my thoughts, but everything I say and everything I do. The connections tumbled onto and through each other, immobilising me at one moment, inspiring me at the next; normal, abnormal, special, regular, mainstream, marginalised. I began to question all that I had come to know about the field of 'emotional/behavioural disorders'. This questioning was not without some pain. I had a position in the field as an 'expert', writing state-wide training materials, presenting at conferences, writing state syllabus materials and policy documents, receiving international visitors to see how it was done correctly. The impact of poststructuralism could have left me out—standing alone in the field. Yet is was from this very position as an 'expert' that I could talk of thinking about things differently; the dominant approaches for students categorised as having 'emotional/behavioural disorders' were generally not as effective as it was once thought they would be. New ways of thinking would move me from my comfortable position as an expert to the position of someone who no longer had the answers. As Edgar says:

> The good old days seemed better. We all knew what we believed (and it was right)...Those days are gone, forever, I hope. First of all we were not right. (If we had been we would not be having this discussion about Behavior Disorders.) Second, I no longer want to be a zealot about anything. I was a zealot in the old days. I believed behaviorism could cure any disability. With my colleagues I shouted down dissent, and our world view won. We had our day in the sun, and it didn't work! Not that all the ideas were wrong, but the notion that we had all the answers for every problem was wrong. (1998, p. 161).

It seems that problem behaviour of children in schools, particularly violence, has come to be a major focus of political agenda. Scheurich (1997, p. 97) asks: "By what process does a social problem gain the 'gaze' of the state, of the society, and, thus, emerge from a kind of social invisibility into visibility?" It is difficult to read the popular press without the issue of school violence being a focus, at least weekly, sometimes daily. While school violence is read as increasing and as more of a social problem now than it was thirty years ago, the issue for me is not whether school violence is on the increase, but how school violence and the behaviour of students in schools has 'naturally' become a societal problem.

In viewing this question from a poststructuralist perspective, I am engaging in a process that involves "refusing the acceptance of social problems as natural occurrences" (Scheurich, 1997, p. 97). In this study, rather than looking at the big picture of policy, I look at the minute detail of our work with violent/problematic children at the special school in order to see how the categories of 'problematic behaviour' and 'violence' are produced, and how those students positioned within these categories perform the behaviours and come to be regulated in and by these categories. In examining the detail of our everyday work at the school, I am able to see the social regularities through which categories are produced, to see, in Scheurich's words, how the "daily human micropractices (at home, at work, at play) are, thus, instantiations of these social regularities" (Scheurich, 1997, p. 100).

One of those regularities, particular to many institutions in the field of emotional/behavioural disorders in NSW over thirty years, is the working, informally, with categories different from the official mental health categories by which the student has been assessed. I cannot remember where I first heard students with 'emotional/behavioural disorders' spoken of as 'mad' or 'bad' or 'sad' but this colloquial naming has been with me for at least thirty years. I re-member these categories as ones by which people tried to avoid the mental health descriptors of a particular disorder or a particular disability. They were an attempt to name the problematic behaviours presented by children some way other than naming the children themselves as 'mad' or 'bad' or 'sad'. Yet I find that the mental health categories, while not so colloquial, do closely parallel this more simplistic naming of children as 'mad' or 'bad' or 'sad'. I use these categories to guide this book. They point to the simplistic, and at the same time deeply ingrained, ways the children who came to our school were positioned as and also took up 'mad' or 'bad' or 'sad'. Through this naming of the un-namable and the use of backstage terms, I am able to make more visible the operations of the power-knowledge about and around these children. The categories of 'mad' and 'bad' are often distinguished from each other in dominant educational/psychological discourses, for example official discourses clearly delineate services for students with emotional disturbance from those for students with behaviour disorders (NSW DET, 1999). The 'sad' category is often used by educators in the field; sometimes it applies to both the 'mad' and the 'bad' (and their circumstances), sometimes it names a whole new category of those caught up in the 'mad/bad' naming through terribly sad circumstances. I argue that the categories serve to brand and mark students as other than 'normal' in similar and overlapping ways. I do not see the category of 'mad' or 'bad' or 'sad' as definable, separate and knowable. Rather I tease out the ways these students are positioned as 'mad' or 'bad' or 'sad', and try to make this positioning more visible. I make it clearer that how these children are read depends on who is doing the reading, who is doing the naming. The work of Michel Foucault is key in helping to make the students' subjection visible, recognisable and self-conscious.

The work of Foucault has also been significant in pointing to the way the social regularities function to brand and marginalise those who are 'poor'. While I hesitate to fall into naming 'the poor' as a category, to fail to acknowledge how the social regularities operate to the advantage of some in society and to the disadvantage of others is, I believe, to participate consciously in such injustice. Scheurich (1997, p. 99) sees that, in relation to the social regularities that are constructed as our social world, "no particular individual or group consciously created them. This does not mean, however, that no individual or group may not benefit from the regularities". It is my experience that it is certainly not the poor who benefit from the social order of things.

Researching

Sam, a fourteen year old male student, has been with us for over three years. He is attending his regular school for two full days each week and doing well there. I sat down beside him in the classroom, as he looked really grumpy.

Cath:	*What's up?*
Sam:	*I'm pissed off that you're leaving.*
Cath:	*I'll be back next year—and I'll be dropping in every week.*
Sam:	*Yeah. Miss Mac told me you were going to do uni—be a doctor.*
Cath:	*Not a medical doctor.*
Sam:	*No, but it sounds pretty hard. Any sort of doctor sounds important.*
Cath:	*To some people—and to me, too.*
Sam:	*Then you'd better do it then. It'll be OK here.*

Cath's Notes

This conversation happened towards the end of my research journey and foregrounds the reflexive and reflective practices present in my work. Such practices are dominant in the selection of the topic, collection of the data, analysis of the data and the writing of this work. For Lather, "methodology is the theory of knowledge and interpretive frame-work that guides a particular research project" (1991, pp. 3-4). My work was guided by poststructuralist theory and approaches to research. To guide both my thinking and the reading of this chapter, I draw on the writing of others about poststructuralist research, in particular Scheurich, Walkerdine, Lather and Davies. Through reading the research of these authors, and through conversations with Davies, who supervised my PhD, I have found ways to make sense of the landscape/waterscape of this research journey. The shape of the journey is influenced by Deleuze and Guattari's concept of rhizomatic research: "A rhizome has no beginning or end; it is always in the middle, between things, interbeing, intermezzo" (1987, p. 25); "a rhizome ceaselessly establishes connections between semiotic chains, organizations of power, and circumstances" (1987, p. 7).

The rhizome has come to mean for me ideas of multiplicities, ruptures, connections, continuities; a rhizome is able to be observed at different points and different times, under the surface, it includes the best and the worst. Like my work. Following the roots of the rhizome as they spread and shoot off in unexpected ways, I am better able to convey the multiple paths of our lives at the special school. Yet rhizomes such as ginger, bamboo and grasses, as much as I like them, do not connect with me. It is the waterlily as rhizome that works for me as an image. I love Monet's water garden—the shape of the pond, the way the waterlilies sit and appear in unexpected ways, around a bend, in the middle of the water, under the bridge. I love the colours and I connect with the beauty of the visible and the work that is happening beneath the surface. I use the metaphor of the rhizome, particularly the waterlily, to situate the process/journey of my research.

One cluster or patch of waterlilies represents my world of work, the method of collecting the data for analysis, the difficulties of working in a poststructuralist way and the issues of anonymity for students at the school. In this cluster is also the theoretical framework used in analysing the data, particularly the work of Foucault. The process of the writing of the work, especially in talking with team members at the school, forms another cluster of plants which are made sense of as part of the methodological process. Up near the bridge is the 'me' who is the researcher/writer; the 'me' in the writing can be read in multiple ways. I will now visit these different clusters, under the surface, tracing how they connect.

AT THE SPECIAL SCHOOL POND

This work is situated in and around my world of work at the special school. It is a world that could be all consuming. In getting it right as a 'professional woman', it seems that the world of work seeps through worlds of home, worlds of pleasure, even worlds of being still and relaxing. I wanted to engage in research that 'mattered', both in terms of my emotional concerns/beliefs and the pedagogy of my work. I did not want to "walk the corridors of academe in search of something familiar" to my lived world (Neilsen, 1996, p. 205). I wanted to work on and through my familiar world of work.

At first I had hoped to make better sense of my world of work and to contribute some knowledge, even some product, that would make a difference to my work and, I told myself, to the lives of those who were in my world of work.

I don't think that we've got it right in helping kids to develop the appropriate social skills they need to survive in the world. I'd like to look at this more deeply and maybe come up with a curriculum that teachers can use and that really works.

Cath's Notes

I made this comment very early in my thinking about my doctoral work. It was before I had even taken up the position at the special school. I had hoped to 'make a difference' for those students whom I had read as being unable to make a difference for themselves. In this rescuing and emancipatory knowingness, I had set out to discover the answers, rise above the water and see it all before me. After all, this is what research is supposed to be about, isn't it? Being able to see the complexities, unravelling them and tracing the threads to their inevitable ends was what I understood research to be. At the same time I suspected that this would not be so simple. After years of my work in schools I guessed that, if things were so simple, then 'the answer' would already have been discovered. 'The answer' had thought itself discovered: the systematic management, mediated by cognitive processes, of stimuli and contingencies around children who cause trouble, are in trouble and are troubled. Yet in spite of my coming to have expertise in the discursive practices of behaviourist management, these theories were insufficient in describing my world of work. I saw things as more complex and layered, and this troubled me.

While I had also taken up action in my work as a feminist, I had limited this action to the world of women and the education of girls. I had compartmentalised feminist theory and thinking—this was in another part of the pond. Ideas around third wave feminism (Kristeva, 1986) opened for me the possibility of seeing what was happening to those, mostly boys, who were positioned as 'emotionally/behaviourally disordered', as their being positioned in similar ways to women and girls—as other than the norm, other than 'normal'. The mechanisms of power work in similar ways for all those who are marginalised and seen as other than powerful, dominant, or 'normal'.

Lather (1991, p. 31) points out that the "complexity of the human situation requires multiple research approaches". The poststructuralist approach that I took up in this research was different to the behaviourist research in which I had previously been involved. Poststructuralism enabled me to set out to find ways to explore these mechanisms of power and how they were played out in my everyday life and the lives of those with whom I worked.

THE GROWTH OF THE DATA

> To think that the journey happened in some way that fits a particular narrative structure that is endemic to modernism itself is to overlay a pre-set structure or pattern onto that which fits and that which does not, to commit inclusions and exclusions. (Scheurich, 1997, p. 3)

In collecting the data to turn over, examine closely, and stand back from in order to try to see how things fitted together, I started exploring the many ways data is collected in poststructuralist approaches. I began by seeing whether I could structure times and ways of collecting data at the school. I tried audiotaping the everyday interactions of the students and teachers. Each time I turned on the tape recorder there would be a 'performance'. Our voices would change from everyday voices to the 'listened to' voices of the radio; or there would be silence; or there would be such continuous profanity emanating from the students that finding any meaning *in* the data would be difficult. The meaning *from* the students was clear and I stopped taping. Perhaps I should have kept taping. After all, would not the performances for the tape constitute enough meaning in themselves? Could not those very performances be scrutinised for multiple readings? While this may have been the case, I decided that taping the everyday would not yield the everyday. More importantly, it intruded on the everyday, made us all feel that we were being stuck with a pin, live, for scrutiny and analysis. As I read more theoretical works, especially those of Foucault, I began to see how the lives of our students were continually under scrutiny and analysis by the very workings of school. To add another piece of apparatus to scrutinise and judge was more than inconvenient. I came to see it as unethical.

If the data on the everyday could not be gathered through taping the everyday, then perhaps it could have been gathered by structuring specific events, carefully recorded through tape or notes, and using this data for analysis. Perhaps showing some key videos and afterwards interviewing the students, individually or as a group, could have yielded some data of interest. Perhaps even interviewing students about an everyday or special school event such as a soccer match with another school could also have yielded data for analysis. Yet interviewing as a way of collecting data also has its problems. Scheurich (1997, p. 72) proposes that we can "look at an interview and conclude that there is dominance of the interviewee by the researcher, resistance of the interviewee to researcher dominance, and chaos/freedom enacted by both the interviewer and the interviewee". It is difficult to imagine another research setting where Scheurich's words could have had more resonance, even 'truth'. As principal of the school I could not have escaped the dominant position. The students, positioned as 'emotionally/behaviourally disordered', could certainly have given an outstanding display of resistance. The chaos/freedom enacted by us all, at a site where chaos/freedom is part of everyday life, could/would have flowed over any attempt at structured interviews. Again, I had what I saw as ethical difficulties with structured interviews that could have been read by students as invasive, even voyeuristic. In addition, the daily life of a school and the lives of those in a school are already events in themselves. To structure the events of a school for the purpose of obtaining research data is almost to have it the wrong way round. In my understanding of poststructuralist research, it is the observation of the everyday that helps the researcher to dip below the surface of the prevailing discursive practices and open them up for scrutiny.

I could have turned to the teachers, and considered inserting the process of collective memory work (Haug, 1987) into our everyday work at the school. It might have been possible to work with the teachers on a project of writing stories of lived experience as special education teachers, that would help to make visible the practices that are produced within prevailing discourses. To structure this into the daily life of the school needed time and thinking space that teachers in schools never seem to have, and I did not want to place this burden on the team at the school.

There were moments when we, as a school team, worked on day-to-day projects that reflected the multiple and contradictory stories of the school. This was particularly evident when we produced a video about the school. The video was intended for use with parents/carers and anyone interested in the programs at the school. The planning around the video involved discussions about needing to present footage of the students engaged in academic work and getting on with each other—those aspects, in fact, of the dominant discourses that would present the students, and the teachers, as 'normal'. The images in the final video did this, but more importantly, the crafting of the video was a time when teachers reflected on the dominant discourses and what it should look like to 'get it right' and be read as 'normal'.

MOVING TO ANOTHER PART OF THE POND

In order to address the ethical issues confronting me as researcher and, at the same time, me as principal, I searched for a way to move in and through the complexity of our world of work. I began making notes of the detail of the daily life of the school: what students were doing and saying and what teachers, including 'me', were doing and saying. I began organising these notes by tracking through events and his-stories of individual children like Sam, Anne and Peter. I used real names at the start and added to each one's story as new and different things happened in their lives at school and their lives at home. This might have been considered a 'journal' where I included reflections on what I understood to be the meaning of the event or interaction.

> We think that the private conversations we have with our selves, our 'I's', are the most precious thing. We typically assume that this self, our individuality, our subjectivity, our agency, exists outside the cultural array, that the individual is an autonomous self largely in control of her/his actions, thoughts, *etc.* (Scheurich, 1997, p. 164).

Yet, through the writing, the collection of data became something different to a journal. The 'I' was present but it started to become an 'I' observed—an 'I' seen to be caught up in the cultural array of the school. This was not an autonomous 'I' who pre-existed the writing, but one embedded in the discursive practices of teacher, principal, human, woman. The writing became a record of events, incidents, conversations, observations and passing glimpses of life at the school through which I was in process of becoming different from my 'self' (Davies, 2010). I began recording these becomings in the finest detail.

After the conversation with Peter today, I jotted down what was said. It was so unbelievable that I knew I had to get it down—word for word. I would write the context stuff later. It seems to me that some of the normal conversations are so incredible that I wonder how I never noticed the way the kids know, really know, what it takes to get it right as a student. Yet we persist with training them as though they didn't.

Cath's Notes

The minutiae of our daily performances could be read in the conversations and the exchanges between teachers, between teachers and students, and between me and students and teachers. I had to be scrupulous in recording the details and many conversations were jotted down so that they could later be recorded accurately. The sense of how things were being said, the emotion, the pauses, the run-ons, had to be remembered and inserted in the re-writing of the notes at night. Perhaps because I also know so well the rational, objective ways of research, I tried to ensure accuracy—albeit an accuracy that reflected the turbulent life of a turbulent school.

> Should we desire, however, to refuse this false order and, instead, foreground the indeterminate ambiguity, how might we redefine or reconceptualize research? (Scheurich, 1997, p. 74).

The notes of the daily events at the school became the data. Rather than structuring the events of the school to collect data, using interviews to explore particular questions that might be thought to need answering, or even using a structured way to collect the lived stories and memories of those in the school, the notes reflected the ambiguity, the contradictions, and the binaries as well as the consistencies, the patterns, and the lived experiences of those at the special school. The notes also reflected my changes in thinking around gathering data and the development of a site for collegial exchange/discussion. Many people in the school team expressed interest in reading the notes/stories and I shared these willingly. Rather than seeing/keeping the notes as separate until the end so that, according to some rationalist notion, they would be untainted and not influence our practice, they became important resources in reflecting on and changing our practice. This reflecting was collegial, in the sense that I often had no idea about what meanings could be made of them—at the time I knew simply that they reflected what I had seen and heard and said. Explorations of possible meanings were shared with the school team, and in this sense the research act became a site of learning for us all. Perhaps, in collecting data this way, I have not redefined research or even reconceptualised it. Yet the process of naming the notes as the data, seeing this as sufficient, was, for me, absolutely consistent with my understandings of poststructuralist methodology and the freedom/chaos available in working/thinking in this way. As Davies (1994, p. 35) says: "The possibility that we might constructively and legitimately think and speak from multiple positions within multiple discourses, not being *identified* with or bound by one is extraordinarily liberating and empowering".

TREADING WATER IN THE POND

But saying that the data/notes were analysed using poststructuralist concepts does not adequately convey the impact of poststructuralist thinking on my thinking, my work, and my life. In saying this, I might seem to suggest some sort of 'religious' experience, a blinding light of truth—revealing that there is no truth. It would be more accurate to say that my journey into poststructuralist theory is one where at times I felt, and continue to feel, totally immobilised, sceptical, disbelieving and, at the same time, an intellectual freedom and challenge that is full of joy to me, and, at times, annoying to others.

On holiday with friends: Cath, I'm not watching television with you any more unless you stop using the 'd' words. It makes my head hurt. (The 'd' words were discourse and deconstruct).

Cath's Notes

As I moved through a process of collecting data, reading theory, and analysing data in relation to theory, I came to see how an "awareness of the complexity, contingency and fragility of the practices" can be paralysing (Lather, 1991, p. 31). My position of 'principal researcher' troubled me in that I worried that it might trouble others or that they, the teachers and students, might have felt themselves to be under some kind of surveillance. Just as paralysing was the tentativeness experienced in 'doing work' differently. This tentativeness was due in part to the complexity of poststructuralist concepts and practices, in part to concern for students, teachers and myself as 'subjects', and in part to concern for the enormity of the risk in operating inside/outside the dominant discourse in such radical ways. Poststructuralist research is about disrupting certainties and seeing possibilities other than 'business as usual' in the cracks/silences opened by such disruption. Schooling, in contrast, is about smoothing over the cracks as they appear, about not disrupting, about ensuring that 'business as usual' goes on. There was no getting away from the risk of being seen as getting it absolutely wrong as a principal/teacher, as I engaged in practices of disruption. Once located inside the pond, however, looking deeply at the waterlilies, there was no possibility of 'objectivity', 'neutrality' or turning away. Although often immobilised, I was/am thoroughly implicated.

VISIBLE/INVISIBLE IN THE POND

In making a commitment to scrutinising our little pond of the special school and taking up the responsibility of being implicated in the work, my own anonymity became an impossibility. But ensuring the anonymity of the students and their families was important to me. I did not want my desire for authenticity in the research to overpower my desire for the anonymity of students and their families. While parents of students appearing in this work signed consent forms, many of the students were too young/disempowered to give 'informed consent'. I tell myself that the research did not involve 'doing unto' students in any rationalist experimental sense. The purpose of the research was to scrutinise the everyday mechanisms that held, and continue to hold, these students at the margins, the workings of these mechanisms, and the workings of other possibilities. My research was not scrutinising the students or the teachers, but the practices around and between the adults and children at the school. Yet I am protective of their stories and cautious that they should not be recognised as 'the objects of study'. Pseudonyms have been used for all students. I have also sometimes added additional 'protection' by changing ages and background information that, through my eyes, would not significantly change the meanings that we have taken from the events I have written about in my notes. The sex of the students in the notes/data has not been changed. Issues and practices around gender are evident in the stories and, consequently, changing the sex of the players would have a significant impact on possible readings and meanings. At the same time, I wonder at the notion of protecting the children in this way, and think that one of the unintended possible outcomes of this 'protection' is that specific issues faced by these children remain hidden and silenced. This is particularly highlighted in the chapter entitled *The Sad: being positioned as 'sad' and counteracting that positioning.* Respecting the confidentiality of those children and young people living in out-of-home care often ensures that the horror and pain of their lives remain largely unknown.

Confidentiality issues were just as important for the school team. The teachers nominated either their real names or pseudonyms to be used in the writing. In the process of the writing, teachers and support personnel reviewed all stories and agreed to stories involving themselves being used in this work. Yet I am mindful of the power relationship between principal and teachers and have used my own judgement in not including some material. I made this judgement on what I would not include both from the perspective of the then and now, and from my anticipation of the possible consequences in five, ten, even twenty years into the future.

In reflecting on this confidentiality, I know that I use data/notes that often do not reflect the levels of violence at the school. This violence from students towards other students and teachers was regular and extreme. Students kicked, punched, bit and head-butted both each other and the teachers. There were times, before I went to the school, when police were called to the school to quell riots and a teacher was stabbed. While this did not happen while I was at the school, I do not fool myself that my presence prevented such incidents. They could have happened at any moment.

Perhaps I could accuse myself of not including these moments in the data/notes as I did not want the teachers, including myself, to be read as not coping, or the students to be read as so violent. Perhaps such silences could be read as even perpetuating the violence in the same way as the legal confidentiality around those living in out-of-home care allows practices to continue unscrutinised. I might also be seen to be caught up in the kinds of responsibility/parenting practices that are most often reserved for women in executive positions and this might be one possible reading of my insistent protectiveness of the students and the school team. Yet it is not possible to talk of these times of extreme violence without the possibility of the incident, and those involved, being recognised by some readers. In spite of the possibilities of how my decision might be read, I remain silent about these times in this work. That is one of the aspects of poststructuralist theory and practice that I find most liberating. To see the traps and the holds does not necessarily mean that I refuse them. I am always implicated in a humanist discourse and so I 'choose' to read this protection as ethical, perhaps even moral.

SCRUTINISING THE POND

What I have tried to enact in my work is a strategy for understanding the lived experiences of everyday life at the special school. I have done this through including data/notes and examining them for the multiple ways that they can be read. In these readings I make more apparent the common storylines that we lived out and that hold us in a place, how they might be read differently, and the possibilities for doing something different. I repeat the earlier conversation with Sam to illustrate the many ways in which it might be read.

Sam, a fourteen year old male student, has been with us for over three years. He is attending his regular school for two full days each week and doing well there. I sat down beside him in the classroom, as he looked really grumpy.

Cath: *What's up?*

Sam: *I'm pissed off that you're leaving.*

Cath: *I'll be back next year—and I'll be dropping in every week.*

Sam: *Yeah. Miss Mac told me you were going to do uni—be a doctor.*

Cath: *Not a medical doctor.*

Sam: *No, but it sounds pretty hard. Any sort of doctor sounds important.*

Cath: *To some people—and to me, too.*

Sam: *Then you'd better do it then. It'll be OK here.*

Cath's Notes

This might read as Sam trying to manipulate, hold me in my place at the school. *Individual manipulates in powerful ways.* It might be read as Sam being concerned about change and not dealing with this well. *Individual shows fear.* It might be read as Sam being impressed at the importance of university and relegating his needs in favour of mine. *Individual recognises his place in the world.* It might be read as him understanding that it was something that I wanted to do and that I should do it if I wanted to. *Individual demonstrates caring and understanding.* It might be read as him, being male, seeing himself as more powerful than even the principal, and demonstrating this power by giving me permission to take leave. *Hegemony in practice.* It might be read as him being a less powerful student, complying with my reasoning. *Subjected student.* It might also be read as him resisting disciplinary practices of school and taking up a different position/being positioned as one who is empowered to interact in the teacher/student binary in different ways. *Possibility of agency.*

In writing the many possibilities of making sense of the conversation with Sam, I use the 'headlines' of 'truth' beside them to illustrate the complexities in analysing the data/notes and the rationalist tendency to have one right answer. When I looked at the data/notes I wrote over seven years, it was difficult to find obvious coherence without the guidance of poststructuralist theory that acknowledges multiple possibilities. The moments of everyday interaction can be read in many ways, all and none of which can be seen as 'true'. The purpose of analysing this data is not to unravel and find a truth or even many truths. It is to trouble, to deconstruct the operations of dominant discourses on our everyday lives. Such thinking through of our everyday practices enabled me to use the data/notes to see better how 'mad/bad/sad' and 'normal' can simultaneously be all three and neither.

I tried to make our everyday experiences at the school productive in relation to theory and practice and used the data/notes to explore both. While I wanted the teachers and students to be recognisable as people at everyday work, I needed to foreground that the sense-making of those everyday lives is only achievable with through the deployment of specific theoretical constructs. The key theoretical concepts used in scrutinising the data in this study include discourse, deconstruction, problematising, subjectivity/subjects, desire, power and agency. It is worthwhile exploring these concepts more closely here as it is they, or my readings of them, which guide the way the data/notes are interrogated in the subsequent chapters. My brief exploration of the terms here is an exploration of the terms *as they are practised in conceptualising* my work at the special school.

Discourse

We, in the western world, are all subject to much the same array of discourses. "Discourses are more than ways of thinking and producing meaning. They constitute the 'nature' of the body, unconscious and conscious mind and emotional life of the subjects they seek to govern" (Weedon, 1987, p. 108). The data/notes are used to examine and bring to light the workings of different discourses and their constitutive forces. While there were many discursive practices at work in the special school, including educational, special educational, psychological, psychiatric and humanist, I see the workings of these as dominating and resonating in similar ways. Consequently, I often refer to the 'dominant discourses' in the analysis of the data/notes as though they are the same, acknowledging that the workings of each will be different according to time and place. In following Foucault, the data is scrutinised to make more evident how any "discourse, whatever it be, is constituted by a set of utterances which are produced each in its place and time, as so many discursive events" (Foucault, 1994, p. 405).

Deconstruction

Often, the way that dominant discourses are explored is through the process of 'deconstruction'. In common with Lather, I see the goal of deconstruction as not to annihilate what is, but to

> keep things in process, to keep the system in play, to set up procedures to demystify continuously the realities we create, to find the tendency for all our categories to congeal. Deconstruction foregrounds the lack of innocence by looking at the textual staging of knowledge, the constitutive effects of our uses of language. (1991, p. 5).

The process of deconstruction is seen to involve "finding the hidden metaphysical binarisms that underlie and structure western thought, finding a way in between the binarisms and breaking them open" (Davies, 1994, p.

39). Through foregrounding the practices that reflect binaries and contradictions, I am better able to illustrate the ways the category 'normal' is only made possible through the categories 'mad/bad/sad'. At times I examine the data/notes in a way that identifies the constructed nature of our practices and our selves. Yet I do not restrict myself to the process of examining binaries. I use deconstruction to engage in a "turning away of the reflexive gaze from the achievement and maintenance of an essential self" (Davies, 2000, p. 170) in order to look at the detailed processes through which we come to think/imagine ourselves as rational individuals.

Problematising

I also examine the ways in which the 'emotionally/behaviourally disordered' have been problematised — how they came to be seen as problematic and how the strategies to deal with the 'problem' have emerged and were played out in our day-to-day work with students. Foucault might have seen this process as one of "critical analysis in which one tries to see how the different solutions to a problem have been constructed: but also how these different solutions result from a specific form of problematization" (Foucault, 2000, pp. 118-119). I attempt to analyse the data/notes in ways that make more visible the solutions/management/treatments that have developed around 'mad/bad/sad' students. At the same time, I explore the ways specific strategies reflect particular ways of making sense of the 'problem' of the 'mad/bad/sad'.

Subjectivity/Subjects

We become subjects/are subjected to the "daily experiences of being in the world, of being constituted in and through various discourses in one or another context" (Davies, 1994, p. 18). In exploring the concept of subjectivity it is important to examine ideas around the "shifting, fragmented, multi-faceted and contradictory" ways in which we are formed (Davies, 1994, p. 3). The data/notes assist in examining the ways we are subjected as teachers, students, good boys/girls, professionals, bad/mad/sad, experts, and/or human beings. Becoming a subject involves being positioned in one way and then another: "We are positioned and position ourselves moment by moment as we make our way through the everyday world" (Davies, 1994, p. 4). And, "[o]nce having taken up a particular position as one's own, a person inevitably sees the world from the vantage point of that position and in terms of the particular images, metaphors, storylines, and concepts that are made relevant within the particular discursive practice in which they are positioned" (Davies and Harré, 2000, p. 89). Through analysing the data/notes, the subject positions of those in the school are made clearer and the different positions we take up are made more transparent.

In particular, I focus on deconstructing the storylines around being positioned/taking up the position as 'mad/bad/sad' students, 'special' teachers, and 'normal' students, and use the data/notes to make these storylines clearer and better understood.

Desire

In the dominant humanist discourses, the desires of individuals are thought to indicate their true selves, their wants and their needs. As Davies states, the "inner quality, what we have come to know as *desire*, is not just a physical inner quality but a psychic quality" (1992, p. 62). In this sense we can come to be seen as desiring love, power, and recognition (by others) as worthwhile, talented, valuable. Our patterns of desire are not easily disrupted, as they come to signify what is taken to be the true, deep down, self.

Yet our desires are not original—they are shaped by the same collective set of images, metaphors and storylines as are the desires of other women, men, children, students. In poststructuralist thinking, desires are discursively produced, and taken up as one's own. "We become not what we have learned to call our true essential selves but that which the various discourses in which we participate define as or make thinkable as a self, or a true self" (Davies, 1992, p. 64).

The way(s) that we came to desire 'getting it right' in the special school as students, as teachers, as 'mad/bad/sad' students and as 'special' teachers are explored in this book in detail, as are the ways that desires come to be "constituted through the narratives and storylines, the metaphors, the very language and patterns of existence" (Davies, 2000, p. 37).

Power

According to Butler, subjection "signifies the process of becoming subordinated by power as well as the process of becoming a subject" (1997, p. 2). In this way I do not see 'power' itself as negative—there can be no subject outside the workings of power. Davies proposes:

> We cannot exist without being subjected through knowledge/discourse, and some of the systems of knowledge through which we are subjected are oppressive to some and give positions of advantage to others (2000, p. 18).

Through the analysis of the data/notes I am able to make more evident the ways that power works with knowledge in a complex relationship so that, for the students in the special school, it is clearer how power "invests them, is transmitted by them and through them" (Foucault, 1977, p. 27). I explore the multiple and contradictory workings of power on the teachers, and on me as researcher and principal.

Agency

The possibilities of agency, as it is conceptualised in a poststructuralist framework, are a key part of this work. It is agreed that

> [a]gency is never freedom from discursive constitution of self but the capacity to recognize that constitution and to resist, subvert, and change the discourses themselves through which one is being constituted (Davies, 2000, p. 67).

Yet, as Butler (1997) suggests, the process of subjection may in itself provide the condition for the possibility of agency. This possibility is explored through using the data/notes to speculate on how this might happen and what agency for marginalised students might look like.

The way I have approached these theoretical concepts is through the work of Michel Foucault. His work has informed almost all that I have written. Walkerdine (1997, p. 60) sees Foucault as important in poststructuralist work because "he allows us to begin to examine truth as a historical production, intimately connected to the regulation and management of populations, deeply tied to the place of the human and social sciences in this process". Foucault's works "raise the necessity to ask why and how certain issues have and have not been addressed, in what historical circumstances, with what truth effects" (Walkerdine, 1997, p. 60). In tracing through the world of my work, asking these questions is, for me, critical.

THE SCHOOL TEAM DOING COLLECTIVE MEMORY WORK

A surprising and unintended moment in my work was enacted in during the writing of it. I took leave from my job at school to perform the original writing. My leave and that writing became a topic of conversation for/between teachers and students. I continued to go to school one day a week and talked with teachers and support personnel. We talked about what I was writing, sharing the data/notes and re-membering the story, what happened before, what happened afterwards. We talked of discourse, deconstruction, processes of problematisation, subjection, desire, power and the possibilities of agency. We discussed memories of desiring to get it right at school, of having independence and freedom at school and what that meant for them, times when they were in trouble, punished, deprived of freedom, times when they had 'played the game' of school and gained the rewards that were on offer. We also talked about how they might read their own experiences of school looking back, and the similarities/differences with/between their experiences and those of the students at our school. We looked at how the data/notes might be read in different ways and, to some extent, were able to "begin to interrogate our own unexamined techniques of sense-making" (Lather, 1991, p. 5).

In this way we talked as if engaged in a 'collective biography' around schooling. I had participated in the writing of a few collective biography papers (Davies et al., 2001; Davies, Britt Flemmen, Gannon, Laws and

Watson, 2002; Davies et al., 2004; Davies, Edwards, Gannon and Laws, 2007; Bansell, Davies, Laws and Linnell, 2009). I found the processes of collective biography exhilarating and important in coming to see the workings of discourses and the possible of agency (Davies et al., 2001). As a result of these experiences, I read the conversations with teachers as 'biographical' in that they drew on memories of the lives of particular individuals, and as 'collective' in the sense that the stories revealed the ways in which we were/are collectively produced as subjects, experiencing ourselves as 'individual' and 'competent'. Through the processes of talking and listening we came to better understand how we are formed as individuals and professionals, and we made more transparent the ways we are subjected as teachers/special teachers. There were moments in these discussions when our individualities seemed to merge and, as 'the team', collective moments of thought developed through our coming to see how we are all constituted as subjects—and how we desire to 'get it right' as teachers, as a team. In this process, the stories become not just our own stories but collective stories through which we recognise ourselves as constituted through similar practices. I had never intended, or anticipated, this part of my work. For the first two years of engaging in this study I was immersed in finding out about poststructuralism and in reading the ideas of others. In the next year I was immobilised by the impact of these ideas on my practice. For the next two years I struggled with trying to read and do things in different ways. This was a struggle with myself and some of those around me—reading and doing things differently can be confronting and dangerous. For the last two years I was joyfully reading and doing things differently. One of the things that made this possible is the collegial sharing and reflection about practice that grew over the years at the school and the feelings of trust among the teachers and support personnel. We had all come to look at our teaching practice reflexively, and this focused for me the possibilities of how research might be thought about and performed differently.

A 'ME' IN THE POND

The process of the research in which this work is grounded is one in which I take myself to be participant and subject. What is the importance of the multiple 'me/s' in this work?

> The crux of the issue is the interpretive moment as it occurs throughout the research process. And, into this moment, the researcher brings considerable conscious and unconscious baggage—other related research, training within a particular discipline (such as anthropology), epistemological inclinations, institutional and funding imperatives, conceptual schemes about story-telling or power, social positionality (the intersection of race, class, gender, sexual-orientation, among other key social locations), macro-cultural or civilizational frames (including the research frame itself); and individual idiosyncrasies, the interactions of which are themselves complex and ambiguous. (Scheurich, 1997, pp. 73-74).

The data/notes of the daily events were not a record of everything that happened in the school. That would have been impossible. In the selection of what was recorded and what was not recorded I was the same as any other researcher. It was not possible for me to free myself from the discourses out of which everyday issues arise. My recounting of the stories can only ever be partial and subject to the discourses of my time and place. I selected to note what was of interest to me and what I considered might be of interest to others. There were a myriad of events in the daily life of the school that I did not notice/note. As Scheurich (1997, p. 40) states, "all perspectives imply political arrangements and invariably exclude some groups, some voices". I am sure there were voices not included in my work—voices unheard because they might have been seen as uninteresting, too difficult, too confronting, and/or too different. I am not obviously aware of where this happened; yet I know that it must have happened. In what I chose to record I aimed for accuracy in recording the event and, at the same time, accuracy in recording my emotional responses as I read them at the time. I could not have been an 'objective' bystander, both because poststructuralist thinking engaged me in seeing 'objectivity' as a particular mode of thinking and feeling in a particular discourse, and because, as principal of the school, I was always emotionally implicated. As Walkerdine writes,

> no matter how many methodological guarantees we attempt to provide to produce objectivity, we all know very well that the subjective intrudes, even in the most so-called rigorous research. (1997, p. 63).

Rather than escaping the subjective, I will now write one version of the 'me' who came to be the principal of the special school and, at the same time, a researcher. I write below these more 'objective' comments, and then additional reflective comments in italics as another version of the experiences.

After finishing high school, I began my engagement with 'higher learning' through completing a three year teacher education course. I was 'qualified' to teach primary school children. My first appointment as a teacher was to a school in the western suburbs of Sydney surrounded by public housing. Here I taught Year 4 (ten year olds) for three years.

The twelve-foot fence around the school cost the Department a fortune to put up. But then they had to leave the gates unlocked. Those who broke in daily did more damage when they couldn't get out.

I 'got out' and transferred to a 'relief' position because I wanted to travel overseas and it would be easier to get leave from such a position. Going to a different school every day, to a different class—I pinpoint this as the time I learnt to 'teach', or at least perform in front of a class and manage them for a day. During this time I completed a Bachelor of Arts degree by correspondence and attendance at residential schools. I went overseas and travelled in 1977 and on my return was appointed to a class for students with intellectual disabilities.

There we all were right at the back of the school, banished, but having so much fun.

I enjoyed working with students with special needs, and so in the next year I applied for and received a scholarship to complete a postgraduate special education course full-time.

My year off—away from the classroom. It felt like I'd been pardoned.

After this training I was appointed to a special school for children with 'emotional/behavioural disorders' where I taught for three years. This school was attached to mental health facility and most of the students in the school resided at the unit.

Meetings and parties. And Rob left in time-out all day when he was put in there at breakfast and there was a shift change. They forgot him. The door was then taken off the time-out room.

During this time I completed a Masters in Education working on the efficacy of social-skills-training with children and young people who were presenting 'emotional/behavioural disorders'. A new way of working with students with 'emotional/behavioural disorders' in the regular school was being explored by employing itinerant teachers to assist regular school teachers develop and implement programs for these students. I worked in such a position for three years. In my last year in this position I 'relieved' as principal of a school attached to a juvenile justice centre.

The girls complained that they were not allowed to wear undies at night—it was an issue of too much washing. I always wear my undies when I stay at someone else's place or a hotel—it is an issue of safety, comfort. I complained. The girls were given that right—reluctantly.

I then worked in a state-wide consultancy position under the national participation and equity program, specifically setting up programs for students with behavioural difficulties.

Blinded by the light and the importance of it all. Writing state-wide materials and training courses—an author of the practices on how to get the special education discourse right.

After the consultancy job, I was appointed as principal of a special school attached to a receiving and assessment centre for those living in out-of-home care and children in need of care and control.

Paralysed by the practices and inhumanity.

I went back into state office and coordinated policy for child protection in NSW for three years.

Seeing myself as making a difference—writing policy and curricula designed to rescue children from abuse.

In the early 1990s with the beginning of rational economic thinking and managerialism in the NSW Government, I moved from state office to work as a training and development consultant in a school district, planning and presenting courses on a range of topics for teachers—outcomes, national profiles, teaching and learning. I also completed a graduate certificate in public policy at this time in an effort to make sense of the changing political landscape—to try to understand managerialism.

Trying to see the big picture, refining the little picture.

I told myself I could not ethically participate around the restructuring/demolition of education and applied for a position as a principal at this school and was selected.

And there I stayed until retirement.

I write myself as the author of 'Cath's notes' so that I can subject my interactions to the same scrutiny as those of the students, teachers and support personnel at the special school, and the moments with the teachers at other schools with whom our students related.

WRITING ABOVE AND BELOW THE WATER

In the writing of this work an exploration of theory and how it might be reflected in the data/notes was undertaken. This exploration/examination involved *writing* the text of this work. I had played with other ideas of representing the work. For example, I could have used the video of the school with images of students and teachers at work and at play. The images of the students show them as something other than 'mad/bad/sad' or even 'normal'. Yet, I knew I had to write—at least present this work in the 'normal' way. Why was I so reluctant to begin the writing? I had gotten pleasure from writing the data/notes. While I could easily have spoken the stories, recounted the incidents onto a tape and then transcribed them, I had enjoyed this type of recount writing. What I was fearful of, when it came to writing up the study, was writing in ways that would communicate the emotions, the 'lived' world of work. Most of my previous writing had been for teachers, bureaucrats, policy-makers, parents and students. I had never thought I was 'allowed' to write the 'me' in the text. I resisted the writing for a long time, fearful of beginning the journey of writing.

> This may be why so many people do not write: because it's terrifying. And conversely, it is what makes certain people write: because it's intoxicating. (Cixous in Cixous and Calle-Gruber, 1997, p. 12).

Once I began to form the detail of the chapters of my work the writing became extremely pleasurable. I came to see the writing itself as an important aspect of the researching. In coming to the writing of my work, I discovered that there was so much more to know, in a theoretical and analytical sense. Through making sense of the theoretical writing of others, I was able to lift the data/notes from the special, localised setting and to conceptualise the practices theoretically. This process began when I wrote a paper about this work with Bronwyn Davies (Laws and Davies, 2000), and collectively wrote another paper on becoming schoolgirls (Davies *et al.*, 2001). Yet these papers were only a beginning to the conceptualising of this work. The intense theoretical analysis that was required to produce this work became a pleasurable journey of thinking. I came to discover a love of writing through the freedom offered to me by researching in this way.

> We always have the belief and the illusion that we are the ones writing, that we are the ones dreaming. Clearly this isn't true. We are not having the dream, the dream has us, carries us, and, at a given moment, it drops us, even if the dream is in the author in the way the text is assumed to be. What we call texts escape us as the dream escapes us on waking, or the dream evades us in dreams. We follow it, things go at top speed, and we are constantly—what a giddy and delicious sensation!—surprised... (Cixous, 1993, p. 98).

ANOTHER 'ME'—BELOW THE SURFACE

> As long as I ignore my own voice, my own experience, I run the risk of being assimilated into the main (male) stream 'objective' view. (Marshall, 1996, p. 88).

When my father returned from the second world war, he was allocated a housing commission house in Westmead, then a new suburb of western Sydney. My parents moved from Annandale, close to the city, to Westmead —a new suburb twenty kilometres from the city. Here they raised their three young children and then the baby 'me' was born. Dad had a job, Mum did not most of the time. I do not remember any pain about growing up in public housing. I do remember the pain of alcohol abuse and domestic violence from a returned soldier—and being invited to find refuge as a small child in the homes of others in the street when Dad came home drunk. But I remember that it was the same for many of my friends. Was I ever scrutinised at school for the signs? Were they? I find it ironic that I lived most of my adult life a street away from where my sisters and brother once lived with my parents in Annandale. A trendy suburb now.

WHAT IS TO FOLLOW—CHAPTER OUTLINES

Chapter 2. Discourses at work: examining the dominant discourses in the special education of students positioned as emotionally/behaviourally disordered

My work involved developing the capacity to apply poststructuralism in a setting where other discourses are dominant. This chapter explores some of those discourses, particularly the ideas and practices around the management of students' behaviour. I scrutinise the dominant practices at work in a special school and in regular schools to better understand the ways children and young people come to be subjected as 'students' and so come to desire to be the best possible students they can be. I then examine the educational/psychological processes used to inform the work of teachers of students who are read as failing to take up appropriate performances as manageable students.

The ideas and practices that are dominant in general education, special education, developmental psychology and therapeutic psychology are discussed. They are presented as an overview to indicate the dominant discursive practices that position both teachers and support personnel in a special setting. I explore the detail of current practices, how these might have come to be regarded as legitimate, and how these current practices are parts of the dominant discourses that constitute the 'nature' of special educational practices. I write about these practices somewhat from a distance—not from the outside as I can never fully escape that which formed me as a 'specialist', a 'principal', a 'teacher', and a person who believes myself to have a social conscience. Yet they are presented critically as I do not call them my own. The process of this work, in looking at these practices and at myself with a critical eye, perhaps even through a different lens, means that I no longer see these practices as 'truth'. One of the difficulties for me is that I still engage in them and teach them at a university in my post-retirement job. I teach about the curriculum, the behaviour management strategies, the ideas around needs and goals, the 'caring discipline'. I now present the dominant practices as only part of the repertoire of techniques available to teachers, and I work with undergraduate and postgraduate teachers in ways that might enable them to use them differently in their work with children and young people.

For me to come to use them differently involved a frightening and joyous journey. Frightening in the sense that I now wonder how I could have even contemplated continuing 'business as usual'; in the realisation of the confusion and even anger from those around me when I engaged in doing something different; and in the sense that doing something different was not only radical but dangerous. At the same time, I remain joyous at being able to better understand the ways we are constructed through multiple and contradictory practices, and at being able to find ways to make this more visible to others and myself.

Chapter 3. The Mad: being positioned as 'mad' and counteracting that positioning

In this chapter the dominant discourses of the special school are made very clear through exploring the practices around children who come to perform as/be read as 'mad'. Using Foucault's (1988) work on madness and civilisation, the practices at the special school and the dominant educational and psychological practices are examined through the detail of the everyday lives of those students who came to be read as more 'mad' than 'bad' or 'sad'. The practices at the special school reflected the dominant discourses and are explored through the data/notes collected. The detail of the data, read in relation to the theoretical framework provided by Foucault, makes it possible to explore the dominance, dangers and chances created when working at the margins with children who are positioned as 'mad'. Through exploring the practices around 'mad' adults as detailed by Foucault, I examine how nearly all of the systems that are put in place for adults named as 'mad' are used with children: confinement to and in the margins, firm and systematic management of behaviour, close surveillance and observation, rewards and punishment, ordering of their lives, and medication. At the same time, in the dominant discourses, childhood is to be read as a time of innocence and so children thought of as 'mad' are not named as 'mad' in the same ways that we name adults as 'mad'. Rather they are to be seen, in the dominant discourses, as demonstrating learned misbehaviour that must be unlearned. There are complex implications for children whose behaviour is read as 'mad', yet not named as such, and at the same time subjected to the same practices as adults who are named as 'mad'. In teasing out the complexity around those children at the special school who are read as 'mad', these students can be read as dangerous in the rationalist discourse because they fail to take up appropriate behaviours, and they display inappropriate behaviour in such a way that clearly marks them as not 'normal' and often wilfully 'abnormal'. I make clear the workings of the dominant discourses in marginalising those children, and the importance, for the smooth functioning of rationalist discourse, in maintaining them at the margins.

Chapter 4. The Bad: being positioned as 'bad' and counteracting that positioning

The practices at work for children positioned as more 'bad' than 'mad' are explored in this chapter. It is extremely challenging to theorise adequately the educational and psychological practices around students who are read as unmanageable and too violent to be maintained in the mainstream school. In the dominant discourses the behaviour of the 'bad' is read differently to the behaviour of the 'mad'. While some 'mad' behaviours are read as wilful, the motivation for such behaviour is read as beyond the fault of the individual whose body is sick. 'Badness' is read as a deliberate, conscious and sane act—a deliberate disruption of the order of things. Those children whose behaviour is read as mostly 'bad', even 'abnormally bad', are read in the dominant discourses as deliberately refusing their subjection as positive, contributing members of our society.

I use the work of Foucault (1977) to explore the ways power and discipline work in schools through normalisation and surveillance, through the specificity of space, place and time, and through the body, to produce the 'student' who desires to get it right, be 'normal'. I then examine the ways punishment works to produce, through individualisation, the construction of codes and consequences, and the ideas/feelings to be taken up as one's own and embodied for the successful performance of 'normal student'. I trace the workings of punishment, in the dominant discourses, used for those students who apparently refuse to take up performing as a 'normal' student and who are read as 'abnormally bad' students. This includes the management of their behaviour, the network of disciplines created around them, and procedures of sending them away even from the margins. The dominant psychological/educational practices of searching for a cause and searching for a conscience in the 'abnormally bad' are also explored. I look at the contradictions between the sympathy and admiration I observed and experienced for those who demonstrate a struggle against/with the norm, and the disgust/helplessness I experienced at some 'abnormally bad' behaviour. Finally, I reflect on the way punishment, in working to categorise the 'abnormally bad', is not intended to rehabilitate but to delineate the possibilities of behaviour.

Chapter 5. The Sad: being positioned as 'sad' and counteracting that positioning

Here I examine the dominant practices around students who are taken into the care of the state and named as living in out-of-home care. I name these children as the 'sad' both because of the sadness we experienced at work about their lives and because of the ways the dominant discourses operate to elicit initial sympathy and sadness for these children. With the help of the work of Foucault (1977, 1988),

Walkerdine (1997) and Burman (1994) I explore how the 'sad' are at first categorised in dominant discourses in terms of their living arrangements, rather than branded by their behaviour/disability. This naming seems to evoke a status of 'other' than 'proper' living arrangements with one's biological family, particularly one's mother. I explore issues around state care for children, the development of a focus on the protection of the child, the positioning of the parent/mother as one who is responsible for the continuous care of the child, and the placement of children in situations most like the fiction of a 'real' family.

I explore the ways in which the dominant discourses permit some sympathy and some acknowledgment of the pain of those who are no longer living with their families. Children are removed from their homes by the state because it is not possible for them to live with their family, usually because of abuse or maltreatment. Yet the dominant discourses seem to double back on them, and the children are the ones who come to be positioned as somehow getting it wrong as appropriate children, not 'getting over' the trauma quickly and thus becoming 'sad'. The practices involved in the dominant discourse around teaching children to get it right, not only as appropriate students, but as appropriately lovable children, are explored. I discuss how the idea that children in out-of-home care should not be seen as damaged, as needing treatment, or as victims helps to distance sadness about their situation. Focussing on their living arrangements also helps to distance sadness and anger and allows children's behaviour, rather than their pain, to be placed under scrutiny.

I also examine the silences around pain, sadness, sexuality and poverty, and the implications of these silences for the 'sad', for the team at the school, and for myself. Walkerdine (1997, p. 36) proposes that "pain is central to working-class lives" and that we are able to "speak of pathology, of difference, of poverty even, but rarely of oppression". In the dominant discourses, it is the specific aberrant behaviours of the 'sad' that must be our focus if we are to get it right as competent special education teachers. Through the silencing of pain and oppression, those whom we contain and pathologise through surveillance and branding come to see themselves as inadequate rather than oppressed. Once again, I do not see it as accidental that the discursive practices of the dominant discourses contain lessons for the poor, for poor mothers and for the children of poor mothers.

Chapter 6. Counteracting dominant discourses: using poststructuralist theory to bring about change

By working in a poststructuralist framework, this final chapter explores the possibilities of students positioned as 'mad/bad/sad' doing something different, not only in the sense of performing as good, appropriate, 'normal' students, but of resisting the discourses that hold them so firmly and consistently in place. I look at ways of developing strategies for working with students and teachers to enable them to become people who can begin to acquire a sense of agency. To do this I ask how might it come to happen that we are able resist being caught up, and able to "do more than reiterate the conditions of subordination" (Butler, 1997, p. 30). The categories that are placed on/taken up by our students in dominant discourses are painful, and to watch their struggle to be something other than 'mad/bad/sad' is also painful. It is difficult to see this without wanting to rescue. Consequently, I try to be careful not to write of/be caught in ideals of humanist emancipation from the chains of subjection. Rather, I explore the kind of agency that comes from recognising the multiple and contradictory discourses shaping oneself and shaping the social world one inhabits. I explore the ways this kind of agency, of reading discursive practices against the grain and of recognising the workings of subjectivities, contains the possibilities of taking up positions other than those made inevitable within dominant discourses.

I examine the ways students in the special school are subjected as 'mad/bad/sad' and the moments, drawn from my notes/data, of resistance to the dominant discourses that hold them in their place at the margins. To make this comprehensible, I present stories/data of resistance to subjection and possible agency in the day-to-day life of the special school. I then use the idea of 'trouble' to reflexively examine what might be known about power-knowledge and the implications of our work at the special school, and the possible contributions of this work to the worlds of general and special education, to the category of 'emotional/behavioural disorders' and to poststructuralist research and theory in action. I examine the aspects of the work that trouble me and may trouble others. In working with students and teachers to rework the ideas of 'special', 'normal' and 'abnormal', I trouble ideas of the ethics of working with teachers and students in such a way that, in a non-threatening environment, we were able to 'get it wrong' under the burning light of the dominant discourses. What might be the implications for students, the school team and myself? Might students be viewed as not undergoing the 'right' process to fix them? Might teachers be viewed as not getting it right as competent teachers? Might I be viewed not only as not getting it right but as wilfully engaging in practices that challenge and even undermine, in damaging ways, the educational chances of students? Might we all be in trouble? Or, through this very writing and practice, might others begin to see the dominant discourses that are not normally visible and begin to open up previously unavailable possibilities of agency?

CONCLUDING AND BEGINNING

The self-reflection of poststructuralism requires that researchers

> attempt to bring to consciousness some of their own reactions, defences, the transferences through which the material brought up by others stirs emotional material of their own. (Walkerdine, 1997, p. 72).

I remain connected to the students and teachers and support personnel at the special school and reflect moment to moment on how their lives stir emotional material of my own. Where I am conscious of it, I write of it. Where I am not conscious of it—will the reader be able to resist seeing the 'real reason' for a particular comment, a particular reading? For this is the crux of the matter, how we are read; how we read ourselves is always confined by particular discourses relating to time and place. This work is about teasing out the particular discourses operating for those at the special school.

In concluding this first chapter, I write almost the 'warning' before the show. I am very aware of the ironic ways in which I write and speak. I say 'very aware' almost ironically, as irony has become such a habit with and for me that I almost find it invisible to myself. I am aware that others are often puzzled by my use of irony. There are many ways this use might be read. At worst it might be read as callous, manipulative, supercilious and unfeeling. It could also be read as a 'defence', a way of dealing with the pain I encounter each day and a pain that is mine. There is resonance for me when Scheurich (1997, p. 90) says that he is "deeply troubled by the anonymous imperial violence that slips quietly and invisibly into our (my) best intentions and practices and, even, into our (my) transformational yearnings". Perhaps my use of irony is a way of 'checking up on' myself in order to catch myself out when I become the valiant rescuer, the all-knowing sage, the righteous judge of those who get it wrong. Irony was one of the main ways that I dealt with the complexity of being not only a researcher but also a principal. As Riley (2000, p. 172) states, "it is not my detachment from my attributed condition that leads to my irony, but on the contrary my deep involvement in it". My use of irony does not free me from my positions but reflects my deep involvement in my positionings.

Yet might not irony serve another purpose? "The raw stuff of verbal irony, this iterability, possesses the odd power to make strange that which it familiarly reflects" (Riley, 2000, p. 158). Might irony be used to pick at the threads of subjectivity, to raise the possibility that what seems to be 'normal' and 'true' might be read differently? I have always found irony useful in drawing attention to the absurdity of the practices of the dominant discourses, and irony saturates my work. Through playing with irony and watching and using it at play, I believe I am better able to still myself and examine the practices around me. The data/stories in my work reflect my habit of questioning in ways that are often read as 'playing dumb'. I sincerely hope that these moments are not read as moments of arrogance or manipulation.

> Irony's studied incomprehension is what permits it to stop its ears to the content of what's being reiterated, and instead to become fascinated by the word made into a thing through the sheer fact of its reiteration. (Riley, 2000, p. 157).

It is this fascination with what is spoken, what is named, how it is named, what is silenced, and the practices around these, that fired my enthusiasm for doing something different than being continually caught up in the practices that positioned me as principal/teacher and positioned the students as 'mad/bad/sad'. There is irony in my selection of the categories of 'mad', 'bad' and 'sad' to structure my analysis of dominant discourses operating with children at the special school. I could have selected any number of categories by which to analyse the details of the positionings of the students. In selecting the common naming of 'mad/bad/sad' I am better able, through irony, to "defuse a hurtful description by deforming it so far towards the grotesque that it becomes a frank travesty and caves in" (Riley, 2000, p. 163). I do not expect that the discursive practices around students in special schools, especially those positioned as 'mad/bad/sad' will simply cave in through my use of irony. Yet in analysing how these practices are played out I do hope for moments of clarity, for moments of seeing the discourses that hold us in our places and, through this visibility, for the possibility of agency.

REFERENCES

American Psychiatric Association. (1994). *Diagnostic and statistical manual of mental disorders* (4th ed.). Washington, DC: Author.

Bansel, P., Davies, B., Laws, C., & Linnell, S. (2009). Bullies, bullying and power in the contexts of schooling. *British Journal of Sociology of Education, 30*(1), 59-60.

Burman, E. (1994). *Deconstructing developmental psychology.* New York: Routledge.

Butler, J. (1997). *The psychic life of power.* Stanford, CA: Stanford University Press.

Cixous, H. (1993). *Three steps on the ladder of writing.* New York: Columbia University Press.

Cixous, H., & Calle-Gruber, M. (1997). *Hélène Cixous rootprints: Memories and life writing.* (E. Prenowitz, Trans.). London: Routledge.

Davies, B. (1992). Women's subjectivity and feminist stories. In C. Ellis & M. Flaherty (Eds.), *Investigating subjectivity: Research on lived experience* (pp. 53-76). Newbury Park, CA: Sage.

Davies, B. (1994). *Poststructuralist theory and classroom practice.* Geelong, Australia: Deakin University Press.

Davies, B. (2000). *A body of writing 1989-1999.* Walnut Creek, CA: AltaMira Press.

Davies, B. (2010). The struggle between the individualised subject of phenomenology and the multiplicities of the poststructuralist subject: the problem of agency. *Reconceptualizing Educational Research Methodology, 1*(1), 54-68.

Davies, B., & Harré, R. (2000). Positioning: conversation and the production of selves. In B. Davies, *A body of writing 1989-1999.* Walnut Creek, CA: AltaMira Press.

Davies, B., Dormer, S., Gannon, S., Laws, C., Rocco, S., Lenz Taguchi, H., & McCann, H. (2001). Becoming schoolgirls: the ambivalent project of subjectification. *Gender and Education, 13*(2), 167-182.

Davies, B., Britt Flemmen, A., Gannon, S., Laws, C., & Watson, B. (2002). Working on the ground. A collective biography of feminine subjectivities: mapping the traces of power and knowledge. *Social Semiotics, 12*(3), 292-313.

Davies, B., Browne, J., Gannon, S., Honan, E., Laws, C., Mueller-Rockstroh, B., & Bendix Petersen, E. (2004). The ambivalent practices of reflexivity. *Qualitative Inquiry, 10*(3), 360-389.

Davies, B., Edwards, J., Gannon, S., & Laws, C. (2007). Neo-liberal subjectivities and the limits of social change in university—community partnerships. *Asia-Pacific Journal of Teacher Education, 35*(1), 27-40.

Deleuze, G., & Guattari, F. (1987). *A thousand plateaus: Capitalism and schizophrenia.* Minneapolis, MN: University of Minnesota Press.

Edgar, E. (1998). Where does the weather come from? A response to behavioral disorders: a postmodern perspective. *Behavioral Disorders, 23*(3), 160-165.

Foucault, M. (1977). *Discipline and punish.* London: Penguin.

Foucault, M. (1988). *Madness and civilisation.* New York: Random House.

Foucault, M. (1994). *Aesthetics, method and epistemology.* London: Penguin.

Foucault, M. (2000). *Ethics: Essential works of Foucault.* P. Rabinow (Ed.). London: Penguin.

Haug, F. *et al.* (1987). *Female sexualization: A collective work of memory.* London: Verso.

Kristeva, J. (1986 [1981]). Women's time. In T. Moi (Ed.), *The Kristeva reader.* Oxford: Blackwell.

Laws, C., & Davies, B. (2000). Poststructuralist theory in practice: working with "behaviourally disturbed" children. *International Journal of Qualitative Studies in Education, 13*(3), 205-221.

Lather, P. (1991). *Feminist research in education: Within/against.* Geelong, Australia: Deakin University.

Marshall, J. (1996). Heavy periods: the process of collusion and compromise in research. In E. Burman, P. Alldred, C.

Bewley, B., Goldberg, C., Heenan, D., Marks, J., Marshall, K., Taylor, R., Ullah & S. Warner, *Challenging women: Psychology's exclusions, feminist possibilities.* Buckingham: Open University Press.

Neilsen, L. (1996). Remaking sense, reshaping inquiry: feminist metaphors and a literacy of the possible. In J. Flood, S. Brice Heath & D. Lapp (Eds.), *Encyclopaedia for teaching in the communicative and visual arts.* New York: Macmillan.

NSW Department of Education and Training. (1999). *Who's going to teach my child?* Sydney: Author.

Riley, D. (2000). *The words of selves: Identification, solidarity, irony.* Stanford, CA: Stanford University Press.

Scheurich, J. J. (1997). *Research methods in the postmodern.* London: Falmer Press.

Walkerdine, V. (1988). *The mastery of reason. Cognitive development and the production of rationality.* London: Routledge.

Walkerdine, V. (1997). *Daddy's girl.* London: Macmillan.

Weedon, C. (1987). *Feminist practice and poststructuralist theory.* Oxford: Blackwell.

CHAPTER 2

Discourses at Work: Examining the Dominant Discourses in the Special Education of Students Positioned as Emotionally/Behaviourally Disordered

Abstract: As detailed in Chapter 1, *Researching special schools: a poststructuralist approach,* this work explores the capacity to apply poststructuralism, in theory and in practice, in a setting where other discourses are dominant. I focus on my own work as principal in the context of a special education school where I worked with students categorised as 'emotionally/behaviourally disordered'. I analyse the discourses that inform this kind of work, both from the position of one who inevitably took them up, even becoming expert in them, and from a Foucauldian position of critique which sets out to render these discourses less able to be taken up.

This chapter explores some of these discourses, in particular the ideas and practices around the management of students' behaviour. I scrutinise the dominant practices at work in a special school, and in regular schools, to understand better the ways children and young people come to be subjected as 'students' and so come to desire to be the best possible students they can be. I then examine the educational/psychological processes used to inform the work of teachers who work with students who are read as failing to take up appropriate performances as manageable students.

Keywords: education, disability, emotional and behavioural disorders, behaviour management, discipline, binary/binaries, psychology, mental health/illness, cognitivist/ism, physical restraint.

Cath:	*I wonder what this means: "secure" and "caring" and "disciplined".*
Lee:	*I guess we can't keep kids safe if there is no discipline.*
Cath:	*So through discipline we show we care?*
Lee:	*It's saying that if there is no order and discipline, then people are unsafe.*
Cath:	*So discipline is the only way to keep kids safe?*
Lee:	*How else could it be done?*
	[Long pause.]
Lee:	*What?*
Cath:	*It's just that—how do we see discipline being done in practice? Is it caring?*
Lee:	*Hmm. I see what you mean—they are almost opposite?*
Cath:	*And yet we speak of them as though they're not—it's so powerful—the way we see things as making sense—yet they don't really.*

Cath's Notes

Examining the ways in which schooling produces "taken-for-granted practices so that they come to seem obvious and unchallenged facts" (Walkerdine, 1989, p. 20) and teasing out the dominant discourses that impact on the work of teachers is complex work. In exploring some of these complexities, it is startling the ways teaching and learning practices reflect the dominant humanist, rationalist discourses—the binaries and contradictions that at one moment seem to be separate, and at another moment seem to be seamless so that teachers and students, together, can ensure that learning takes place as prescribed.

In Chapter 1, *Researching special schools: a poststructuralist approach,* I describe the special school used in this study and discuss my role as researcher and as principal. My focus in this chapter is to trace the dominant educational and psychological approaches at play in making sense of the problematic behaviour

Cath Laws

of students. I explore what happens when children fail to get it right as students in persistent, extreme and disturbing ways, and come to be categorised as 'emotionally/behaviourally disordered'. I examine how, and the extent to which, the problematic behaviour of these students is mostly and/or partly attributed to the child, and also to parents, peers, faulty learning, teachers, schools, a disability or an inequitable society. It seems that the dominant educational treatment/interventions are mostly on/with the child; in this chapter I explore some of the dominant treatment/interventions used for students categorised as 'emotionally/behaviourally disordered' and the complex work of the teachers and children at the special school.

In one sense this chapter is written as a literature review wherein I scrutinise the multiple and contradictory approaches, ideas, theories and practices that seemed to fly around me and have shaped me, and continue to shape me, in such ways that I have come to see myself in some coherent way as a 'special educator'. Yet I am aware that these approaches, ideas, theories and practices cannot be taken to be truths and need to be carefully examined and questioned.

LEARNING AND TEACHING

The dominant discourses around schooling are full of contradictions. Yet teachers seem to fold these contradictions in on each other and blend them into apparently rational educational practices. There is no right or wrong discourse—all discourses can be critiqued and questioned. One way of critiquing the discourses in question here is to tease out their contradictions and binaries. Some of the contradictions that confront teachers are clear binaries, established as though they are opposite to, and exclude each other: good/bad, teacher/student, normal/abnormal. Here, the first term "is the privileged term and is often equated in an unstated way with humanness, normality" (Davies and Hunt, 2000, p. 108). Other binaries are more complex and are often seen as exclusive to each other at one moment and as bound together at the next moment: theory/practice, learning/teaching, directed/investigative, developmental/individual, unique/social, equity/quality. In order to be seen as performing effectively as teachers, and as demonstrating appropriate subjection as teachers, we often do not even see the possibility of these pairs being played out as binaries. For example, there is supposedly a smooth flow from theory to practice, yet children learning to read is a site of continuing debate and controversy. There are several theories that can be contradictory and the practices emanating from each theory differ significantly. Even within each theory there can be contradictory prescriptions for practice (Nicholson, 1992).

Teaching-learning is often placed on a continuum where more formal and traditional teachers are seen as the 'sage on the stage' and less formal teachers are seen as 'the guide on the side' (NSW DET, 1993). Teachers are required to organise learning activities that direct students in their acquisition of basic skills and that at the same time ensure students investigate and think inductively using concrete materials. Teaching is supposed to be organised around the proposition of sequential development of skills. Yet, at the same time, teachers need to know about, and step into, different learning approaches in order to cater for individual students who may not fit into such sequenced learning patterns. It seems that teachers struggle to be 'good' teachers and to exist on the right side of different binaries at different times. For example, teachers have been encouraged through educational research and policy to be the 'guide on the side' to facilitate learning rather than being the 'sage on stage' (Jones, 2006). For at least twenty years student centred learning was seen to provide the most effective environment for students to learn effectively (Cannon, 2000). Yet more recently, Dinham and Scott (2007) argue that 'good teachers' always knew that teaching requires both approaches—being the guide and at the same time being the sage. Teaching is complex, and many teachers do not have access to the reflexive and critical practices that might enable them to see the contradictory discourses acting on and through them.

POLICIES OF EDUCATING

Educational policies reflect contradictory prescriptions for teachers. In government education systems strategies for education are articulated in various strategic directions documents distributed to schools by those who coordinate the particular school systems. For example, at the time of my work in schools, teachers in special schools were asked "to build on a heritage" (look to the past) while at the same time to prepare "a new generation for the future" (NSW DET, 2000, p. 1). There were also ideas that being "productive" leads to "rewarding lives", that an "educated" society leads to a "just society", and that it is possible to "provide a broad range of educational choices to meet diverse aspirations" leading to a "socially cohesive" society (NSW DET, 2000). There were "agreed and explicit educational outcomes" that had been developed through a "partnership with students, parents and the wider community" (NSW DET, 2000, p. 1). It is doubtful that students, parents or the wider community had been engaged in specifying these explicit educational outcomes. An education system's outcomes are prescribed in mandatory policies, yet teachers are expected to act as though they are 'agreed', 'just' and 'right' outcomes for students. In spite of the possibility of such language being read as empty, idealistic metaphors with little relation to practice, teachers are expected to read such directions as meaningful to them in their everyday practices in schools.

At the turn of the century on the other side of the world, the British Department for Education and Employment (DFEE) was concentrating on the ambition that all young people, upon reaching the age of sixteen years, would have "the skills, attitudes and personal qualities that will give them a secure foundation for lifelong learning, work and citizenship in a rapidly changing world" (2000, p. 6). This policy envisaged its goal as being achieved through "substantially improving literacy and numeracy skills in primary schools" and "pupil achievement in secondary schools" (2000, p. 6). In the dominant educational discourses across the world, the focus is on teachers working in ways to increase students' basic skills, and this is seen to be the pathway to lifelong learning. This lifelong learning is entwined with, and even limited to, the world of work. The overall aims of the British DFEE include giving "everyone a chance to realise their full potential, and thus build an inclusive and fair society and a competitive economy" (2000, p. 6). "Inclusive", "fair" and "competitive" are not seen in this policy as possibly contradictory but as seamless goals within the rationalist educational discourse. Bird Claiborne, Cornforth, Davies, Milligan and White (2009) consider that teachers need to learn to tease out the ways dominant discourses are at work in their own and others' speech and practices. For example, they have analysed the ways in which ideas of 'inclusion' and 'mastery' have become linked in complex ways.

The links between education and employment are now more specifically stated in NSW, where the NSW DET (2010a) "strongly promotes lifelong learning, and aims to provide students with a smooth transition from school to work or further study, and from post-compulsory education and training to work or further study". The rhetoric now focuses on "lifelong learning", an approach that is about learning how to learn and getting pleasure and insight from learning (Hargreaves and Fullan, 1998). Yet it is operationalised as "further education and training for employment", thus attaching an explanation that converts the idea of lifelong learning to getting work, and to becoming and changing into whatever kind of worker the society wants.

LEARNING

The dominant discourse of working with students in schools is said to be one of 'learning'. It is a discourse in which teachers are charged with the responsibility of teaching students, and students (and teachers) with the responsibility of learning. Teachers are asked to guide students through the learning process. If students refuse to be guided, then, in the dominant discourses, teachers are expected to 'ensure' that learning takes place. Through this 'ensuring', more 'direct' teaching is thought to be required if teachers are to be considered, and see themselves as, effective. While 'guiding' and 'facilitating' learning is sometimes the stated required practice, there is also a contradictory expectation that teachers 'make' students learn. Yet this ensuring of learning needs to be seen as being done in a *democratic* way—learning must not be *forced*. The 'effective teaching' discourse expects teachers to empower students, invite them into decision-making about their learning, and ensure that teaching is a democratic process. Walkerdine (1990, p. 24) sees this democracy as a "fantasy of liberation", the cost of which is borne by the teacher.

To get teaching right in the dominant discourses, teachers come to see themselves as responsible and accountable for students' learning. Walkerdine talks about schooling as a mimicry of the 'scientific process' and the schoolroom as having become a "laboratory where development could be watched, monitored and set along the right path" (Walkerdine, 1990, p. 21). Students' development is the *responsibility* of teachers. In this sense 'responsibility' is seen as a privilege—a calling—one that is to be embraced with dedication. Teaching may not, however, become a *passion*—that could be read as being 'over-involved'. Walkerdine concludes that teachers are really losers in this discourse, and that "the happy classroom is a place where passion is transformed into the safety of reason" (1990, p. 23). In contradictory ways, teaching is supposed to be performed with love, and with caring concern for students as students, not students as children. Teaching is expected to be performed as though it is a science, but this science is expected to be performed as though it is a 'craft'—imaginatively, carefully and skillfully. Teachers are expected to craft their students' learning so that it can be measured, and to do it in such a way that students also want it to be this way, desire it, desire achievement, desire teachers' reinforcement and approval. Students are expected to learn as a group yet at the same time to perform that learning as an individual, to both give over their power and demonstrate their power through self-control and self-discipline. For the most part, these contradictory expectations are not seen by teachers as they go about their daily work in schools as contradictory (even impossible) expectations.

CARE AND DISCIPLINE

The NSW Department of Education and Training (NSW DET, 2010c) advises teachers regarding the 'care and discipline' they are to provide for students. The dominant educational discourse exhorts that this care and discipline be exercised so that effective learning can take place and so that students may receive a quality education in a safe environment. This care and discipline is thought to ensure that thirty young individuals can work together in a confined space and learn what is defined as relevant within a specified timeframe.

In working with young children, teachers are advised to make sure that the power they have as teachers is covert and that they have a non-confrontational behaviour management style. With young children in particular, teachers are advised to nurture each child's self esteem, wellbeing and development (NSW DET, 2010c). "One of the hidden aspects of our cultural ideas about human development concerns our norms and expectations of people at different ages" (Bird and Drewery, 2000, p. 25) and, in line with these ideas, young children are seen to need nurturing. Teachers are expected to be "passive to the child's active" (Walkerdine, 1990, p.24) and to gradually transform the child into a student and themselves from mother to teacher. For the young child it is the teacher as mother who teaches children about the practices of power in the classroom (Walkerdine, 1990). Teachers are expected to empower children to make the right choices and to suppress overt demonstrations of their own power. Teachers' 'control' of students is expected to be achieved through a range strategies such as focussing on the positive, redirecting children from engaging in those behaviours seen as 'inappropriate', praising the good, and reprimanding the bad. This is to be done in a caring, loving yet *teacherly* way, focussing on the "work" of the teacher and, through "play", the learning of the child (Walkerdine, 1990, p. 22).

As children get older and make the transition from early learning to Primary settings, the teacher-as-mother role is expected to be abandoned by teachers, as in the dominant educational discourses an older child must not be 'molly-coddled' and inhibited from becoming an independent learner. It is now the teacher as sterner parent (perhaps father) who is expected to remind children of the rules and the learning required, and to use more overt power to discipline students' behaviour and learning. In secondary schools, students are expected to be students—independent yet part of the school group, creative yet scientific, caring yet strong. They are also permitted to use power in more overt ways to demonstrate their independence and strength. Secondary teachers are expected to focus both on disciplining and controlling students, and also on their own discipline—their teaching expertise. The focus is expected to be on demonstrating that students are learning what is prescribed for them to learn, when they are supposed to learn it. Bird and Drewery point to the "many practices which allow children to compare their performance with that of others of their age" (2000, p. 120). In spite of there being "not enough evidence to support the idea that all humans go through a universal sequence in the development of their thinking" (Bird and Drewery, 2000, p. 127), the dominant educational discourses require teachers to behave as though this evidence exists. They are expected to perform their teaching in a sequenced, rigorous and developmental way, and this teaching is subject to public scrutiny through standardised testing. With older students the power of teachers seems to be permitted to be more overt, perhaps to demonstrate that the school is an environment where learning is happening—as shown by the level of control of teachers over students.

Within the dominant educational discourses compliance of students is often read as an indication that learning is taking place. Teachers are expected to find ways to ensure that a child complies with requests so that effective learning can be seen to be taking place. While policies emphasise caring, there is also discipline, and all the contradictions that this pairing can bring. Discipline brings to my mind ideas about order and following of rules—using strategies that result in children doing as they are told so that a school is an ordered environment. Presumably, it is this order that will enhance, and even produce, learning. Certainly policy statements reinforce this belief (NSW DET 2006a). While discipline can be seen to be about an adult using discipline to control the child, the expectation placed on teachers is that this process of control cannot be too overt, as discipline can easily become punishment, and punishment is seen to have negative effects on children's self-esteem. Teachers are expected to build self-esteem, not damage it. The goal in the dominant discourses is for the child to be self-disciplined—to take on the rules and the behaviours required by the rules as though they are their own, and to control any actions, or even thoughts, that are against those rules. In the dominant discourses, being self-disciplined is thought to be a goal worthy of praise and reward, since it shows responsible, civilised behaviour. In the dominant, rationalist, humanist discourse, self-discipline (control of desires and emotions) is the sign of a caring and responsible individual.

The practice of school discipline leading to self-discipline involves power. Students are expected to acknowledge the rights of adults in schools to have power and to use that power to control them. Students are expected to give over their own power in the interest of harmony. The practice of discipline also involves demonstrating a kind of power in controlling oneself: this is seen in the dominant educational discourses as a 'good' sort of power. But in the dominant discourses, while teachers are expected to use their power, limits are placed on this use of power. Teachers' power cannot be too overt; they are expected to ensure that the power they have over students so that students will do their learning is both covert and caring.

In the regular school setting, these underlying expectations that everyone is being disciplined, and even self-disciplined, are not transparent. Children are taught that they have choices about how to behave, and that learning to make the right choices is demonstrating self-control, self-discipline. Children are to observe others making the right choices, and they are coached, both by teachers and other children, to make these right choices. Children soon learn to be *students* in schools—learning when they must work, when they must play, how they must learn, when they can be creative and in what environment, when to be silent, when to speak and "what can be spoken" (Walkerdine, 1990, p. 31).

Throughout their schooling, students can also exercise their power by the ways that they refuse to comply, or are abusive, or refuse to learn what they are told they need to learn. This power is also often covert, but the limits to its use are clearly defined in the dominant discourses. Students covertly demonstrate their power over teachers who are considered 'poor/weak/bad teachers'—those who cannot control a class, who are weak and not strong, who do not get results and whose students do not demonstrate learning. Students also demonstrate their power over teachers who are 'casual/substitute' and are not really part of the school but might be filling in for the 'real' teacher. While there are times when students are able, even expected, to exercise their power, there seem to be unspoken limits agreed upon between students and perhaps even students and teachers. Even being 'out of control' has to be performed in a controlled way.

Students who are 'out of control' too much, or perform being out of control with 'skilled/strong/good' teachers, stand out and come to be seen in the dominant educational discourses as being in need of strong discipline, lacking in self-discipline, poor students, problems. If these students do not respond to strong discipline and continue their misbehaviour then they come to be seen as having a 'poor grasp of reality', as being 'pathological' and in need of special help, as being disturbed. Too much activity, passion, anger, refusal, or resistance is pathologised. That children in schools who are "so obviously watched and monitored might still rebel" (Walkerdine, 1990, p. 31) is defined, in the dominant discourses, as a significant problem.

DEFINING PROBLEMATIC BEHAVIOURS

A review of students with special needs in NSW schools identified the behaviour of students as the issue that is the "most troublesome for schools, the most stressful for staff and the most unsettling for other students"

(McRae, 1996, p. 86). Problematic behaviour is seen as a significant issue for schools and a variety of terms are used to describe and sometimes identify antisocial, defiant, disruptive and/or aggressive behaviour. Terminology used includes antisocial, conduct disordered, behaviourally disturbed or disordered, socially or behaviourally maladjusted, disruptive, delinquent or pre-delinquent, and severely emotional disturbed (Breen and Alterpeter, 1990; Davies, 1996; Kauffman, 1993; Walker, Colvin and Ramsey, 1995). There is a lack of consensus in definition and terminology in this area (Laughlin, 1998) and there is no universally accepted definition of emotional and/or behavioural disorders and/or disturbances and/or difficulties.

The very label ascribed to the 'problem' carries with it implications for how the 'problem' is being made sense of, solved. The label ascribed in the dominant discourses also defines the believed solutions. If the term 'behaviour' is used, then the ideas around such a definition include that it is the action and the effect of the action that are the focus, not the intent of the behaviour, or the mental or emotional state of the person performing the behaviour, or the social setting in which the behaviour takes place. If the term 'emotional' is used, then there is thought to be a sense of the involvement of the individual and the state of her/his emotions while the behaviour is happening. The term 'disorder' brings to mind a medical approach, 'disturbance' a mental health approach, and 'difficulties' a seemingly more 'objective' view of the impact of the behaviour on others and also on the individual.

Kauffman (1999) proposed that 'emotional/behavioural disorders' be the common term used, and for the purposes of beginning this discussion, I will use this term. It blends the medical/psychiatric terms 'emotional' and 'disorders' with a learning theory approach involving 'behaviour'. This is indicative of the blending of discursive practices through which these children are 'diagnosed' and 'treated'.

Kauffman (1993) also proposed that many agree on a common set of persistent characteristics of those children with 'emotional/behavioural disorders'. These include: problems with learning at school; poor interpersonal relationships; inappropriate behaviour including antisocial, defiant, disruptive and aggressive behaviours; pervasive unhappiness or depression; and physical symptoms or fears associated with school or personal problems. While the school in my study provided enrolment for students with a range of difficulties/disorders/disturbances, almost all students had a clinical diagnosis of 'conduct disorder' or 'oppositional defiant disorder'. These labels come from a mental health framework and are defined in the Diagnostic and Statistical Manual of Mental Disorders, Fourth Edition (DSM-IV) (American Psychiatric Association, 1994).

DEFINING THE PROBLEM—MENTAL HEALTH FRAMEWORK

How children with 'emotional/behavioural disorders' are identified in the twenty first century is important since it is the definition that results in the provision of services. While it is estimated that up to 20% of students have difficulties with behaviour at some time in their schooling, prevalence estimates suggest that 3-6% of school-aged children have 'emotional/behavioural disorders' requiring professional attention. However, less than 1% are identified and provided with services (Eber and Nelson, 1997; Walker *et al.*, 1995). Kauffman (1999) estimates that for perhaps 5-10% of students in general education, intensive individualised intervention is needed. But to access services such as those provided by the school in this study, a mental health diagnosis is required. To be 'treated', the dominant discourses require that children must first be named as 'ill'.

Some researchers claim that aggressive behaviour is a relatively stable human characteristic throughout the lifespan, second only to IQ in its enduring nature (Davison and Neale, 1990; Kauffman, 1993). The early indicators of aggressive and oppositional behaviour are thought to be apparent in the preschool years, and if not effectively 'treated' by time the child is about eight years old, are considered likely to continue (and worsen) into adolescence (Campbell, 1995; Sanders, Markie-Dadds and Turner, 1994). Children with 'emotional/behavioural disorders' are seen to follow a developmental trajectory in which the antisocial acts they engage in become more and more serious, and intervention becomes less and less effective (Walker *et al.*, 1998; Gentleman, Burtt and D'Arcy, 1996). Consequently, it is thought that with earlier identification and intervention, it is likelier that serious antisocial acts will be prevented (Kauffman, 1999). Thus, in the dominant discourses, identification of these children is seen as important, not only so that they gain access to services but also because, in failing to identify them, these children are thought to be put at risk of never 'getting better'.

DIAGNOSTIC AND STATISTICAL MANUAL OF MENTAL DISORDERS (DSM-IV)

DSM-IV provides the diagnostic criteria for the clinical diagnosis of conduct disorder (CD), oppositional defiant disorder (ODD), and disruptive behaviour disorder not otherwise specified (DBD). Diagnoses of these disorders are deemed to be made reliably only by trained clinicians (American Psychiatric Association, 1994), generally psychiatrists and clinical psychologists. While diagnoses are generally made through interviews with children and their parents, information from other sources, such as schools, is often sought to give a complete picture of the problematic behaviour. Standardised behavioural checklists completed by a number of people (child, family, teachers, peers) are thought to provide the most reliable assessment, when combined with interviews and behavioural observations made over multiple settings (Achenbach, 1991; Hart, Lahey, Loeber and Hanson, 1994).

DSM-IV defines the essential feature of conduct disorder as

> a repetitive and persistent pattern of behaviour in which the basic rights of others or major age-appropriate societal norms or rules are violated. (American Psychiatric Association, 1994, p. 85).

Four groups of behaviours are defined: being aggressive, deliberate property destruction, deceitfulness/theft, and serious rule violation. To confirm a diagnosis, three or more behaviours must have been present during the past twelve months, with at least one present in the past six months, and the behaviour disturbance must seriously impair social, academic or occupational functioning. DSM-IV outlines two subtypes of conduct disorder, childhood onset (onset prior to ten years of age) and adolescent onset (onset in adolescence with the absence of any criteria prior to ten years of age). Each of these subtypes is further specified by three levels of severity: mild, moderate and severe.

Although oppositional defiant disorder includes some of the criteria for conduct disorder, in medical discourses it is seen to differ due to the proposed absence of serious violations of societal rules and of the rights of others. DSM-IV defines the essential feature of oppositional defiant disorder as

> a recurrent pattern of negativistic, defiant, disobedient and hostile behaviour towards authority figures that persists for at least six months. (American Psychiatric Association, 1994, p. 91).

Behaviours include losing temper, arguing and non-compliance with adults, and deliberately annoying others. For a diagnosis of oppositional defiant disorder to be made, the behaviours must occur more frequently than those typically observed in age-equivalent peers, and must seriously impair functioning in social, academic or occupational spheres.

Males dominate the field of 'emotional/behavioural disorders', with DSM-IV reporting the prevalence of conduct disorder as 2-16% of males under the age of eighteen years, and 2-9% of females under the age of eighteen years (American Psychiatric Association, 1994).

While it is considered that many children and adolescents will, at some time in their development, engage in antisocial, defiant, disruptive and/or aggressive behaviour, few will ever attract a label of a 'disorder'. What is considered to distinguish 'disordered' from 'normal' behaviour, in the dominant psychological discourses, is the magnitude, frequency, intensity and duration of the behaviours (Breen and Alterpeter, 1990; Cole and Visser, 1999; Cooper, Smith and Upton, 1994; Walker *et al.*, 1995). By placing behaviour on such a continuum—frequency, intensity and duration —the dominant psychological discourses ensures that there will always be a population of those who are to be categorised as outside the norm: the abnormal.

Rarely is one disorder considered to occur alone. In the dominant psychological discourses there is seen to be considerable overlap, for example, between conduct disorder, oppositional defiant disorder and attention deficit hyperactivity disorder (Breen and Alterpeter, 1990), and also a developmental *progression* from early oppositional/defiant behaviour to later conduct problems (Caron and Rutter, 1991). The aggressive and oppositional behaviours associated with 'emotional/behavioural disorders' are often referred to as *externalising* behaviours (Achenbach, 1991). Thus, it is the impact of the behaviour on other people and things *external* to the child that is of most concern in the dominant psychological discourses. Yet there is considered to be a high co-occurrence of conduct and oppositional defiant disorders and depression, anxiety and learning difficulties (Caron and Rutter, 1991). In spite of this, the focus is on behaviours that are seen to violate societal norms through their negative impact upon others, rather than on depression. The aggressive and non-compliant behaviours of children with 'emotional/behavioural disorders' and the negative impact of these behaviours on those around them generally ensure that these children become a focus for treatment services.

HISTORICAL ASPECTS

A mental health framework for defining and providing services for children with 'emotional/behavioural disorders' is a relatively recent phenomenon of the twentieth century. Children presenting problematic behaviour have been executed, incarcerated, cared for, treated, punished or educated depending on the approach of the time. For example, in 1684 a hospital for boys and girls under twenty five years of age was created in Paris. It specified that work must occupy the greater part of the day, accompanied by reading pious books, with children made to work long and hard. Every fault was to be punished by a reduction of food, an increase of work, imprisonment and other punishments (Foucault, 1988). In England in 1785, 90% of those executed were under twenty one years of age (West, 1967). For those who were not dealt with in this way, exorcisms, physical restraints, bloodletting, as well as regular beatings were considered appropriate (Davison and Neale, 1990). This way of dealing with young people who did not fit was replaced in the mid-nineteenth century with a more sympathetic movement towards children and the establishment of large, residential industrial schools (Cole, 1989). Here, those who did not fit were placed in large institutions and prepared for work in factories. Towards the end of the nineteenth century, along with the moves for universal education, the large institutions began to be seen as too punishing and smaller cottages and homes were set up for children. The vast majority of these children were from families living in poverty. At the same time some children were placed into adult asylums. In the early twentieth century, children in England presenting problematic behaviour came to be seen as 'maladjusted'. There was more of a focus on democratic settings as providing the best way to help 'maladjusted' children adjust to a supportive, democratic society, as well as on seeing the children as having 'mental health needs'.

After the second world war, 'maladjusted' children continued to be placed in settings separate from regular schools and a more humane, caring view of these children was apparent. They were seen as unhappy individuals who

> fail in their personal relationships. Receiving is difficult for them as well as giving, and they appear unable to respond to simple measures of love, comfort and reassurance. At the same time, they are not readily capable of improvement by ordinary discipline. (Ministry of Education (Britain), 1955, p. 22).

In the 1960s and 1970s the dominant educational practices around maladjusted students involved a humanist approach, with a focus on developing relationships with teachers that would lead to students learning life skills and self-management skills (Wilson and Evans, 1980). In the 1980s maladjusted children were seen as basically 'normal' children reacting in sometimes extreme and unsocial ways to abnormal childhood experiences (Cole and Visser, 1999). It began to be thought that a structured education in a location separate from regular school students with small class sizes but with the same curricula might be all that was required. This thinking was accompanied by a more behaviourist approach, the problem being constructed as outside the child and the problem *behaviour* being separate from the identity of the child. Through such a separation the problem could be worked on through behaviourist technology that looked at managing the events that were seen to provide stimuli for the problematic behaviour (and its positive and negative consequences), and that sought to manipulate and extinguish inappropriate responses from the child. Such a 'scientific' approach was moderated toward the end of the decade by a cognitivist-behaviourist approach, including the child's thinking in the equation. This meant that, as well as managing the stimuli and responses through events contingent on the responses, what children were saying inside their heads was also seen as contributing to inappropriate behaviour, and training to change an individual's 'self-talk' was implemented. At this time there was a focus on equity; the curriculum that students were receiving needed to be in line with that received by students in regular schools so that 'disturbed/disordered' students had the same access to educational success as non-disturbed/disordered students.

In the latter part of the twentieth century the focus was still on the *behaviour* being disordered or disturbed, but these behaviours were often understood as learned in response to imperfect school environments or flawed teaching. This was in line with the school effectiveness literature (Cuttance, 1994) that saw differences in outcomes between schools as independent of the students and more to do with the school culture and performance of the teachers. The ways that children presenting problematic behaviour have been viewed, and the responses to these views, parallel the ways children in general have been viewed, the ways we have searched for explanations of behaviour in general, the ways disciplines such as psychology, sociology and education have developed, and the sociopolitical thinking of the times.

In the early part of the twenty first century, in the dominant educational discourses the focus for teaching is on producing students who can "compete in the global economy on knowledge and innovation" (MCEETYA, 2008, p. 4). This is thought to be achieved through explicit and visible teaching (Hattie, 2009), as are the results of teaching made visible by the publication of student assessment results. There is thought to be "agreement on and consistency around what constitutes quality teaching" (MCEECDYA, 2003, p. 2), so as well as being explicit about what they are teaching, teachers are also required to incorporate values education and subject learning at the same time, linking with each other as some type of double helix (Lovat and Clement, 2008). In the field of special education, the New South Wales Parliament Legislative Council (2010, p. 141) believes better individualised learning programs are an answer to the challenge of teaching students with disabilities. There is a contradictory double bind of inclusion: on the one hand, dominant educational discourses propose that students with special needs should be educated within regular or mainstream classrooms rather than in segregated settings (NSW Government, 2010, p. 8); at the same time students with challenging behaviours are to be excluded from regular schools because of their violence (NSW DET, 2010b).

No phase of this development in beliefs about teaching children has presented a clear abandoning of a previous view. Rather, the contradictions seem to blend together to form seemingly cohesive discourses. Inevitably, then, the education of students presenting problematic behaviours is a site of much debate and of strongly held views similar to those held about the whole area of education. In spite of the differences in views, the thinking is fixed firmly within a rationalist, humanist discourse.

PROBLEM—MOSTLY THE FAULT OF THE CHILD

Medical/psychiatric discourses are dominant in making sense of the behaviour of children categorised as 'emotionally/behaviourally disordered'. While there are certainly different approaches, such as those offered by critical psychology, seeing the problem *within* the child is the main way problematic behaviour is constituted through the dominant educational and psychological discourses. This is evidenced by policy documents (NSW DET, 1999b) and the training and support available to schools through school mental health programs (Commonwealth of Australia, 2005). The dominant educational and psychological discourses include biological explanations such as inherited chromosomal abnormalities, chemical malfunctions and other physical factors. Lytton (1990) asserts the primacy of biological explanations, putting forward evidence of these students' under-responsiveness to punishment and social reinforcement, lower galvanic skin response to intense or threatening stimuli, and a range of biochemical differences, as well as the effect of temperament. In addition, Lytton draws evidence from the "relatively high incidence" of minor physical abnormalities, such as "curved fifth finger or wide gap between the first and second toe" (Lytton, 1990, p. 691). While Lytton's claims are strongly disputed (Dodge, 1990), some support remains for a level of biological/neurobiological causality, and this is indicated by the level of medication prescribed for children presenting problematic behaviours. Drugs such as Ritalin and dexamphetamines are increasingly prescribed for children who have been diagnosed as having an attention deficit (Livingstone, 1997; Runnheim, Frankenberger and Hazelkorn, 1996; Mackey and Kopras, 2001).

PROBLEM—MOSTLY THE FAULT OF THE PARENTS

In the pursuit of causal explanations for problematic behaviour there has been much debate about the relative effects of within-child factors and also of environmental factors, largely parenting and family factors (Kauffman, 1993). There seems to be general consensus in the dominant discourses that parenting/family factors reciprocally influence child factors in the development of 'emotional/behavioural disorders'. Parental factors include psychopathology, paternal criminality, marital conflict, alcohol abuse, harsh and inconsistent discipline practices, poor supervision and monitoring of the child's behaviour, large family size, and socioeconomic disadvantage (Sanders *et al.*, 1994) as well as low warmth and responsiveness, and insecure or disorganised attachment patterns (Campbell, 1995).

In deconstructing these dominant discourses, a different reading might focus on issues of extreme poverty in the lives of many students categorised as 'emotionally/behaviourally disordered'. Yet such a focus is made almost invisible through the ways in which the dominant discourses focus on the lack of appropriate parenting skills. Parent training programs, or behaviourist family interventions, are seen in the dominant discourses as an effective prevention and/or treatment of behaviour problems in children. Interventions generally aim to develop parents' skills in teaching their children core social and behavioural competencies (Sanders and Markie-Dadds, 1996, pp. 69-70).

An approach that tries not to blame solely the parents or solely the child involves the child and his/her environment reciprocally influencing each other (Dodge, 1990). The most influential within-child factor is considered to be a child being 'born with a difficult temperament', although the child's temperament is not seen to automatically predict an outcome of an 'emotional/behavioural disorder'. Thomas and Chess (1986) proposed the concept of 'goodness of fit' between the child's temperament and the parenting style employed, in the development of aversive or optimal outcomes.

There is also a growing perspective that childhood abuse (physical, psychological, sexual and/or neglectful) contributes to the development of problematic behaviour. Petit and Brook (1998) propose that cognitive distortions, as well as many of the behaviours that are later displayed toward others, are developed through exposure to abuse. Proponents of the theory of emotional intelligence describe how early abuse not only teaches aggression, but leads to "the extinction of empathy" (Goleman, 1996, p. 196).

PROBLEM—MOSTLY FAULTY LEARNING

In the behaviourist psychological discourse, children presenting problematic behaviour can be thought to have deficits in the skills required to interact with others positively, deal with their anger, control their emotions and/or care about themselves or others. They are seen as either not knowing the skills or not knowing how or when to perform the skills (or both), and so intensive teaching of these skills is required (Elksnin and Elksnin, 1995). According to Dodge (1986, in Walker *et al.*, 1995), children with behaviour problems have deficits in processing social information, and make frequent errors in interpreting the social cues and behaviour of other children and adults. They are likely to attribute hostile intentions to accidental or ambiguous behaviour and, as a result, respond inappropriately, thus affecting responses of others, and so on. Children with emotional/behavioural disorders are seen as either being deficient in specific areas (such as reading social cues or reading intentions) or as having an excess of extreme responses. In either case, in the dominant discourses, teaching the unlearned (self-control) skills is seen as fundamental to changing problematic behaviour. The teaching of these skills could involve a process of training in the performance of skills, and/or the use of a cognitive framework of self-talk to change children's thinking about, and therefore their responses to, situations that elicit negative behaviour (Goldstein, 1988).

Although there is a persistent belief that a social skills training approach can stop problematic behaviour,

Gresham (1998), in his overview of the research into social skills training, found weak evidence for the efficacy of social skills training, particularly on direct measures of social behaviour in naturalistic settings. The greatest weakness revealed in the social skills training literature is the absence of consistent, durable gains across situations and settings over time (Gresham, 1998, p. 20). Although the literature is replete with suggestions and tactics for promoting the transfer of social skills, students trained in these skills nevertheless seem to fail to perform these skills in the 'real' world (Mathur and Rutherford, 1996). That children know the appropriate social skills, but fail to perform them in the regular school setting, is explained as a deficit in performance or generalisation (Stokes and Baer, 1977; Gresham, 1998). The focus, following this reasoning, moved to training of skills in the regular setting, and/or training in a way that promotes generalisation. While even in the dominant behaviourist psychological discourse there is little evidence for the efficacy of social skills training, the strategy is persistently refined and revised. The journals that specialise in behaviour management generally publish only on aspects of the one approach and, in the special education discourse, problematising the behaviour of students in any other way remains almost invisible.

PROBLEM—PARTLY THE FAULT OF FRIENDSHIPS

In the dominant discourses, children presenting problematic behaviours are often seen as being rejected by other children because of the inappropriate social and sometimes violent behaviour that they exhibit (Cullinan, Sabornie and Crossland, 1992). Social status problems in relation to peers early in a child's school career are thought to correlate with later juvenile delinquency (Cullinan *et al.*, 1992). Consequently, ways of facilitating positive interactions with peers are sought. Schools are seen as key places where children interact with their peers, and are seen as important places where children with 'emotional/behavioural disorders' can learn to get along with others and make friends. Teachers are asked to construct situations where children with 'emotional/behavioural disorders' can be socially accepted by peers, have at least one reciprocal friendship, and be "active and equal participants in activities" performed by the peer group (Cullinan *et al.*, 1992, p. 340).

While children with problematic behaviours can be rejected by those 'without' behaviour problems, they can also be considered at risk from others with worse behaviour problems. It is seen as typical for antisocial children to associate with other antisocial children at school, as their 'regular' peers reject or avoid them (Conway, 1994b; Walker *et al.*, 1995). It is also supposed that association with difficult peers is strongly influential in the further development of difficult behaviours (Alloy, Acocella and Bottzin, 1996). In this way, relationships with particular types of peers are read in the dominant discourses as either increasing or decreasing problematic behaviour. Yet there are many possible ways to read the dynamics of behaviour of students in schools. The behaviour of the 'regular' students who reject the problem students is not viewed, as it might be, as aggressive behaviour or bullying. Rather, aggression towards and rejection of those students positioned as disturbed by 'regular/normal' students can be read as regular students engaging in constructing the 'right' kind of social order (Ellwood and Davies, 2010).

PROBLEM—PARTLY THE FAULT OF TEACHERS

Within dominant educational and psychological discourses 'poor fit' between a teacher's style and a child's temperament is seen to exacerbate problematic behaviours. Much of the 'expert' advice for teachers positions teachers as critical, even instrumental in exacerbating or reducing problematic behaviour. Difficulties of children with 'emotional/behavioural disorders' in regular classrooms are thus often attributed to incompatibilities between students and teachers. Effective classrooms for difficult students are conceptually constructed as those where the environment is "nurturing, consistent and fair" (Kauffman, 1993, p. 346). Hall, Williams and Hall advise that effective classroom interventions should focus on "comfort, not confrontation; support, not shaming; and bonding, not belittling" (2000, p. 21). Ineffective instructional practices, unmonitored repeated academic failure, and low levels of academic engagement are also seen to generate negative behaviours. A teacher's tolerance of a child's behaviour is seen as influential in labelling a behaviour, the expectations and the consequent behaviours displayed (Conway, 1994b; Safran and Safran, 1988). Implicit in this view is the belief that ineffective teachers confront, shame and belittle, and that this not only exacerbates the difficulties of children with 'emotional/behavioural disorders', but might even cause them. In contrast, effective teachers engineer the learning situation such that students acquire appropriate behaviours.

Teachers are therefore asked to increase their positive interactions with students, deliver more positive consequences and praise students more (Shores, 1992). As well as being confident in their ability to help students learn and behave appropriately, and believing that teaching can change children, teachers are advised to use interventions that teach students how to behave and praise them for doing so (Cole and Visser, 1999). The dominant educational discourses position effective teachers as those who can possibly prevent, if not the development, then the exacerbation of problematic behaviour.

To be read as 'good' teachers in the dominant educational discourses, teachers are expected to develop an effective behaviour management program that meets the needs of all students and, at the same time, meets the specific needs of students presenting problematic behaviours. Teachers are required to be consistent, yet fair, in their application of behaviourist and cognitivist-behaviourist management techniques, to structure the use of antecedents that promote appropriate behaviour, and to avoid the use of antecedents that increase problem behaviour. 'Good' teachers also use structured teaching, set routines and clear rules with contingent consequences (Hall *et al.*, 2000). At the same time they ensure that instruction is effective and the curriculum is appropriate to students' needs—as well as comforting, supporting and bonding with students. The prescriptions for getting it right as effective teachers might seem impossible to fulfill. Yet if these prescriptions are not at least attempted, or seen by students, parents, other teachers and supervisors to be attempted, then teachers are at risk of being read not only as ineffective but also as exacerbating and even causing the problematic behaviour of some students.

PROBLEM—MOSTLY THE FAULT OF SCHOOLS

In the dominant special education discourse, students with 'emotional/behavioural disorders' are read as demonstrating learned behaviours or responses to imperfect school environments and flawed teaching rather than expressing within-child emotional factors (Cole and Visser, 1999, p. 61). Conway (1994b, p. 306, citing Kauffman, 1985) suggests that schools might contribute to behaviour disorders through: teachers' and peers' insensitivity to a child's individuality; inappropriate expectations of students on the part of teachers; inconsistent behaviour management; instruction in irrelevant skills; inappropriate contingencies of reinforcement; and teachers and/or peers modelling undesirable behaviour. This view seems to be supported by the work of people such as Rutter (Rutter, Maughan, Mortimer and Ousten, 1979), who questioned why schools differ in their number of difficulties when their student populations are similar (Rutter *et al.*, 1979). Hence 'problem behaviour' can be seen as a social construct that appropriate school cultures can significantly deal with.

NOT A PROBLEM BUT A DISABILITY

Children with behavior problems can sometimes be seen as having a disability, especially if they have been given a label under the DSM-IV as having a mental health problem. Under the NSW Anti-Discrimination Act 1977 and amendments (NSW Government, 1977) the term disability includes a disorder, illness or disease that affects a person's thought processes. This legislation applies to 'emotionally/behaviourally disordered' students as they could be seen to have a disorder, a malfunction and/or to learn differently.

The NSW legislation also applies to education in that it is unlawful in NSW to refuse an application from a person with a disability for admission as a student, or to discriminate in the terms or conditions on which a school is prepared to admit a person (NSW Government, 1977). It is also unlawful for an educational authority to discriminate against a student on grounds of the student's disability by denying or limiting access to any benefit provided by the educational authority, or by expelling the student, or by subjecting the student to any other detriment. It is policy in NSW that people with disabilities should be able to live in and be educated within their own communities. This policy is based on the principle of 'normalisation', that is, the creation of a lifestyle and set of living conditions for people with disabilities that are as close as possible to those enjoyed by the rest of the population.

Students with an 'emotional/behavioural disorder' are considered to have the right to access regular schools. There is, in policy, a belief that all students with disabilities have the right to 'normalisation' and that those with disabilities will be provided with the same range of educational opportunities as other people (NSW DET, 2005). This is reinforced nationally by disability standards, which "provide a framework to ensure that students with disability are able to access and participate in education on the same basis as other students" (Australian Government, 2005, p. iii). However, the NSW Enrolment of Students policy (NSW DET, 1996a) states that principals need not enrol a student who has a record of violence unless the student has participated in a program to decrease the violence. As violent behaviour is often displayed by students with 'emotional/behaviour disorders' (this being the basis of their classification), their access to enrolment in regular school is, in practice, precarious. The precariousness of continuing enrolment for difficult students has become even more of a focus in terms of the occupational health and safety of school personnel. The legal requirement of providing safe workplaces for students and staff means that students who have a history of violence may not be enrolled in government schools in NSW unless a risk assessment indicates that the school can satisfactorily manage potential safety issues (NSW DET, 2007). By the very definition of 'emotional/behaviour disorders', the behaviour of disordered students can be seen to violate the idea that other students have the right to expect that they will spend the school day free from the fear of bullying, harassment, intimidation and victimisation (NSW DET, 2006). At the same time, the Council of Australian Governments (COAG, 2008) has agreed to place people with disability, their families and carers at the centre of services across Australia. Being an inclusive school is seen by policy makers to be positive: "an inclusive school is measured by the degree to which each and every student in it is provided for and is successfully achieving, rather than by its type or category" (NSW DET, 1999a, p. 5). Regular schools are required to keep children safe, not tolerate violence, and yet be inclusive of those who perform violence.

NOT A PROBLEM BUT A DISADVANTAGE

Issues for students categorised as 'emotionally/behaviourally disordered' can also be cast in a sociopolitical framework. The overwhelming majority of these children are boys (American Psychiatric Association, 1994) from socially and economically disadvantaged groups (Sanders *et al.*, 1994). In America, African-American students are one and a half times more likely to be identified as having a 'severe emotional disturbance' than non-African-American students (Coutinho and Oswald, 1998), and African-American males are placed in special education services more often than African-American females (Harry, 1994). If this is viewed from a perspective of identifying the social structures and ideologies that influence society (Habermas, 1971), then identification and categorising of the 'disturbed' could be seen more as a social and a class issue than a mental health issue. Rather than being seen as disturbed, the inappropriate behaviours might be seen as understandable responses to extreme situations. The sociopolitical issues around students with 'emotional/behavioural disorders' are seldom explored. While the statistics are not hidden, they are made almost invisible; they are seldom a focus for discussion. Yet in a recent discussion in a journal of behavioral disorders, Harry, Hart, Klingner and Cramer (2008, p. 169) "highlight the arbitrary and detrimental decision making that results in inappropriate placement of minorities in special education". The response from an editor of the journal countered that a "world without labels and categories for educational purposes would be chaotic and brutal" (Kauffman, Simpson and Mock, 2009, p. 177). A child not having a label and hence access to services can be read as inequitable; a society's desire to be non-discriminatory leads to failure to identify children in need and to deliver to them specialist services. The desire to be non-discriminatory can derive from a fear that labelling the poor as disturbed will further position them as a group to be despised, even feared. In spite of the over-representation of the poor in emotional/behavioural disorder categorisation, their behaviour is seldom constructed as an issue predominantly relating to poverty, marginalisation and oppression in a society.

TREATING THE PROBLEM

The ways that problematic behaviour of children is made sense of in the dominant discourses are multiple and contradictory. The 'problem' can be seen as belonging to/the fault of parents, peers, poor learning and teaching, schooling itself, social class, or as the construction of disadvantage or disability—and often all at the same time. Yet the dominant solution to the problem remains the treatment of the individual child. Students who exhibit behaviour(s) characteristic of mental health problems, at a level of frequency, duration and intensity that seriously affects their educational functioning and emotional wellbeing, are referred by regular schools to specialist educational programs (NSW DET, 1999b). While regular schools are encouraged in policy to use all their resources before referring a child for specialist intervention, early intervention is also encouraged, as it is believed that it may be better to use off-site intervention early in order to "prevent incarceration strategies later on" (Kauffman, 1999, p. 453).

Special classes for 'emotionally disordered/disturbed' students in regular schools provide short to medium term segregated programs, with varying degrees of integration into regular classes. They aim to return the students to a regular classroom. Special units and schools, residential schools, and classes for 'emotionally disordered/disturbed' students require that students have a clinical diagnosis, and anticipate the student's gradual, supported return to the regular setting. Some residential schools operate joint programs with Department of Health personnel, and so provide interventions such as family therapy and psychological and psychiatric interventions (NSW DET, 1996b, 1999a). In addition, the NSW Department of Education and Training operates special schools for students with severe behaviour disorders and histories of violence and unsuccessful intervention programs. At these schools, medium to long term placements are available to students with little specific requirement for their return to the mainstream setting.

'Best practice' for students with 'emotional/behavioural disorders' was identified in a NSW Department of Education and Training review by Laughlin in 1998. These best practices were facilitated by teachers who were trained in behaviourist management techniques, and who provided continuously assessed and monitored programs. Best practice was defined as involving a continuum of services, and interagency co-ordination and co-operation. Kauffman (1999, p. 450) summarised the research and concluded that programs for students with 'emotional/behavioural disorders' should be based on rewarding of desirable behaviour, non-violent punishment of inappropriate behaviour, effective instruction in basic skills and social skills, and correction of environmental (for example familial/residential/peer) conditions that foster deviant behaviour. This special education discourse focuses on learning, with teachers responsible for ensuring that students learn different (better) ways to behave so that they can comply with the requirements of the regular school environment.

Throughout the past decade this approach has moved from the specialist environment to the regular school environment, where there have been emphases on behaviour management strategies and school-wide positive behaviour support, as influenced by the work of Lewis and Sugai (1999). In this approach there is also a strong emphasis on collecting data, hypothesising a function of the misbehaviour (usually constructed as a desire to escape or access something), and then developing a plan to intervene and change the misbehaviour. The plans commonly involve teaching the 'desired' replacement behaviours to students, and changing the environment in order to decrease reinforcement of the undesired behaviours. The instructional environment needs to be organised to reinforce the pro-social replacement responses.

Sugai and Horner (2006) refer to the growing attention to adopting practices that represent "what we know about the science of human behaviour" (p. 246) and the growing adoption of the 'positive behaviour support' approach. They acknowledge that this approach has been established for many years within the behaviour field and has an extensive empirical history. They also discuss the importance of system wide support, and funding for training and coaching as well as political support, as key to the ongoing success of this approach in schools. In a country dominated by economic rationalist discourse, where there is a focus on data and evidence, it is not surprising to see this recent increase in the implementation of behavioural interventions to deal with the challenging behaviour of students.

Current specialist services for students with problem behaviours are intended to provide even more intensive, individualised educational and behaviour management programs. The 'intensive' nature of the program is considered by education authorities to be provided by the child:adult ratio in specialist settings, that is, six to seven students to each teacher. The ratio is designed to allow more time to be spent with each child in order to 'individualise' instruction. Most children with 'emotional/behavioural disorders' are assessed as below the average in performance in basic numeracy and literacy skills, and poor educational performance is linked to difficulties with behaviour (Coleman, 1996). In 'special' education the specialised teaching strategies used, such as direct instruction (Englemann and Carnine, 1992), are developed for individualised instruction. The cornerstone of direct instruction is the systematic, explicit teaching of academic strategies to students (Gersten, Woodward and Darch, 1986). In practice, this means using explicit step-by-step strategies (and/or modelling effective performance) where students are required to develop mastery at each step in the process through systematic practice with a range of examples (Gersten *et al.*, 1986).

While special education is supposed to be special in its use of more precise teaching technologies, the curriculum applying to general education is also mandated by education authorities. For example, in the teaching of reading this means special educators also need to take into account general education approaches including: understanding what the reader brings to the process; increasing time spent in regular classrooms on a range of literacy and writing tasks, especially those that develop comprehension and analytic skills; and knowing the way regular students often direct and plan their own learning tasks (Gersten and Dimino, 1993). As well as using 'special' approaches, special education teachers are also required to use strategies that will enable students to connect with regular classroom practice (NSW DET, 2003).

The dominant special education discourse also requires teachers to provide the same caring environment for all students (NSW DET, 1996c). This 'caring' is enacted in the special school through strategies that closely watch the students and their behaviour. Perhaps the close surveillance of children and their behaviour is the way special programs are expected to perform their caring. At the same time as being caring, special education teachers are expected to implement programs that change inappropriate behaviour through individual *behaviour management* programs. While the general 'caring and disciplined' approaches are the same for both regular and special schools, the special school's way of doing this is more specific and detailed. The broad culture of caring and discipline is added to in the special school by the use of detailed behaviour management strategies based on individual behaviours for each child. Students in the special school operate in a context of these strategies and come to know the ways of getting the reinforcement they desire for completing tasks and performing required behaviours.

Individualised behaviour management programs are based on as much information as possible about the child's behaviour—defining the specific behaviours, discovering the stimuli for the behaviours and identifying the reinforcers for the behaviours. Teachers in specialist settings are advised through policy and research to observe children's misbehavior to see how the behaviour is performed, how often it occurs, where it occurs, with whom it occurs, how long it lasts, and how damaging/destructive it is (O'Neill, Horner, Albin, Sprague, Storey and Newton, 1997). Once such a functional assessment has operationally defined all the problem behaviours of concern, a specific plan to manage the behaviours is developed. Such a plan includes identifying the critical features that shape all of the elements of the intervention, the specific changes that need to occur in the behaviour of teachers, and any changes in physical setting, timetable, or teacher behaviour. The dominant special education discourse stipulates that effective plans should be logical and consistent with assessment assumptions. The plan for behaviour-change must involve procedures that are socially acceptable, likely to be both effective and possible within the local context. There must be monitoring procedures to assess both the problem behaviours and the larger lifestyle patterns of the student, and also an evaluation component with regular assessment of the effects of the plan (Horner, O'Neill and Flannery, 1993).

An intensive behaviour management plan needs to include carefully thought out and inscribed consequences —both positive and negative. Often extreme forms of 'consequences' can be used in special settings. Sometimes 'time-out' is used as a consequence for non-compliance. During this time-out—this isolation—students are asked to speculate on ways that they can get it right—get it right as a student and make better choices. Physical restraint of students with 'emotional/behavioural disorders' is a practice sometimes used in special settings, yet rarely observed in regular school settings.

There appear to be three main ways of making sense of physical restraint of children with 'emotional/behavioural disorders'. The first way is in the context of cognitivist-behaviourist psychology that is applicable to students in both regular and specialist settings. Here students' freedom to move around the classroom or the school is restrained. Glasser (1986), for example, outlines ten steps to classroom discipline wherein students who present problematic behaviours are required to go to an isolation area in the classroom. If the problematic behaviour continues they are then required to go to an isolation area in the school, and may possibly be required to leave the school if problematic behaviour still continues. These ideas are based on restricting students' access to desired activities in class and with peers. The isolation and restraint of movement is thought to give students time to reflect on their poor behaviour and make a plan to get their behaviour right.

A second way of making sense of physical restraint relates to the idea of a 'duty of care,' where physical restraint is associated with extreme risk and teachers have duty of care to intervene to prevent injury. Teachers have a duty to act reasonably in the interests of maintaining order and/or preserving the safety of persons or property (NSW DET, 1983).

The third view of physical restraint comes from the ideas around therapeutic intervention. While this can be in the context of behaviour management strategies (Ross, 1981), more often it has a psychological/psychiatric base. The ideas about therapeutic communities seem to arise from a number of theories but particularly those of Laing (1969), whose interventions in a therapeutic community in a psychiatric hospital focused on the positive outcomes of therapeutic relationships between therapists and clients. In this context patients may be held and physically restrained when they are out of control. Therapists and allied personnel work with the clients—taking control for them—holding them until they can get back in control. The strength of the helping relationship is thought to be a key therapeutic intervention for clients—one that can help lead to patients taking control for themselves and to recovery. Many teachers in special education sites are trained in physical restraint that can be defined as "the forcible and involuntary deprivation of the liberty to move about" (Smith, Johnson, Fox, Nihart, Schindler and Smiar, 1993, p. 29). Physical restraint is only recommended when all other techniques have been exhausted and when the individual presents a danger to him/herself or to others. "Taking physical control of a person when he has lost complete control of himself is the most therapeutic process possible" (Crisis Prevention Institute, 1987, p. 9s).

It is only recently that physical restraint in either its therapeutic or behaviour learning guise has come to be seriously questioned in the field of 'emotional/behavioural disorders'. The Council for Children with Behavioral Disorders (CCBDa, 2009, p. 224) claims that the current purpose of physical restraint is to control the behaviour of a student in an emergency situation in order to prevent immediate danger or possible injuries to that student or to others. The Council also claims that most professionals believe that seclusion is warranted only when a student's behaviour is so out of control or so dangerous that, in the current environment, it poses a risk of injury to the student or to others (CCBDb, 2009, p. 234). However, because the idea of time-out from positive reinforcement can be employed without the use of seclusion, a limit on seclusion does not prevent the use of time-out from positive reinforcement as a behaviour-change strategy when employed correctly (CCBDb, 2009, p. 239). While seclusion is not a teaching strategy adopted by the Council, its continued use can only be seen as a learning strategy for students—in terms of their learning to get their behaviour right.

In the special education discourse, the behaviours targetted in a behaviour management program are placed in a framework of stimuli and reinforcements. At the same time, in the dominant special education discourse teachers must also help students to acquire the pro-social behaviours that replace the negative behaviours. This is usually done through teaching students appropriate social skills. While the efficacy of social skills training programs continues to be debated, Gresham (1998) advises that we should persist with the approach, using a combination of modelling, coaching and reinforcement procedures, thus combining cognitivist and behaviourist models of training. In the current dominant cognitivist-behaviourist framework, the search for cause, including a mental health cause, a child abuse cause or a cause related to poverty, is discouraged. Faith in the validity, reliability and scientific truth of the intervention techniques that must be implemented in the prescribed way is all that should be required. There is also a less impersonal way of making sense of behaviour, and a cognitivist-behaviourist approach is often combined with ideas about needs and choices that are made about ways to meet those needs. The ideas about needs and choices are embedded in prominent educational/psychological approaches, particularly those of William Glasser, whose original 'Control Theory'

(Glasser, 1986) has been renamed as 'Choice Theory' (Glasser, 1996). Choice Theory is the most frequently cited basis for the programs provided for 'emotionally/behaviourally disordered' students in NSW government schools (Conway, 1994a). Glasser originally developed the theory and therapeutic processes when working with delinquent adolescent girls in a specialist setting. His approach talks about universal motivation—that we all have the basic needs of fun, freedom, belonging and power as well as the basic survival needs. This places the motivation for behaviour as internal to individuals who go through life finding ways to meet their basic needs. For some people these needs are not met in a satisfactory way, and so they find socially 'inappropriate' ways to meet their needs. For example, students who act-out in class to get attention from other students might be meeting their need for recognition or even love.

This notion of the needs of students is fairly universal in education. The existence of internal needs that people try to meet is referred to in many documents from the NSW Department of Education and Training, particularly the Student Welfare Policy (NSW DET, 1996c). For example, schools develop practices in student welfare so that they can meet the personal and social needs of students. Also, in a national context, school programs are required to be responsive to students' developmental and learning needs (MCEETYA, 2008 p.12). Glasser (1996) specifies those needs and gives a detailed sequence of how the environment is perceived and mediated by needs, and how we have ideal pictures about meeting these needs. He claims that our behaviour is centred on finding ways to attain these idealised pictures, or to deal with the fact that we may not have attained them. By observing students' behaviour and speech, teachers are expected to get an idea of which needs the students are trying to meet, and to discuss with students more appropriate ways of getting their needs met. Ways to help students change their behaviours are based on helping students recognise that they are responsible for their own behaviour and their own satisfactory need-fulfillment, and then helping them to recognise that their current behaviours are ineffective in meeting their needs. This creates an impetus to change current behaviours. Most teachers in NSW schools have received some training in the cognitivist-behaviourist ideas of Glasser, where everyone is defined as acting to fill their 'buckets' of 'needs'. The prescription for the specialist teacher is often to help children to find more acceptable ways of meeting these needs: these individualised, personal buckets that children go about trying to get filled in the 'wrong' ways. In this dominant cognitivist-behaviourist approach, teachers are required to show students how to get them filled up in the 'right' ways.

'Choice' is also dominant in such educational/psychological thinking. That we all have the choice to behave in right or wrong ways is fundamental to the humanist discourse. In the cognitivist-behaviourist psychological discourse dominant in education, children are believed to choose to misbehave—they choose the wrong ways of getting their needs met. Because they have conscious choice, they can also choose to behave in the right ways. In order for children to be humanised they must be responsive in the right way and become non-violent, rational beings—make the right choices, the safe choices. This should happen in a way that children take up the idea that they have a choice. A lot of work is put into structuring children's desires—learning to desire what schools offer—learning to value achievement awards—and to take up the idea that they can choose to behave in a way that will get them what they are convinced they want.

This idea that we have 'free' choice is embedded in moral and even western religious thinking. It is a technology of power that works to bind us to the idea that as individuals we are responsible for our own actions and that the things that happen to us do so as a result of those actions. Talking with students about their choices and their needs is the dominant therapeutic approach used in special education settings for students with 'emotional/behavioural disorders'. Therapeutic success is sometimes thought to be achieved specifically through 'talking through' with students the difficulties they are having. Whether through the steps of Glasser (1996) or Life Space Interviewing (Long, 1991), teachers are trained to work with students to help them to identify helpful/unhelpful choices, in the hope that they will come to make the right choices, break aggressive conflict cycles, disengage from self-defeating patterns and develop responsible pro-social values and behaviour (Brendtro and Ness, 1983; Long, 1991).

More specific training in the required pro-social behaviours is promoted by 'positive psychology' (Seligman and Csikszentmihalyi, 2000) and this approach has had a significant impact on schools' work with their students. Many of the components of positive psychology are not new but attempt to bring together a range of ideas about what makes young people flourish and what makes their lives satisfying. While positive psychology sees itself as being firmly grounded in empirical research, McDonald and O'Callahan (2008) put forward a Foucauldian critique of positive psychology as tied to a neo-liberal economic and political discourse.

The mental health labelling of students with 'emotional/behavioural disorders' indicates that they are somehow ill/damaged/broken/negative and that this illness or breakage needs to be dealt with through some type of therapeutic treatment/intervention. Despite the psychological discourse's positioning of these students as in need of therapy, the treatment for school-age dysfunction is usually limited to behaviour management, behaviour and socials skills training, and talking about needs and choices. A child positioned as having an emotional/behavioural disorder is not generally able to access a psychoanalytic approach.

In the dominant special education discourse, in addition to talking through needs, consequences and goals of behaviour, behaviour management plans and social skills training, other resources and approaches are also considered necessary for success. In contexts in which risk and protective factors arise, it has been found that interventions targeting factors beyond the individual student may be more effective than focusing solely on building students' strengths or remediating areas of risk (Gresham, Kern and Vanderwood, 2007, p. 72). Consequently the special education discourse requires teachers to extend their work outside the school setting and consider family and community factors. Eber and Nelson (1997) promote a 'wraparound' process for planning unique and flexible services for meeting the range of needs of students with 'emotional/behavioural disorders'. Such services include social and community services agencies, police, counsellors, social workers, and extended family members.

Sometimes, in the special education discourse, a wilderness experience is considered appropriate as a catalyst for behavioural change. Such an approach aims to bring about attitudinal, perceptual and behavioural changes by giving students challenging experiences where disequilibrium and dissonance occur. In the bush or wilderness, students face real problems/risks to which personal solutions must be found or survival itself will be threatened. Leaders (whilst always bound by duty of care) must maintain a carefully constructed role of perceived non-involvement, and non-direct intervention (Handley, 1994). Such an approach is considered to initiate the change process in students often considered as 'too late or too hard' for intervention.

While objectively implementing programs that are designed to measure and change behaviour, the special education discourse requires teachers to show young people that they are being "looked after and educated by trustworthy, empathetic adults, who are willing to make personal sacrifices on the child's behalf—people who are human and forgiving, yet demanding in terms of their expectations because they believe in the child's innate potential" (Cole and Visser, 1999, p. 62). More than being humane and making sacrifices, if the special education teacher gets it right they can help to heal children or at least lessen the impact of abuse and trauma by helping children to be more resilient. Some research has indicated that children who are resilient in spite of multiple risk factors have had 'buffering' experiences of positive relationships with adults (for example, parents/relatives/teachers) who care for, support and encourage them (Katz, 1997). The dominant special education discourse expects a special education teacher to be such a person and special education teachers come to expect this of themselves.

At the same time, the equity/rights discourse specifies that the ultimate goal for special educators to ensure the 'special' child returns to the regular school as soon as possible. In the equity/rights discourse staying in a special school can be seen as condemning children to lives of difference, discrimination and inequality. Consequently, special education teachers measure their success as teachers in terms of children's integration into the regular school. Facilitating a child's journey back to the regular school setting has come to be a priority for special education teachers, despite the limited success of the students once they return to the regular school setting. A report by Bradshaw (1997) presents the results of a longitudinal study of thirty Australian children with 'emotional/behavioural disorders' who were integrated into fifteen regular primary schools in Victoria and NSW. The results of the study indicate that, two years after the initial survey, over 70% of the students in Victorian schools were no longer enrolled in their surveyed school. In NSW, over 33% of the students no longer attended the surveyed school one year after the initial survey. Bradshaw concluded that, for many children with behaviour disorders, placement in the regular school might not be the most appropriate educational placement. The factor that appeared to assist in the length of placement of the child in a regular school was a close working relationship with a special school. For the special education teacher to increase the chances of success for 'special' students, they must not only get their special education discourse right but also understand regular education and develop close working relationships with regular school teachers.

CONCLUSION

In working at a special school for children classified as 'emotionally/behaviourally disordered', one that is not linked with a mental health facility or situated as an addendum to a regular school, the teachers in this study were required by dominant education and special education discourses to know and do all that is required in the regular school—the learning, the teaching, the curriculum and the dominant culture operating in regular schools. Teachers in special schools are expected to know this, often better than the regular school teachers, because the goal is for their students to return to the regular school and behave appropriately, sometimes even more appropriately, than other students in the regular school. They are required do this because dominant discourses inform them that it is just and fair for their students to have an equal chance of being successful in regular schools.

They are also required to know special education techniques, as many of their students have learning difficulties that must be remediated if they are to have a chance of success in the regular school. Remediation, fixing up the learning, is an imperative of the special education discourse; to be read as, and to read themselves as, effective, special education teachers must ensure that their students are at least 'average' learners. In this remediation that involves 'special' approaches, they are required to work with regular curriculum and approaches that are current. But they are then required to implement a behaviour change discourse that often conflicts with the covert power structure in the regular school setting, especially in relation to rewards, sanctions and restraints. They are required to know how to train pro-social behaviours using behavioural and cognitivist-behaviourist approaches. They must be constructed as humane and so must also know psychological thinking—such as working with students' needs and goals in a therapeutic community—and apply this well. They are required to identify the needs of their students and to help students to find 'better' regular ways of getting their needs met. They are required to keep abreast of educational and psychological thinking and use current, positive approaches. For example, they must blur and not read as contradictory two current, dominant and different approaches such as positive psychology (Seligman and Csikszentmihalyi, 2000) and positive behaviour support (Sugai and Horner, 2006), and provide a cohesive approach to the management and support of students. They are required to be innovative in finding ways to change the behaviour of the most difficult and violent students, including taking the students camping and helping them face challenges that will provide the impetus for change. They are required to understand about violence in the home and child abuse and be supportive and sympathetic to students. They are required to work with parents and gain their support even though, for many parents, relationships with schools have been negative, even volatile. They are required to know and work with the community services and supports and work in a team relationship with them. And they must be constructed as being the one person who is going to make a difference in the life of a child—to save children from themselves, their abuse, their thinking, and their own behaviour. All this is required to be done with enthusiasm, commitment and caring—but with not so much caring that they might be constructed as being enmeshed in the child's problem, or as manipulated by them; this is not read as helpful. Teachers are required to keep their emotional distance while doing their job. All these strategies are required to be implemented as though they are seamless and not informed by deeply contradictory discourses.

The next three chapters examine these discourses operating for students positioned as 'mad', 'bad' and 'sad'.

Chapter 3. The Mad: being positioned as 'mad' and counteracting that positioning

This chapter explores the practices around children at a special school who come to be read as/perform as 'mad'. Using Foucault's work on madness and civilisation, I examine the everyday educational practices around these children and tease out the dangers and chances created when working at the margins. Through exploring the practices around 'mad' adults, as detailed by Foucault, I examine how these same practices are used with children in covert and complex ways and explore the dominant and marginalising discourses positioning children whose behaviour is read as 'mad'.

Chapter 4. The Bad: being positioned as 'bad' and counteracting that positioning

In this chapter I use Foucault's work on discipline and punishment to make sense of the discipline practices that are at work in schools such that most students in mainstream schools 'get it right' at being good students and come to desire getting it right. I then explore the workings of punishment for those students in mainstream schools who perform 'bad' behaviour yet remain in mainstream/regular schools. This exploration is used to gain insight into the ways students in the special school, in contrast, perform 'bad' behaviour in such ways that they are read as 'abnormally bad', and confined even to the margins in a special school.

Chapter 5. The Sad: being positioned as 'sad' and counteracting that positioning

In this chapter I examine the discourses that have informed the way we think about children who do not fit into the normal school system. I explore my own embeddedness in these same discourses when I work with these children, and I subject the discourses to critique—to make them visible and analysable, showing the (often negative) effects they have on the children's lives. These are powerful discourses with powerful effects, and what I set out to do here is show how we are inevitably constituted by them and constitute the children within/by them, even while learning to distance ourselves from prevailing discourse and no longer hold it as revealing 'the truth' about the individual children we work with.

REFERENCES

Achenbach, T. M. (1991). *Manual for the Child Behaviour Checklist / 4-18 and 1991 profile.* Burlington, VT: University of Vermont, Department of Psychiatry.

Alloy, L., Acocella, J., & Bottzin, R. (1996). *Abnormal psychology—current perspectives.* New York: McGraw Hill.

American Psychiatric Association. (1994). *Diagnostic and statistical manual of mental disorders* (4th ed.). Washington, DC: Author.

Australian Government. (2005). *Disability standards.* Canberra: Author.

Bird, L., & Drewery, W. (2000). *Human development in Aotearoa.* Auckland, New Zealand: McGraw-Hill.

Bird Claiborne, L., Cornforth, S., Davies, B., Milligan, A., & White, E. J. (2009). Inclusion and mastery: variations on the theme of subjection. *Gender and Education, 21*(1), 47-61.

Bradshaw, K. (1997). The integration of children with behaviour disorders: a longitudinal study. *Australasian Journal of Special Education, 21*(2), 115-123.

Breen, M. J., & Alterpeter, T. S. (1990). *Disruptive behavior disorders in children: A treatment-focused assessment.* New York: The Guildford Press.

Brendtro, L., & Ness, A. E. (1983). *Re-educating troubled youth.* New York: Aldine de Gruyter.

Campbell, S. B. (1995). Behavior problems in preschool children: a review of recent research. *Journal of Child Psychology and Psychiatry, 36*(1), 114-119.

Cannon, R. (2000). *A guide to improving teaching methods.* Hamstead: Simon & Schuster Education.

Caron, C., & Rutter, M. (1991). Comorbidity in child psychopathology: concepts, issues and research strategies. *Journal of Child Psychology and Psychiatry, 32*, 1063-1080.

Cole, T. (1989). *Apart or a part? Integration and the growth of British special education.* Milton Keynes, UK: Open University Press.

Cole, T., & Visser, J. (1999). The history of special provision for pupils with emotional or behavioral difficulties in England: what has proved effective? *Behavioral Disorders, 25*(1), 56-64.

Coleman, M. C. (1996). *Behaviour disorders: Theory and practice* (3rd ed.). Boston: Allyn & Bacon.

Commonwealth of Australia. (2005). *Education connect: Occasional papers about social and emotional wellbeing in education. Issue 1.* Canberra: Author.

Conway, R. N. F. (1994a). Meeting the needs of adolescents with conduct disorders. In M. Tainsh & J. Izard (Eds.), *Widening horizons: New challenges, directions and achievements.* Camberwell: ACER.

Conway, R. N. F. (1994b). Teaching students with behaviour problems. In A. F. Ashman & J. Elkins (Eds.), *Educating children with special needs* (2nd ed.) (pp. 291-343). Sydney: Prentice Hall.

Cooper, P., Smith, C. J., & Upton, G. (1994). *Emotional and behavioural difficulties: Theory to practice.* London: Routledge.

Council of Australian Governments (COAG). (2008). *National disability agreement.* Canberra: Author.

Council for Children with Behavioral Disorders (CCBD). (2009a). Position summary on the use of physical restraint procedures in school settings. *Behavioral Disorders, 34*(4), 223-234.

Council for Children with Behavioral Disorders (CCBD). (2009b). Position summary on the use of seclusion in school settings. *Behavioral Disorders, 34*(4), 235-243.

Coutinho, M. J., & Oswald, D. P. (1998). Ethnicity and special education research: identifying questions and methods. *Behavioral Disorders*, *24*, 66-73.

Crisis Prevention Institute. (1987). *Nonviolent crisis intervention.* Brookfield, Wisconsin: Author.

Cullinan, D., Sabornie, E. J., & Crossland, C. L. (1992). Social mainstreaming of mildly handicapped students. *The Elementary School Journal*, *92*(3), 339-351.

Cuttance, P. (1994). Monitoring educational quality through performance indicators for school practice. *School Effectiveness and School Improvement*, *5*(2), 101-126.

Davison, G. C., & Neale, J. M. (1990). *Abnormal psychology* (5th ed.). New York: John Wiley & Sons.

Davies, B., & Hunt, R. (2000). Classroom competencies and marginal positionings. In B. Davies, *A Body of Writing 1989-1999.* Walnut Creek, CA: AltaMira Press.

Davies, T. (1996). Overview of provisions for students with severe behaviour difficulties in New Zealand. In J. Izard & J. Evans (Eds.), *Student behaviour: Policies, interventions and evaluations.* Camberwell: ACER.

Davison, G. C., & Neale, J. M. (1990). *Abnormal psychology* (5th ed.). New York: John Wiley & Sons.

Department for Education and Employment and Office for Standards in Education. (2000). *Departmental report: The Government's expenditure plans 2000-01 to 2001-02.* London: Author.

Dinham, S., & Scott, C. (2007). Parenting, teaching and leadership styles. *The Australian Educational Leader*, *29*(1), 30-32; 45.

Dodge, K. A. (1990). Nature versus nurture in childhood conduct disorder: it is time to ask a different question. *Developmental Psychology*, *26*(5), 698-701.

Eber, L., & Nelson, C. M. (1997). School-based wraparound planning: integrating services for students with emotional and behavioral needs. *American Journal of Orthopsychiatry*, *6*(3), 385-395.

Elksnin, L., & Elksnin, N. (1995). *Assessment and instruction of social skills.* London: Singular.

Ellwood, C., & Davies, B. (2010). Violence and the moral order in contemporary schooling: a discursive analysis. *Qualitative Research in Psychology, 7*(2), 85-98.

Engelmann, S., & Carnine, D. (1992). Analysis of basic communications. In S. Engelmann & D. Carnine, *Theory of instruction: Principles and applications.* New York: Irvington.

Foucault, M. (1988). *Madness and civilisation.* New York: Random House.

Gentleman, L., Burtt, A., & D'Arcy, Y. (1996). Itinerant support teacher (behaviour and learning): kindergarten to year two program in western Sydney. In J. Izard & J. Evans (Eds.), *Student behaviour: Policies, interventions and evaluations*. Camberwell: ACER.

Gersten, R., Woodward, J., & Darch, C. (1986). Direct instruction: a research-based approach to curriculum design and teaching. *Exceptional Children*, *53*, 17-31.

Gersten, R., & Dimino, J. (1993). Visions and revisions: a special education perspective on the whole language controversy. *Remedial and Special Education*, *14*(4), 5-13.

Glasser, W. (1986). *Control theory in the classroom.* New York: Harper & Row.

Glasser, W. (1996). Then and now. The theory of choice. *Learning*, *25*(3), 20-22.

Goldstein, A. P. (1988). PREPARE: A prosocial curriculum for aggressive youth. In R. B. Rutherford, C. M. Nelson & S. R. Forness (Eds.), *Bases of severe behavioral disorders in children and youth.* Boston: College-Hill Press.

Goleman, D. (1996). *Emotional intelligence: Why it can matter more than IQ.* London: Bloomsbury.

Gresham, F. M. (1998). Social skills training: should we raze, remodel or rebuild? *Behavioral Disorders*, *24*(1), 19-25.

Gresham, F. M., Kern, L., & Vanderwood, M. (2007). Risk and protective factors of emotional and/or behavioral disorders in children and adolescents: a mega-analytic synthesis. *Behavioral Disorders, 32*(2), 64-77.

Habermas, J. (1971). *Knowledge and human interest.* Boston: Beacon Press.

Hall, N., Williams, J., & Hall, P. S. (2000). Fresh approaches with oppositional students. *Reclaiming Children and Youth: The Journal of Strength-based Intervention*, *10*(2), 15-22.

Handley, R. (1994). Out of the bush—into the wilderness: tension and change. In M. Tainsh & J. Izard (Eds.), *Widening horizons: New challenges, directions and achievements.* Camberwell: ACER.

Hargreaves, A., & Fullan, M. (1998). *What's worth fighting for out there?* New York: Teacher's College Press.

Hart, E. L., Lahey, B. B., Loeber, R., & Hanson, K. (1994). Criterion validity of informants in the diagnosis of disruptive behavior disorders in children: a preliminary study. *Journal of Consulting and Clinical Psychology, 62*(2), 410-414.

Harry, B. (1994). *The disproportionate representation of minority students in special education: Theories and recommendations.* Washington, DC: US Department of Education.

Harry, B., Hart, J. E., Klingner, J., & Cramer, E. (2008). Response to Kauffman, Mock, & Simpson, (2007): Problems related to underservice of students with emotional or behavioral disorders. *Behavioral Disorders, 34*(3), 164-171.

Hattie, J. (2009). *Visible learning: A synthesis of over 800 meta-analyses relating to achievement.* London: Routledge.

Horner, R. H., O'Neill, R. E., & Flannery, K. B. (1993). Effective behavior support plans. In M. Snell (Ed.), *Instruction of students with severe disabilities* (4th ed.) (pp. 184-214). New York: Merrill.

Jones, A. N. (2006). From the sage on the stage to the guide on the side: the challenge for educators today. *ABAC Journal, 26*(1), 1-18.

Katz, M. (1997). Overcoming childhood adversity: lessons learned from those who have 'beat the odds'. *Interventions in the School Clinic, 32*, 205-210.

Kauffman, J. M. (1993). *Characteristics of emotional and behavioural disorders in children and youth* (5th ed.). Englewood Cliffs: McMillan.

Kauffman, J. M. (1999). How we prevent the prevention of emotional and behavioral disorders. *Exceptional Children, 65*(4), 448-468.

Kauffman, J. M., Simpson, R. L., & Mock, D. R. (2009). Problems related to underservice: a rejoinder. *Behavioral Disorders, 34*(3), 172-180.

Laing, R. D. (1969). *Self and others.* London: Penguin.

Laughlin, A. (1998). *Review of services for students with emotional disturbance and behaviour disorders.* Sydney: NSW Department of Education and Training.

Lewis, T., & Sugai, G. (1999). Effective behaviour support: a systems approach to proactive schoolwide management. *Exceptional Children, 31*(6), 1-24.

Livingstone, K. (1997). Ritalin: miracle drug or cop-out? *Public Interest, 127*, 3-18.

Long, N. J. (1991). What Fritz Redl taught me about aggression: understanding the dynamics of aggression and counter-aggression in students and staff. In W. C. Morse (Ed.), *Crisis intervention in residential treatment: The clinical innovations of Fritz Redl.* New York: The Hawthorn Press.

Lovat, T., & Clement, N. (2008). Quality teaching and values education: coalescing for effective learning. *Journal of Moral Education, 37*, 1-16.

Lytton, H. (1990). Child and parent effects in boys' conduct disorder: a reinterpretation. *Developmental Psychology, 26*(5), 683-697.

Mackey, P., & Kopras, A. (2001). Medication for attention deficit hyperactivity disorder (ADHD): an analysis by Federal Electorate. Canberra: Federal Parliament.

Mathur, S. R., & Rutherford, R. B. (1996). Is social skills training effective for students with emotional or behavioral disorders? Research issues and needs. *Behavioral Disorders, 22*(1), 21-28.

McDonald, M., & O'Callaghan, J. (2008). Positive psychology: a Foucauldian critique. *The Humanistic Psychologist, 36*, 127-142.

McRae, D. (1996). *The integration/inclusion feasibility study.* Sydney: NSW Department of School Education.

Ministerial Council for Education, Early Childhood Development and Youth Affairs (MCEECDYA). (2003). *A national framework for professional teaching standards for teachers.* Melbourne, Victoria: Curriculum Corporation.

Ministerial Council on Education, Employment, Training and Youth Affairs (MCEETYA). (2008). *Melbourne declaration on educational goals for young Australians.* Melbourne, Victoria: Curriculum Corporation.

Ministry of Education (Britain). (1955). *Report of the committee on maladjusted children (Underwood Report).* London: Her Majesty's Stationery Office.

Nicholson, T. (1992). Reading wars: a brief history and an update. *International Journal of Disability, Development and Education, 29*(3), 173-184.

NSW Department of Education and Training (DET). (1983). *Physical restraint of school pupils.* DET Memorandum.

Sydney: Author.

NSW Department of Education and Training (DET). (1993). *Quality teaching training—course materials.* Sydney: Author.

NSW Department of Education and Training (DET). (1996a). *Enrolment policy.* Sydney: Author.

NSW Department of Education and Training (DET). (1996b). *Special education handbook.* Sydney: Author.

NSW Department of Education and Training (DET). (1996c). *Student welfare policy.* Sydney: Author.

NSW Department of Education and Training (DET). (1999a). *Learning together: A discussion paper for school communities.* Sydney: Author.

NSW Department of Education and Training (DET). (1999b). *Who's going to teach my child?* Sydney: Author.

NSW Department of Education and Training (DET). (2000). *NSW public schools strategic directions 2000-2002.* Sydney: Author.

NSW Department of Education and Training (DET). (2003). *NSW quality teaching in NSW public schools: Discussion paper.* Sydney: Author.

NSW Department of Education and Training (DET). (2005). *People with disabilities—statement of commitment.* Sydney: Author.

NSW Department of Education and Training (DET). (2006). *Anti-bullying plan for schools.* Sydney: Author.

NSW Department of Education and Training (DET). (2007). *Legal issues bulletin, number 43.* Sydney: Author.

NSW Department of Education and Training (DET). (2010a). *About us.* Sydney: Author. Retrieved May 3, 2010 from https://www.det.nsw.edu.au/aboutus/ index.htm

NSW Department of Education and Training (DET). (2010b). *Management of health and safety risks posed to schools by students' violent behaviour.* Sydney: Author.

NSW Department of Education and Training (DET). (2010c). *Recruitment and employment: Professional responsibilities.* Sydney: Author. Retrieved May 3, 2010 from https://www.det.nsw.edu.au/employment/recruit/casualteachers/profrespons.htm

NSW Government Information Service. (1977). *Anti-Discrimination Act.* Sydney: Author.

NSW Government. (2010). *Submission to inquiry into the provision of education for students with a disability or special needs.* Sydney: Author.

New South Wales Parliament Legislative Council. (2010). *The provision of education to students with a disability or special needs.* General Purpose Standing Committee no. 2. Sydney: NSW Parliament.

O'Neill, R. E., Horner, R. H., Albin, R. W., Sprague, J. R., Storey, K., & Newton, J. S. (1997). *Functional assessment and program development for problem behaviour: A practical handbook* (2nd ed.). Pacific Grove, CA: Brooks Cole Publishing Company.

Petit, M., & Brook, T. (1998). Abuse and delinquency: two sides of the same coin. *Reclaiming Children and Youth: The Journal of Strength-based Intervention, 7*(2), 47-56.

Ross, A. (1981). *Child behaviour therapy.* New York: Wiley & Sons.

Runnheim, V. A., Frankenberger, W. R., & Hazelkorn, M. N. (1996). Medicating students with emotional and behavioral disorders and ADHD: a state survey. *Behavioral Disorders, 21*(4), 306-314.

Rutter, M., Maughan, B., Mortimer, P., & Ousten, J. (1979). *Fifteen thousand hours: Secondary schools and their effects on children.* London: Open Books.

Safran, S. P., & Safran, J. S. (1988). Perception of problem behaviours: a review and analysis of research. In R. B. Rutherford, C. M. Nelson & S. R. Forness (Eds.), *Bases of severe behavioral disorders in children and youth.* Boston: College-Hill Press.

Sanders, M., Markie-Dadds, C., & Turner, K. M. T. (1994). Childhood disruptive behaviour disorders. *General Practitioner, 2*(20), 18-21.

Sanders, M. R., & Markie-Dadds, C. (1996). Triple P: a multilevel family intervention program for children with disruptive behaviour disorders. In P. Cotton & H. Jackson (Eds.), *Early intervention and prevention in mental health. NSW DET in Western Sydney.* Carlton, Victoria: Australian Psychological Society.

Seligman, M. E. P., & Csikszentmihalyi, M. (2000). Positive psychology: an introduction. *American Psychologist, 55,* 5-14.

Shores, R. E. (1992). *Analysis of aggression of children with severe behaviour disorders in school environments. Final report.* ERIC No: ED408783.

Smith, P. A., Johnson, L., Fox, L., Nihart, M. A., Schindler, M., & Smiar, N. (1993). *Professional assault response training* (Australian ed.). Ringwood, Victoria: Professional Group Facilitators Pty.

Stokes, T. F., & Baer, D. M. (1977). An implicit technology of generalization. *Journal of Applied Behaviour Analysis,*

10, 349-367.

Sugai, G., & Horner, R. R. (2006). A promising approach for expanding and sustaining school-wide positive behaviour support. *School Psychology Review, 35*(2), 245-249.

Thomas, A., & Chess, S. (1986). Goodness of fit: control and mastery versus controlling parent or child. In T. F. Dugan & R. Coles (Eds.), *The child in our times: Studies in the development of resiliency.* New York: Brunner Mazel.

Walker, H. M., Colvin, G., & Ramsey, E. (1995). *Antisocial behavior in school: Strategies and best practices.* Pacific Grove: Brooks Cole Publishing Company.

Walker, H. M., Kavanagh, K., Stiller, B., Golly, A., Severson, H. H., & Feil, E. G. (1998). First step to success: an early intervention approach for preventing school antisocial behaviour. *Journal of Emotional and Behavioral Disorders*, *6*, 66-80.

Walkerdine, V., & The Girls and Mathematics Unit, Institute of Education. (1989). *Counting girls out.* London: Virago Press.

Walkerdine, V. (1990). *Schoolgirl fictions.* London: Verso.

West, D. (1967). *The young offender.* Harmondsworth: Pelican.

Wilson, M., & Evans, M. (1980). *Education of disturbed pupils.* London: Methuen.

CHAPTER 3

The Mad: Being Positioned as 'Mad' and Counteracting that Positioning

Abstract: As detailed in Chapter 1, *Researching special schools: a poststructuralist approach*, this work explores the capacity to apply poststructuralism, in theory and in practice, in a setting where other discourses are dominant. I focus on my own work as principal in the context of a special education school where I worked with students categorised as 'emotionally/behaviourally disordered'. I analyse the discourses that inform this kind of work, both from the position of one who inevitably took them up, even becoming expert in them, and from a Foucauldian position of critique which sets out to render these discourses less able to be taken up.

This chapter explores the discourses and practices used with children at a special school who come to be read as/perform as 'mad'. Using Foucault's work on madness and civilisation, I examine the everyday educational practices through which these children are constituted, and tease out the dangers and chances created for teachers and students working at the margins. Through exploring the practices around 'mad' adults, as detailed by Foucault, I examine how these same practices are used with children in covert and complex ways, and I explore the dominant and marginalising discourses positioning children and young people as 'mad'.

Keywords: education, disability, emotional and behavioural disorders, binary/binaries, psychology, psychiatry, mental health/illness, cognitivist/ism, Foucault, poststructuralist research, deconstruction.

I was out in the real world with three kids. Going up the lift in the shopping mall. The kids started fighting and swearing and the other adults in the lift looked at me as if to say, "Can't you control your children?"

Cath:	*Come on everyone, settle down. We'll be back at the hospital soon.*
Student 1:	*(singing and raising his hands as though a bird in flight) The hospital, the hospital, we're going to the hospital. The hospital, the hospital, we're going to the hospital.*
Student 2:	*What fucking hospital?*
	[Student 3 sits on floor in corner of lift.]
Student 1:	*(still singing and flapping his arms) The hospital, the hospital, we're going to the hospital. The hospital, we're going to the hospital.*

The others in the lift looked at me and smiled, knowingly. Once I had rescued myself from being seen as incompetent, once I had mentioned the hospital, everything the students could do or say could only have them seen as mad. I had rescued myself from being seen as incompetent and them from being seen as bad. Being seen as mad is far more tolerable than being seen as bad.

Cath's Notes

The confinement of madness is more than a physical confinement in a place away from society's mainstream. In the dominant rationalist discourses, the reasonable person does not have an excess of feelings and emotions. Reasonable people do not display their feelings inappropriately or have a disturbance of their emotions. The reason of the reasonable person manages and suppresses feelings and emotions. Knowledge "forms around feeling a milieu of abstract relationships" and such knowledge and rationality detaches us from feeling (Foucault, 1988, p. 218). To be read as reasonable within the terms of the dominant discourses, we must detach ourselves from an excess of emotions/feelings.

Children categorised as having 'emotional/behavioural disorders' are confined to and in the margins through their positioning within dominant rationalist/educational/psychological/humanist discourses. They

Cath Laws

are confined to the margins by the positioning of them as having a mental illness, a disturbance of the emotions. This chapter explores the development of this type of confinement by looking at the history and civilising of madness as traced by Michel Foucault (1988). Our practices at the special school reflected the dominant discourses and these practices are explored by means of the detailed data collected being read in relation to the theoretical framework provided by Foucault. This makes it possible to explore the dominance, dangers and chances created when working at the margins with children positioned as 'mad'. Over time the take-up of Foucauldian concepts changed how we saw what we were doing and led to important changes in our practices.

The following stories of the teachers and students at the school are full of irony and I am aware that others are often puzzled by my use of irony, which might be read as callous or unfeeling. My use of irony, however, is a way of 'checking up' on myself to catch myself out when I become the valiant rescuer and/or the righteous judge. Irony was one of the main ways that I dealt with the complexity of being not only a researcher but also a principal. My use of irony does not free me from my positions but reflects my deep involvement in my positionings.

CONFINING MADNESS

In his history of the 'mad' in civilisation Foucault (1988) wrote about the expulsion of the 'mad' from civilised society as one of a number of ritual exiles of those whose visibility was considered unsuitable. The practice of confinement—expulsion from the mainstream of society, known or thought of as the regular or the 'normal'—continues today and is evident in the placement of children who are too different in special schools. While this confinement of the child with an 'emotional/behavioural disorder' is not articulated as confinement, their banishment to another place, separate from those who are 'normal', is a type of confinement. This is not a physical locking away in the sense of confinement in an asylum. Today's confinement is multiple: confinement in a special school with limited access to the regular school, and confinement of the expression of emotions with the privileging of reason. One might say that 'madness' is an invention of the dominant discourses intended to separate off the correctly achieved 'humans' from those who fail to achieve and accomplish their humanist selves. An excess of emotions and a lack of reasonable behaviour can be read as 'madness' in the dominant discourses and, as such, 'madness' is something that is confined, silenced. Often to even speak of 'madness' in children is outside the dominant discourses. The way we think about and position children with problematic behaviour is as innocent/untamed/uncivilised but not 'mad'. 'Madness' is the domain of adults. Yet traces of the practices around 'madness' over the centuries can be found in the ways we thought about, talked with, managed and helped children at the special school. Even the way I talk about children rather than students in this chapter reminds me that the positioning of 'emotionally disturbed' is something that permeates all parts of one's life and is not restricted to life at school.

Foucault argues that the confinement of 'madness' has nothing to do with any medical concept. It is an instance of order. Once 'madness' could only be dealt with by bringing it into the open—making it public and thus warning about the darkness that could befall us all. Confinement means that 'madness' is to be locked away and separated from the 'normal'. In this "great confinement, the mad are assigned the same homeland as the poor, the unemployed and prisoners" (Foucault, 1988, p. 39). The community has acquired an ethical power to eject, from the world of the 'normal', all forms of those who are read as 'abnormal'. At the same time, confinement, in locking away 'madness', also organised "into a complex unity a new sensibility to poverty and to the duties of assistance, new forms of reaction to the economic problems of unemployment and idleness, a new ethic of work, and also the dream of a city where moral obligation was joined to civil law, within the authoritarian forms of constraint" (Foucault, 1988, p. 46). It seems that confinement may have little to do with curing the sick, or providing a refuge for 'madness', but more to do with an imperative of ensuring a workable labour force.

The traces of practices of confining poverty and 'madness' together, and even reading the poor as 'mad', can be found in the current practices of the dominant discourses. All of the students at our school were from lower socioeconomic backgrounds; most were from single parent families; most lived in public housing; a third of our students were Aboriginal; a third were living in out-of-home care situations. If 'emotional/behavioural disorders', as a medical/mental illness, were distributed on a 'normal' curve, then our students might have come from a range of backgrounds. They did not. They came from the most marginalised groups in our society and, more than simply existing at the margins, they are confined there.

I have to take the kids to the camp slowly to give the other teachers time to set up the tents. So three cars packed with kids drop in to my sister's house. The kids swim and play pool in the poolroom upstairs. She has a full sized table, cues and balls and even chalk. Chris is really interested in how someone could get so rich. I said that they had both worked hard at school and got careers and continued to work hard. Strive for the middle class Chris—it could happen to you. He knows that it is not likely.

Cath's Notes

The type of confinement that our students experienced was not one that locked them away to be forgotten or left at peace. The repressive function of societal confinement came to include giving work to those who had been confined "thus making them contribute to the prosperity of all" (Foucault, 1988, p. 51). If the 'mad' were not contributing, they were idle, and being idle was something that could not be tolerated. Those that are confined need to work, know that they need to work to contribute to society and know that, to be moral humans, they need to be seen to contribute their share. In the case of students positioned as 'mad' in the special school, the work they must do is: academic learning; working at learning to control themselves; working at being peaceful students responding to the order of society; and working at controlling and eliminating any sort of 'madness'. They must work as if it is possible to move away from the margins. Yet it is likely that the poor will always be confined to the margins. This confinement is not a planned, deliberate exclusion of the poor by the rich. As Foucault states: "One should not assume a massive and primal condition of domination, a binary structure with 'dominators' on one side and 'dominated' on the other, but rather a multiform production of relations of domination" (1980, p. 142). Yet confinement does benefit the rich. Just as, in the asylum, 'madness' took on a structure in which were symbolised "the massive structures of bourgeois society and its values" (Foucault, 1988, p. 274), so it is with the special school. The symbols of schoolwork, being polite, respecting ourselves and each other, working to build our esteem, limiting our desires and curbing our greed are all required of students in schools. These are taught, focussed on and reinforced as if those who get it wrong might not know just how wrong they are getting it.

FASCINATION WITH MADNESS

In tracing the stories of 'madness', and of its confinement, Foucault proposed that what came to be "confined was not only an abstract unreason which mingled madmen and libertines, invalids, and criminals but also an enormous reservoir of the fantastic, a dormant world of monsters supposedly engulfed in the darkness" (Foucault, 1988, p. 209). There was a time when 'madness' could be seen as folly—as a "sort of great unreason for which nothing, in fact, is exactly responsible, but which involves everyone in a kind of secret complicity" (Foucault, 1988, p. 13). In the special school, traces of 'madness' that presented as bizarre and fascinating could be observed.

Louise: *Have you seen Arthur today?*

Cath: *No, why?*

Louise: *He filed down his eyeteeth last night so that they are really pointy. He said he did it for Halloween.*

Cath: *Right. Of course, makes perfect sense to me. Did I tell you when we were on camp last year that he starting kissing the fish? Picking them up one by one from the bucket and kissing each one on their little lips and putting his tongue right in.*

Louise: *Oh, no! What did the kids do?*

Cath: *They were pretty stunned really. It was so bizarre that they didn't pick on him.*

Cath's Notes

Filing down one's teeth so that one can present as a more realistic vampire can be considered quite bizarre, even an act of 'madness'. Particularly so when this event took place six months before the celebration of Halloween. Yet in this story, as special school teachers, Louise and I are not shocked by or fearful of this behaviour. The behaviour 'makes perfect sense' for the 'mad'. This act of 'madness' separated Arthur from the other students, his difference resulting in him being avoided by them. Yet it was tolerated. He did not become a victim of their fear or intolerance. Teachers could read what Arthur did as amusing, sensible acts, and respond to them in a 'business as usual' way. There was also an admiration for the bizarre: an admiration for the bravery of one who is outside the limits of the 'normal'. While "morality, in complicity with medicine, has tried to defend itself against the dangers" of 'madness', these same dangers can continue to fascinate people's imaginations (Foucault, 1988, p. 207).

Cath: *So Noel, what did you do last night?*

Noel: *I am working on a big job at the moment and I am really tired. I didn't get home until three a.m.*

Cath: *So what are you working on?*

Noel: *I have to work with the police—we're working on a big case.*

Cath: *Are you allowed to talk about it?*

Noel: *No. I'm not allowed to talk about it. My tigers were really hungry when I got home and I had to feed them.*

Frank: *He's just lying, Miss.*

Cath: *You might think that he is but you will never know. He's got a very important job and he's not allowed to talk about it to anyone. I'm sorry, Noel, for even asking you. I know that you can get into big trouble for even talking about it to me.*

Noel: *That's right—I could get the sack.*

Frank: *Yeah, right.*

Cath: *You might have your doubts Frank, but Noel leads an interesting life.*

Noel: *I also twisted my ankle trying to stop them getting away.*

Cath: *Really? Well you must be pretty tired and sore. Let's see what work we can get done so that you can have a rest.*

[Frank looks disgusted and shakes his head.]

Cath's Notes

The conversations with Noel were a joy: a total immersion in the fantasy life of this six year old who daily told us stories of nightly adventures. Frank found my acceptance of Noel's imaginings surprising and pointed out to me that they were not true. Joining with a student like Noel in his world of imagination, even 'madness' as these imaginings formed the bulk of Noel's conversations with people, often results in the non-mad being disgusted. Frank did not find the imaginings of Noel fascinating. The 'mad' are supposed to be confronted by the realities of life. They are to be told the truth and to be realistic about life. Living in a world of imaginings is frightening for others. Perhaps traces of the ideas that 'madness' is out there and can befall anyone at anytime can be found in this attitude. Perhaps there are also traces of the fear of 'madness', not only because it could happen to you, but also because 'madness' has to be separated from, confined away from, others. Engaging with 'madness' goes against being a rational, moral human. However, the dominant discourses include traces of finding 'madness' fascinating, even brave, and these could also be observed at the special school.

[Teacher] Steve was saying how Bob is a hero to his class—small but mad and powerful. The bullies who know [what's good for them] keep away from him.

Cath's Notes

Bob was seen as heroic to the younger children as he was able to confront the bullies and beat them at their own game of violence. The bullies were fearful of him and this gave heart to the younger students that they could aspire to be in a position where the bullies also left them alone. There is power in 'madness'—a power to fascinate and to sometimes frighten.

The teachers, including me, are afraid of Peter. He has no limits and he is so unpredictable. I have seen him hold a grudge for over a week to get a kid back—wait until he sees a chance and then destroying something he knows that the kid really values. If a kid takes him on he will use anything—scissors, pencils, to stab and win. He will even bite. Biting is seen as so wrong by the other kids but Peter doesn't seem to care. He does whatever it takes to win. The kids stay right away from him and then he whinges that he has no friends.

Cath's Notes

I wrote extensively of Peter in my data, giving an indication of both my fear of the violence he could perform toward others, and my confusion about understanding his behaviour. Consequently, the times with Peter were full of dread. This fear of 'madness' as well as the dread of unreason was shared by all teachers. We saw it as unreasonable to hold a grudge for this long as we expect that children have short memories and get over things quickly. The fact that Peter ensured his own justice, in his own way, was read by us as being unpredictable, without reason. This view was confirmed, to us, by his use of weapons beyond the usual, reasonable use of the body. Biting, as if an animal, nearly always resulted in other students leaving the fight. They were shocked at Peter not getting aggression right. Being so far over the edge, and resorting to unpredictable and extreme means to win was, and remains, frightening.

I was working with both Peter and Adam on some maths when Adam took his life into his hands. Peter was complaining to me that he had no friends. There are only three other students in the class with him and they find ways to get into another class as soon as Peter comes into the room. They know that Peter is dangerous to be around and that he will find a way to make them suffer if they cross him. Peter was talking to me about wanting kids to be with him in the class when Adam, who was across the room, dropped his bomb. Adam told Peter that the reason no one wanted to be in the room with him was because he hurt everyone and no one could trust him—that he would probably never have any friends. Adam said it in a matter of fact sort of way—not nasty and not crawling. Adam had no idea of the [possible] consequences. I saw the look on Peter's face. No one in his right mind would have said that! We'll have to make sure that Adam is safe over the next couple of days.

Cath's Notes

In teasing out the story of Peter I read myself as skeptical that Peter was not seeing the consequences of his actions—surely he could see why he had no friends. Perhaps I expected him to have a rational understanding of this and, in a contradictory way, talked of him being beyond reason. I expected, in this unreason, that there would be violent consequences for Adam and I was afraid of this. Yet teachers, especially principals, are not supposed to be afraid of students. Strong feelings indicate lack of professional distance, not being able to be objective and being too involved. Fear is considered, in the dominant discourses, to be too extreme an emotion to be expressed by rational teachers. Yet it is fear that I felt in the face of Peter's extreme violence, fear for the safety of students and fear of the unreasonable violence itself. There was even a fear of acknowledging that I experienced this fear—a fear that I was not getting it right as a principal. I should have been managing the situation so that teachers and support personnel, students and myself did not get to experience fear.

The binaries reason/unreason and fear/control were not only at play with me but with the students. I expected 'reason' from Peter in having insight into his behaviour and understanding why other students stayed away from him. At the same time, I expected unreasonable violence from him. The 'mad' seem to be caught in being read as being expected to see the effects of their behaviour in a rational way. At the same time, their behaviour is expected to be unreasonable, irrational. Adam was seen by me as brave, as having insight but also as not 'being in his right mind'—exhibiting 'madness' by confronting Peter with information about why other students would have nothing to do with him. I thought I had the knowledge about the effects of Peter's behaviour as a rational adult. I had not expected that Adam, as an unreasoning child, also had an understanding of the possible consequences of Peter's behaviour both then and in the probable future. I was surprised at Adam's insight into Peter's behaviour as this kind of knowledge is usually reserved for knowing adults. In analysing this data, the contradictions of expecting reason and understanding from children and, at the same time, being surprised when it is displayed are apparent.

In tracing through lives of 'madness', Foucault (1988) talks of fascination because the 'mad' were seen to hold a knowledge not readily accessible to others. In the depths of 'madness', in the eye of the storm, there is sometimes thought to be a clarity that gives the 'mad' access to truth. For example, Ophelia, in her 'madness', tells the truth of the murder of Hamlet's father. A fool, such as the one in King Lear, sees the truth of what is happening while "the man of reason perceives only fragmentary and all the more unnerving images of it" (Foucault, 1988, p. 22). The old and senile, those close to 'madness', are also seen as not being guarded by reason and to make observations about which those with reason would keep silent. Children, in their innocence, might also be seen to have access to the 'truth'.

Lee talked to me about her 'conversation' with Ian today. It was not really a conversation—there was no room for her comment and no expectation from Ian that she was expected to comment. Ian was in the classroom alone with Lee. Ian had chosen not to go out on the excursion and so stayed back to work on the computer. Lee was supervising him. He was pacing up and down the room and then started talking to himself and to Lee, very rapidly.

Ian: *I am not a human being. I am a machine. I have no heart.*

He took some chalk and drew a person with a heart inside. Underneath this he wrote 'normal' in big letters and underlined it. Beside the person with the heart inside, he drew a person with a computer inside. Underneath he wrote in big, capital letters 'ME'.

Ian: *See this is a human being. They have a heart inside. They are normal. They have a heart. They are normal. This is me. I have no heart inside. I have a computer inside me. I am not human because I have no heart. I am not normal. I have a computer inside me. When mum is making lunch for me, she doesn't make a sandwich she makes a 1765413 because I have no heart, I am a computer, when mum gets clothes for me she gets a [computer] chip, when...*

He went on this way for at least ten minutes. Then he seemed to be exhausted and went to work on the computer.

Lee said that all she could do was say "Right", "Mmm", and "I see" as the 'conversation' was to her but not with her.

Cath's Notes

Ian could be read as having given Lee a presentation of a possible theory of himself and why he thought he was the way he was. His talk could also be read as a symptom of his mental illness, involving being this automaton with no emotion. In whatever way Ian's speech is made sense of, it affected Lee. In the dominant discourses in which we worked, we were trained to see 'mad' behaviour as learned behaviour and the task of those in the special school is as to persuade students to learn new, better, more appropriate, more 'normal' behaviours. In the story above there was perhaps a moment when Ian handed Lee a piece of knowledge that he had acquired about himself, about his emotions, and about how he, and his emotions, were to be positioned in a mental health/illness discourse.

Lee said she had never heard anyone give such a detailed analysis of what he thought was wrong with him.

She found it really eerie. She said there seemed to be none of the usual emotion in it—he was just saying it like a robot—yet he was really agitated. She said she had never thought about it before with him—that he does act like a computer—the way he always gives all the facts about everything he knows. It stunned her.

Cath's Notes

Perhaps Lee had not thought a child possible of coming up with such a theory about the disturbance of their emotions and proposing that their emotions are so difficult that they no longer existed. What could be observed in the special school environment of Ian's behaviour could have fitted in with his theory of his being a boy without a heart but a computer chip, and that without a heart, there could be no emotions. (Emotions, and the disturbance of emotions, were too much to bear.) This information about emotions, particularly coming from a child, was information to which Lee had not previously had access. Dipping into a world of psychology is not something dominant education discourses allows teachers to do—they are not trained psychologists and must keep to their education world. Yet the psychotherapeutic world is a contested world. Linnell (2010, p. 24) writes of the ways different therapeutic approaches can de-throne the therapist's authority or can "reinstall the therapist as a 'ritual master'". As a teacher, Lee was aware of the mastery of psychological discourses over educational discourses. What Ian had said was both fascinating and fearful.

The traces of 'madness' that produce fascination, fear, and the idea of a deep truth can be both surprising and disturbing. When these traces confront the rational mind it seems they must be made sense of in a rational way—almost as if to read them other than rationally may signify a 'madness' in those doing the reading. In the story below, Shane's attempts at suicide, and his previous talking of voices in his head, positioned him firmly as irrational, and yet the way he was able to see the humour in this positioning was surprising.

Shane had a really hard night last night. Attempted suicide again. He was sticking to me like glue but I needed to go to the shops to get some things.

Cath: *Shane, I really need to go out for a little while. You're more than welcome to come with me. How do you think you will go out in the real world?*

Shane: *Just a minute, let me check.*

Shane put his head in his hands and was there for at least a minute. Then he looked up.

Shane: *I think it will be all right.*

Cath: *What did you do, Shane? Take a vote?*

We both roared laughing.

Cath's Notes

This was a surprising moment for me—both because of what I said and because of Shane's reaction to it. One reading of this is as a moment of complicity with/in the 'madness'. Shane's attempted suicides were genuine yet could be read as 'attention-seeking'. The way he spent so long deciding about whether he would be able to stay safe, even keep 'sane', outside the confines of the school, surprised me. And touched me. And troubled me. The state he was in was so difficult for him and while he had his head in his hands, I felt him to be falling away. If I had added 'into the darkness' to this last reading, I know that I would be seen to have been too enmeshed, too psychiatric, buying into his behaviour and, worse, possibly seeing a 'madness' that was so dark that I might have been thought to be there. For those who even see extreme pain and emotional turmoil there is a doubling-back on them that means they may be seen as possibly 'mad'. So rather than being seen in this way, I turned it into a joke. My use of humour could be read as inappropriate. Yet in the face of such pain and confusion, the connection that was made through humour could be almost outside, or at least going against the grain of, the dominant discourses. We were both aware of the ideas around 'multiple personality' and found a space to see the idea of taking a vote amusing. Yet, in analysing this story I still cringe at the possibilities of what could have happened. The fear of the possibility of a rational person's action pushing 'madness' to and 'over the edge', to a place where 'sanity' can never be retrieved, is with/in me. Even though, as the researcher/author/collaborator, I understand sanity as a socially functional category constituted in a particular time and serving a particular purpose (Foucault, 1988), ideas of 'madness' possibly being a truth and real are with me. Consequently, there is danger in speaking of 'madness', of seeing humour in its practices and in the practices around it. We left the school and returned, both safe.

The surprising learning that can happen when working with times of 'madness' could also have the effect of the teachers and support personnel learning more about themselves and their own emotions.

Very early in the year Frank tried to be friends with the bullies. For a lot of the time they found him amusing and he often joined with them in talking about cars and television shows that they liked, and even harassing others. Yet he was never really one of them, accepted by them. I remember one recess so clearly when they turned on him. He had gone to recess wearing a Power Ranger cape from the dress-up box. Such dressing up was meant for the younger students, not for students in Year 5, but Frank loved to dress up. Two of the bullies were chasing him, calling him a range of names, throwing stones at him. They had pushed him over and stood over him, threatening to hurt him more. He ran and they kept chasing him. They found it amusing. He ran and hid in my office—crawled right up under the table. He was scared of the boys who were after him and furious that he couldn't understand why they had turned. What had he done? Why couldn't he get it right? He started screaming at me about my being a bitch, a slut—the usual abuse. I really felt for him. It hurts being rejected by people who you want to accept you. I remembered the same feeling, a specific time in Year 8 in high school. This happens to everyone at some time—but I had never remembered it so clearly for myself as with Frank. This really hurts and you never really understand why you are being rejected.

Cath's Notes

'Madness', in the dominant discourses, is supposed to be confined to, and to stay within, the margins. When it stays in its place, 'madness' can be left alone, feared and sometimes admired. The non-mad, the simply bad and violent, generally stay away from 'madness'. Arthur's fish-kissing, Noel's nightlife, Bob's extremes, Peter's strange violence, Adam's bravery, Ian's computer-speak and Shane's voices were all able to go on unpunished by the bad. The 'mad' have to stay separate from the 'bad'. While there were some moments when Frank was able/allowed to move out of 'madness' and join with the not-mad bullies, in the end he was actively rejected by them. I see this as very sad and connect it with times of being rejected at school. But this is not the same fear and confusion as Frank experienced. I have never known this despair, and perhaps the boys who chased him have never known it either.

In the history of confinement, the presence of the 'mad' has appeared as an injustice, not for the 'mad', but for others. The 'mad' have been seen to defile those with whom they are confined. In the nineteenth century there was indignation that the 'mad' were confined with the 'bad', and calls to separate the "innocence of unreason from the guilt of crime" (Foucault, 1988, p. 222). This indignation did not arise primarily from concern about the 'mad' but from concern that the "mad defile those with whom they have been imprudently confined" (Foucault, 1988, p. 236). This seems to be tied to ideas about the innocence of the 'mad' in that 'madness' is read as an illness—something that cannot be helped, yet is contagious. There is fear that the 'bad' will go 'mad' when confined with the 'mad' and a belief that the 'bad' are rational, since they choose to be bad.

Chris is doing really well at his regular school—he said he is sick of being here with all the weirdos.

Cath's Notes

When I compare the previous story of Frank with this story of Chris the differences are stark. Chris was on the way to being read as 'normal' in his regular school and perhaps we at the school might even have read his 'normal' to be at-risk by his proximity to the 'weirdos/mad', such as Frank in the previous story. I constructed Frank as unknowing and innocent in the rejection by the 'bad', reflecting my immersion in discourses that read 'madness' as innocent and 'badness' as guilty. Perhaps the 'bad' boys saw his 'madness' as deserving of punishment and the victimisation of 'madness' as reasonable. Perhaps I could read the 'bad' boys' abuse of Frank, while leaving others alone, as the 'bad' making sure that the 'mad' come to know that the 'mad' are not to mix with the 'bad'—Frank was to be confined separately from the bullies. Perhaps, as in the prisons described by Foucault, the 'bad' see themselves as being, and are seen to be, defiled by the 'mad'. In resonance with the ideas expressed by Foucault about prisons, I found myself feeling immense sadness for Frank that in doing/being 'mad' he was to be confined only with the 'mad'. All the students at the school had a label of problems with mental health and, while all were confined together, the different performances of the 'mad' and the 'bad' could be clearly observed and their intermingling often led to difficulty, and even violence, as described in the notes about Frank.

The historical fascination with 'madness' has left traces in the current discourses. But, in the dominant discourse, limits are placed on how fascinating madness is permitted to be and how one performs fascination with 'madness'. While Foucault (1988, p. 69) reminded us that 'madness' was once put on show and "became pure spectacle", such an act is now clearly unacceptable from a humanitarian view. The team at the school was sensitive to those who watched the children at their work for what we saw as the wrong reasons.

The visitor at school today really annoyed the teachers. Voyeuristic. He wanted to know all the gory details of the kids. Made us feel really uncomfortable. I think it is important that we have as many visitors as possible. Sometimes in these places, practices can develop that are really not OK and it helps to have visitors observing our practices—asking why we do something. The down side of that is you do get the voyeurs.

Cath's Notes

The school team accepted, and even encouraged, visitors to the school. Learning about the behaviours of special children and how to work with, and modify, those behaviours is appropriate at work in the special school. The dominant discourses often constitute special children as specimens in the scientific laboratory of learning. While the school team accepted, and even expected, visitors to come to the school to watch, work and play with the children, they were not accepting of those who simply came to watch the 'show'. There should be no trace of viewing the behaviour as a spectacle, no trace of voyeurism. 'Mad' behaviour is to be treated and modified, not left alone and simply watched.

Foucault (1988) has traced the movement of 'madness' and 'unreason' around each other. Madness no longer threatens us with "being swallowed up by the darkness" (Foucault, 1988, p. 84). In the dominant rationalist discourses 'madness' is now constituted by ideas of determinism, as having specific causes and treatment. Yet even though madness is something that can be rationalised and treated in the dominant discourses, it is still something to be feared. Perhaps it is because of this fear that children are not generally read as 'mad'. Perhaps it is because childhood is seen as a time of irrationality anyway. In spite of the children at the special school having been labelled as possessing mental health problems, the dominant discourses usually exclude children from being seen to be in any world of 'madness'. But the possibility of 'madness' in children, in some rare cases, does exist in the dominant discourses, and so we were cautious in case we were dealing with 'real madness'.

Arthur is the kid that has really had me stumped all year. We manage him but I think he has single-handedly broken more windows than anyone else. I have consciously avoided writing about him as he had me so confused for so long and it is only as I start to write this—as I start to select the things that are in my mind about him that some sort of understanding starts to emerge.

Arthur has this need to be all-powerful—as his psychiatrist once said. His teacher has one way of making sense of it but I am not so sure that the 'management' of him will work. His teacher is concerned that I am being 'too psychiatric' and that this is dangerous. In a way she is right. I was not operating in the same discourse as she was.

Cath's Notes

I was stumped by Arthur's behaviour, confused and silenced. Understanding the history of how 'madness' has been constructed can assist in understanding the development of the dominant discourses in which I was positioned. The rational, objective, non-emotional way of making sense of and working with students in the special schools is privileged. Thinking around extreme emotions and behaviour that occur seemingly without reason, in any other but a rational way, is usually silenced and not accessible to teachers. It is silenced both through constructing madness and its treatment in a rationalist discourse and at the same time medicalising madness and placing its diagnosis and treatment in the hands of the medical profession. In the face of such extreme confusion and unreason as is expressed in these stories, it is to the expert psychiatrist that teachers must turn. It is, therefore, not surprising that I was confused by Arthur's behaviour and made sense of his behaviour through the eyes of his psychiatrist: he is a child who has a need to be powerful, possibly having a delusional disorder. Yet in special education thinking it is psychiatry, and its way of engaging with 'madness' as even an aberration of nature, that must not be accessed, as psychiatry is seen as the opposite to rational, behaviourist theory and its approaches. In seeing possibilities other than those associated with behaviour theory, in doubting that these approaches will work with Arthur, I was positioned as 'too psychiatric'. Burman (1994, p. 13) points to the "clear lines of demarcation" between psychology (rational, conscious) and psychoanalysis (emotional, unconscious). If I was not behaviourist then I must have been psychiatric as these are the only possibilities available in the dominant discourses for making sense of extreme behaviour. Foucault writes that behaviourist psychology has its basis in a 'madness' relating to animality, as the ideas of mechanistic psychology are linked with the notion that the "forms of madness can be referred to the great structures of animal life" (Foucault, 1988, p. 76). To get it right as a special educator, I should have been using the behaviourist approach—managing the stimuli and responses and mediating the negative thinking that must be causing Arthur's inappropriate behaviour, training him in alternative behaviours, taming him.

Yet I no longer slip into the behaviourist approaches as easily as I once did. Looking at different ways of making sense of behaviour, particularly those that are non-behaviourist, can be seen as dangerous in the dominant special education discourses. This danger is present both because I may have been seen to get special education wrong and because, paradoxically, there are fragments of belief, even in behaviourist practices, that there may be some truth in psychiatry and its practices around 'madness'. Consequently, a 'layman' engaging in this could be dangerous for the child as only medical/psychiatric personnel are trained to engage with 'madness' in a way that cannot damage the child. I did not see myself as speaking with a psychiatric voice, and yet because I was not immersed in behaviourist practices I was read as engaging in psychiatric thinking. The behaviourist/psychiatric binary was the only possibility available to Arthur's teacher at this time. I understood her concerns and I saw the possibilities of engaging in poststructuralism being read as even more dangerous. In seeing all truths as constructed, and behaviourism/psychiatry as a binary in the dominant discourses, I might be read as having no beliefs and even no values—as anti-ethical. While the reading of poststructuralism as relativist is discussed in Chapter 6, *Counteracting dominant discourses: using poststructuralist theory to bring about change,* not seeing the dominant discourses as constituting the only legitimate reality is, at the very least, confusing to others.

To the extent that I am also constituted as inside the dominant discourses, I found myself worrying that there may be secrets of psychiatry to which I had no access, and believing, therefore, that I should be cautious.

I was talking to Arthur's psychiatrist and taking his perspective just to be on the safe side—to make sure that we weren't damaging Arthur.

Cath's Notes

'Madness' is seen in the dominant discourses as a medical issue requiring the special status of medical persons who are in charge of entry to the asylum. This is so much so that medical personnel, either psychiatrists or clinical psychologists, had to give our children their labels, their classifications, in order that the children could gain entry into the school. Yet, for the children at the margins, it was extremely rare (perhaps for less than 3% of our students) that there was any ongoing therapeutic relationship with a psychiatrist or clinical psychologist. The engagement with the medical world was maintained for about 30% of our students in the form of drug therapy. While concerns are raised about the administration to children of drugs designed for adults, such as lithium, drug therapy continues to be seen to be an important part of treatment regimes (NSW Government Committee on Children and Young People, 2002).

Foucault (1988, p. 270) believed that the "medical enterprise is only a part of an enormous moral task that must be accomplished at the asylum and… which alone can ensure the cure of the insane". It is not possible to totally escape the dominant discourses and there were times when I caught myself believing that, for extreme 'madness' that is puzzling and does not respond to behaviourist management, medically trained personnel might have been the only ones who possessed the 'cure'. Yet, for children, it is not a psychoanalytic therapy that is offered as the cure. The dominant discourses offer children a therapy that almost exclusively involves "Order, Authority and Punishment" (Foucault, 1988, p. 272).

MADNESS ORDERED

The dominant discourses of the world of the special school positioned 'madness' as almost an issue of morality. In the historical confinement of the 'mad', hospitals became moral institutions responsible for punishing and correcting a certain moral abeyance. Though we were not a hospital, aspects of this way of viewing 'madness' as a mental health problem were dominant for us. Foucault (1988, p. 60) proposed that 'madness' as an issue of morality is an important aspect of the dominant discourses: "this invention of a site of constraint, where morality castigates by means of administrative enforcement" is where "morality permitted itself to be administered like a trade or economy" (Foucault, 1988, p. 61). Being virtuous and good is now an affair of the state and the authority of the state is established to make sure it is respected. In placing the special students at the margins, 'madness' is confined and tied to reason and to the rules of morality.

We too, as teachers in the special school, were required to engage in the ordering of life and conscience in ways not totally divorced from the asylums of the 1700s (Foucault, 1988). This thread can be traced in the detail of the rules, the consequences, the choices that are not choices and the goals that can never be reached. In teaching about getting on with others, doing the right thing, citizenship, fixing things, and apologies we were not far from the situation Foucault draws attention to through a quote from St Vincent de Paul:

> Experience convinces us only too unhappily that the source of the misrule triumphant today among the young lies entirely in the lack of instruction and of obedience in spiritual matters, since they much prefer to follow their evil inclinations than the holy inspiration of God and the charitable advice of their parents. (1988, p. 62).

As we went about a daily work of making rules and implementing positive and negative consequences, of helping students to get their behaviour right, there was a sense that this was a moral duty. Foucault (1988, p. 257) saw that the asylum assimilated those aspects of religion that relate to religion's "moral power of consolation, of confidence and a docile fidelity to nature". The asylum became "a religious domain without religion, a domain of pure morality". In this same way, religion was not visible in the education discourses at our school, yet 'madness', as a breach of rational humanity, has aspects of breaching moral codes and hence its treatment requires a moral commitment. The 'mad' are represented to society as failures and, in this sense, they are read as immoral.

For the 'mad' confined to asylums everything was/is organised so that they knew/know that they are being "watched, judged and condemned; from transgression to punishment the connection must be evident, as guilt recognized by all" (Foucault, 1988, p. 267). Rather than leaving the 'mad' alone in their 'madness', they are subjected to a system of rewards and punishments, and asked to display a moral consciousness of their acts that includes regret. And so it was for those placed in a special school for the 'emotionally/behaviourally disordered'.

There is something really confusing about Frank. When he makes it, achieves something, gets his rewards, when people are most pleased with him and he seems to be most pleased with himself, he blows it. He always has to ask for more than he's got—two vouchers, extra food—something special—additional for him—more than anyone else would get. Some team members get really angry with him for this because he is being greedy—asking for too much—not being satisfied with what he has got. There are limits that we are supposed to teach him and we get angry with him for wanting more. Then he gets angry with us for not giving in to him and we get angry with him for being 'ungrateful'. He really doesn't seem to get this being grateful thing right.

Cath's Notes

In this story, the practices that judge, watch and condemn can be seen. As part of our behaviourist technology we gave rewards for doing the right thing—vouchers, food, praise. The limits on gaining these rewards were also clear. In this moral context the recipients of the rewards need to demonstrate appreciation, even gratitude. They must experience the reward as satisfying. Frank did not get it right in demonstrating appropriate gratitude or being satisfied. In the moral context of schooling, children are required to come to know the limits of what they can receive, and 'get it right' in showing appreciation for the rewards, the praise. Those 'special' children often received more than 'normal' children do and because of this 'more', they were required to show more appreciation, more gratitude, as well as modifying their behaviour to get the rewards in the first place. Frank did neither of these. He got it wrong as a 'special' child, and this was confusing because the systems were in place to teach him to get it right. In spite of the tight system surrounding his behaviour, Frank did not 'play the game'. Frank's behaviour, from the view of behaviour management practices, can be seen as a conscious, deliberate act which elicits anger; that he should so deliberately choose not to play by the rules, and even exploit the rules, is at the least annoying. From the psychiatric view, his 'getting it wrong' might not seen as 'bad', but read as more to do with his lack of reason and reasonableness. Frank got it wrong in both points of the behaviourist/psychiatric binary. While behaviourism dominates the practice of the special school, the possibility of rare but 'real madness' must also be entertained to get it right as special teachers in the dominant discourses. Perhaps our confusion at Frank's behaviour could be read as a belief that his lack of reason indicated a possible 'madness' that must be acknowledged yet seen as a rarity.

That we could detail, count and observe Frank's behaviour so carefully is not unusual. Observation pursues in the 'madman' "the least perceptible signs of his madness" (Foucault, 1988, p. 249). Our special school was small. There were two double classrooms, one single classroom and an office area. While there were some trees in the playground, they were thin and students could easily be seen behind or up a tree. There was a small toilet block but there were no locks on the doors. There was a small wash-shed with palings that were far enough apart so that they could be seen through. While the buildings themselves had not been altered so that they were different from regular schools, the strong wire fencing preventing access to the underneath of the buildings was unusual. The only place that students could possibly be that teachers or support personnel could not easily access was the roof of the third building. Access to this roof was limited by removal of anything that could be used for climbing. If children were successful at accessing this roof then they knew that it was likely that they would be suspended from school; it became the 'suspension roof'. The visibility of students was important as it allowed teachers to observe students and make sure that they were safe. This was an important issue as, sometimes, younger students who had been sexually assaulted in the past are read as being in patterns of inviting and receiving sexual experiences. It was seen as essential that these patterns are not repeated. Some children had previously attempted suicide and it was seen as essential that they could be observed so that further attempts could be prevented. Some children were extremely violent and it was seen as important that we were able to observe students so that no-one was hurt.

If we were to be seen to get it right as responsible teachers, fulfilling our duty of care in being concerned for the safety of our students, then observing students and their behaviour was one of our jobs. Such observation also ties in with the idea that 'madness' must be continually observed, surveilled and judged. But, as Foucault indicated, this observation is not reciprocal. Teachers had their own space, a staff room, where students could not observe their behaviour. Such close observation on the part of students might have led to students coming to know the detail of teachers' lives in the same way we got to know the detail of students' lives. But this was not the case. Teachers' observation of students does not allow such reciprocity, only the nearness of the observer who watches, and almost spies, so that one group's behaviour can be observed. For our thirty six students we had three team members on duty at each break time, and a team member would follow and observe any student who left the room, sometimes waiting an appropriate distance outside the students' toilet area. We made sense of this to ourselves as ensuring the safety of our students, as getting our job, as responsible teachers, right. Perhaps we were also, though not consciously, ensuring the close observation of 'madness' that is constantly required so that "it is judged only by its acts; it is not accused of intentions, nor are its secrets to be fathomed. Madness is responsible only for that part of itself which is visible. All the rest is reduced to silence. Madness no longer exists except as *seen*" (Foucault, 1988, p. 250). 'Madness', under this continual surveillance, is objectified and behaviour is scrutinised and judged to be appropriate/inappropriate, mad/sane, normal/abnormal, special/regular.

It is interesting how Allison, a teacher, has re-positioned the word 'special' with David. He is so unpredictable and dangerous and so violent. She's started to get him to see some of his most outrageous behaviour as 'special'. He seems to be taking it on board. I took him to go and get lunch for the kids today and we were waiting in the shop for it to be cooked. There were a lot of other people in the shop and he started offering them some prawn chips from the plate that was there. Everyone said, very politely, "No, thanks" and moved so that there was considerable distance between him and them. He came very close to me and we had a whispered conversation.

David: *That was being a bit 'special' wasn't it? They are all looking at me.*

Cath: *Yes, it was a bit special. People in shops like this usually don't talk to each other. They are just here to get their lunch.*

David: *I think I'll go and wait outside.*

Cath: *OK.*

Cath's Notes

David was confronted by his behaviour out in the 'real' world and was learning to judge his own behaviour, to monitor himself. It is interesting that 'special' is used paradoxically for inappropriate behaviour rather than as a positive attribute. The students at the school were categorised as 'special' and they came to a 'special' school. 'Special' is usually thought of, in the special education discourse, as a more positive term than disturbed/disabled. In this story it was used ironically —as a way of not pretending that 'special' is anything other than a category of abnormal. David showed that he was taking on the discourses of judging his own behaviour, acquiring 'appropriate' guilt at displaying any signs of the inappropriate and was well on the way to silencing 'madness'. In the rational, educational management of children, this is the task of the special educator.

There were also times for students at the school when being 'normal', and having the freedom to select the spaces in which to perform this, were evident.

We had some performers come to the school today. They were going to do a dance performance for the kids. I was with Karl putting out chairs for the kids to sit on.

Karl: *Miss, aren't you worried about having these people here?*

Cath: *Why should I be worried?*

Karl: *You know—the kids—what if they do something?*

Cath: *No, I'm not worried. It's like when we go out in the real world and you guys do 'normal'. It will be the same having them at the school.*

And they were all perfectly behaved.

Cath's Notes

In conversations such as these, it can be seen that the ideas of 'normal' and 'not normal' were known by teachers and students and talked about. The special school is not the 'real world'—it is different from the world out there. At the school, extreme emotions and behaviour could be displayed at times and not read as 'mad' or 'bad'. In the real world such extremities are not permitted and, if they are performed, they will be read by observers as extremely 'mad' or 'bad'. But in this place of confinement, the special school, the relentless ordering of behaviour was not always done. There was space to be something other than 'normal'. Karl knew this and was possibly concerned for me that I might have been embarrassed or let down in some way by the kids doing behaviour that should not be seen by people from the 'real world'. He knew that I should get it right in being principal, and that by allowing outsiders to see students doing/being 'mad' or 'bad' I would not have been getting it right as a principal. I was not worried. I knew that the students knew the appropriate skills, knew what was 'normal' and that they would do this for the time that the outside/real world was present at the school. I am reminded in this of the afternoon teas held in the historical asylums (Foucault, 1988), when the mad were required to act as if they were totally socialised. In that situation the 'mad' were put on display to show their normality and the effects of socialisation. In this situation with Karl both the students and teachers became complicit in putting on a display for the real world, knowing that it was only a display and that when the visitors were gone, all could return to their 'normal'.

That 'normal', however, could be quite disturbing, particularly when it came to the level of aggression the students displayed towards each other, the school team, and especially 'mothers'. Foucault (1988, p. 254) argues that the asylum "keeps the imperative fiction of the family", with the 'mad' being seen as children and reason containing an aspect of the father. Reason, order and control are delivered in a firm, kindly and paternal way. The mother appears to be absent—perhaps labelled as causing 'madness'. This has resonance for me with our students' verbal abuse of 'the mother'.

The next day was the last day of camp. It's my experience that this is always a bad day and the fights start. Bill is silly enough to say to Bob, "You fuck your mother". Bob loses it and kicks Bill in the face.

Cath's Notes

Insulting another's mother was standard practice between our boys. It is a gendered practice where boys are required to belittle another's mother, preferably sexually. This was usually done by one child stating that another child 'fucks' his mother. In this gendered practice of boys getting it right as tough boys, one child says to another that one's mother is considered to get it so wrong as a mother, and to be so sexually indiscriminate, that she will fuck her own children. The recipient of the insult is expected, if he is to get it right as a boy, to respond 'like a man' and physically engage with the insulter. After all, it seems that even a six year old boy is expected to act to defend his mother, thus positioning mothers as somehow unable to defend or protect themselves—their young male child must do it for them. This may seem an absurdity, but it was nevertheless a common practice that we observed not only amongst our boys but also amongst 'normal' boys in regular schools.

Chris and David had a fight just before lunch. They were getting along really well until Chris asked David if he could do something with the Lego that David had been playing with but wasn't playing with at the time. Share! No way! Chris told David he was a dickhead and David told Chris he fucked his mother, or to go fuck his mother. The ultimate insult. And then it was on. The usual fighting but this had a different twist. Chris did a perfect right cross to the jaw and David dropped to the ground, stunned. Chris then walked out saying that he knew his mother was a slut but that he was the only one who could say that. Instead of going after him, David rubbed his jaw and said, in great surprise, even awe, that "Chris has a really good punch, hasn't he, Miss?"

Cath's Notes

David was very impressed with Chris's response. He got it right in defending his mother in an impressive way, showing that he could fight 'like a man'. He also revealed something of his mother and was even more heroic by acknowledging his mother's possible flaws and still defended her in an impressive, manly way. There is also another possible practice at play in this gendered mother-abuse-defend pattern. In the dominant gendered discourses, boys are seen to get it right by defending their mothers. Perhaps they had learned that aggression in response to negative comments about family members is considered justifiable in some situations—defending one's mother may be accepted as a legitimate, morally good reason for engaging in violence. Perhaps the boys had come to know this in their history of violence in the wider community and regular schools. By saying they had got into a fight in defense of their mother they had experienced lesser consequences. This moral stand, this extenuating circumstance, had worked to get them out of trouble with school authorities. In my observations, I found that engaging in violence in defense of the mother is seen as legitimate by boys at the special school, and they performed it repeatedly, this patterned minuet of violence.

MADNESS RESTRAINED

The organising and "purifying" of asylums in the context of positivism was seen by Foucault (1988, p. 206) as a way of gaining a protection against 'madness', its disease and even its evil. Confinement protected society and, within that confinement, practices developed so that those confined were also protected from possible scorn, manipulation or abuse by those in normal society. Just as in the nineteenth century, this authority to confine was used in the interest of protection at our work.

Peter really lost it today. One of the other kids denied him something—have no idea what it was. He started swearing at the teacher, threw chairs, turned tables over. One of the bigger kids told him to stop it and Peter went for him. He knew that he was going to get hurt but he did it anyway. We pulled the bigger kid off him and then he started on us. Had to put him into time-out. Couldn't stay in there with him as he kept going for us. It took him at least ten minutes before he stopped kicking at the walls and screaming at us. He then went into the corner and just started crying. I got him some water and he stayed in my office, curled up on the chairs and went to sleep. Losing it takes a lot out of you.

Cath's Notes

This description of Peter 'losing it' indicates the violence and dangerous behaviour of some of the students. It also differentiates 'losing it' from deliberate acts of violence towards others that were designed to gain something, such as hurting someone else in a controlled way and then stopping once the victim has been removed or there is no longer easy access to the victim. For us, 'losing it' meant that no amount of change of place, warning, deprivation of rewards, or reminders to use self-talk strategies could calm the child. If the attempted violence continued, escalated, then everyone was put at risk. In this situation there was the added problem of Peter also being at risk from the retaliation of the bigger child who could have really hurt him. So Peter was confined in our time-out room. I used this time-out room not for punishing the 'bad' but giving space to the 'mad' so they could get back in control. It was a large room, the size of a normal classroom. The walls had paintings done by the children—paintings of superheroes, dinosaurs, streams, rivers, mountains; one wall had a number of paintings of Aboriginal symbols including the Rainbow Serpent. All the windows were Perspex and the walls with the paintings were double thickness, so if they were kicked, holes could not usually be made. There was no furniture in the room. While it was used for time-out when someone had 'lost it', the room was also used to play indoor soccer. It was also the room in which we held a weekly assembly where students received special awards for keeping the rules and making changes towards keeping the rules. Because of the way the room looked, and the multiple purposes of the room, it was hoped that the room would not be seen as a place where students could be confined within their confinement. To avoid the room being seen as having trappings of confinement from the days of the asylum, a team member usually went into the room with the student. Reasoned talk was then usually used to calm the child so that the child could then leave the room and join the other students. Putting a child in time-out came to be rarely implemented at the school as team members read it as a confinement and were very reluctant to do it. In the early days of my work there, it happened at least once daily as it was read at the time as a reasonable consequence for violent behaviour.

On this particular occasion with Peter, a teacher could not go into the room with him as he kept attacking them. Peter was left in the room, being observed by a team member through the window. It took about ten minutes for Peter to give the signs that he was back in control, that he had found his self-control again and was ready to come out. He showed this by crying which was read as an indication of his remorse. Foucault (1988) talks of the controlling practices in the asylum needing to persist until there is real remorse. Once Peter curled up and cried, this was a sufficient sign of remorse. While Peter's crying could have been read as another way of showing his frustration, or could have indicated his emotional exhaustion, crying by children after chastisement for an inappropriate behaviour is often read by adults as the child regretting the behaviour and being sorry. Peter's perceived contrition was sufficient to indicate that the intervention, being placed in time-out, was effective. There was once a time when I read it in this way. Now what I read as effective is not that Peter had seen the error of his ways and was contrite, but that no one was hurt in the incident and that he did not hurt someone once he was out of the room.

In the asylum of previous times there were instruments of control in addition to locking people away in isolation. When particularly dangerous, the 'mad' were confined in order to limit the physical locus of the raging frenzy. Placing the 'mad' in showers was also commonly used to deal with 'mad' ideas.

Foucault (1988, p. 267) quotes Pinel (1836):

> …if the idea persisted, the shower was repeated. Care was taken to avoid using a hard tone or terms that would cause rebellion. The mad needed to be made to understand that it is for their sake and reluctantly that such measures are resorted to, sometimes adding a joke, taking care not to go too far with it.

This has resonance for me in our work, particularly in relation to the use of physical restraint. I can trace the different ways that we, as a team, viewed physical restraint over my time the special school. These stories reflect the unfolding and evolving way we explored making sense of physical restraint. In this unfolding, we came to understand what Foucault might have meant when he said "to do criticism is to make harder those acts which are now too easy" (Foucault, 2000, p. 456).

In the practices of the dominant discourses, particularly those special education practices around the 'emotionally/behaviourally disordered', physical restraint or confinement in time-out was once done as a part of systematic behaviour intervention. Such restraint came to be seen as more of a safety issue and was usually done when students were out of control in that they were hurting other students or teachers and/or would not stop even when other students and teachers left the classroom. It also happened if students were trying to hurt themselves, for example trying to cut themselves with a knife or trying to strangle themselves with computer cords.

While having a basis in the practices of the asylum, the beliefs around physical restraint seem to come from two main ideas. The first idea involves a 'duty of care', where physical restraint is associated with extreme risk and the teacher's legal duty of care (NSW DET, 1983) is to intervene to prevent injury. This idea is present in the guidelines produced by the American Council for Children with Behavioral Disorders (CCBD, 2009, p. 224) wherein the current purpose of physical restraint is to control the behaviour of a student in an emergency situation to prevent immediate danger or possible injuries to that student or others.

The second idea of physical restraint comes not from special education discourses but from psychological discourses. This idea involves taking physical control when a person has lost complete control: 'therapeutically' taking control of them until they are in control of themselves. The strength of the expert/client relationship is thought to be a key therapeutic intervention for clients—one that can help lead to the patient taking control for themselves and to recovery (Laing, 1969). Teachers at our school came to know these more psychological ideas through training organised by the NSW Department of Education and Training. The workbook for this training states: "Taking physical control of a person when he has lost complete control of himself is the most therapeutic process possible" (Crisis Prevention Institute, 1987, p. 9s). Consequently, in the dominant discourses, physical restraint is not viewed as intrusive or as a punishment, but as a responsibility and as therapeutic.

Peter was being held by three team members. I joined and there were four of us—one on each leg and one on each arm. He was being held because he had a lighter and was starting fires when he was let go. He had slipped the lighter down his pants. I said to him 'all' he had to do was give us the lighter and he would be let go. For Peter, that 'all' was too much.

Cath's Notes

While holding Peter could have be seen as therapeutic, all involved, including Peter, would have difficulty in seeing this physical restraint and confinement as anything other than control. Of course, there was an issue of safety with the fires, and we were all immersed in this being the only way to prevent a fire being lit. This was not confining the limits of a raging frenzy; it was controlling and ordering the behaviour of Peter.

I remember a time when some team members were really unhappy with what I was doing. Things were changing—from my view I wanted less physical restraint and time-out. From their view the kids were out of control—there wasn't enough discipline. So the taming of Frank became almost a test case. The firmness, the discipline, the holding, the time-out worked for a while—at least the first few weeks. But then he started to really hurt the teachers—laying on of hands results in this.

Cath's Notes

Seeing physical restraint as at the least unhelpful, I opened myself to being seen as unable to manage and control the students and not getting it right as a keeper/teacher/principal. This story of Frank indicated my reluctance to be engaged in 'taming' of students and my belief that such taming would result in retaliation from the students. I wrote of retaliation as an inevitable consequence.

Steve, a teacher, has decided to do a project on physical restraint because he hates to do it—he has said that he wonders how taking all the control away from someone can be seen as therapeutic—he feels disgusted when he has to do it. I think I understand how he feels. I told him about Sarah, a twelve year old girl who was a fabulous athlete I was working with in another school about ten years ago. She had moved on to another place. At a conference I saw the principal of her new place and asked how she was going. He said she was settled now but it took her a while. He talked of a specific time when she had to be physically restrained for a long time but he knew that he had 'broken' her when she started to sob. She was well behaved now. I too felt disgusted.

Cath's Notes

While physical restraint was minimised because of the way our teachers came to understand its history and purpose, we continued to engage in promoting in children a 'self-restraint', encouraging them to control their own behaviour, to 'tame' their own temper. Foucault (1988, p. 250) sees the essential element of 'self-restraint' as one where freedom is curbed and the person, once 'mad', who has now become the 'patient', is "engaged by work and the observation of others" and is now "ceaselessly threatened by the recognition of guilt". In this moral restructuring of 'madness' the "free terror of madness" is replaced with "the stifling anguish of responsibility" (Foucault, 1988, p. 247). In this way guilt organises for the 'mad' a consciousness of themselves and, in non-reciprocal relation to the keeper/teacher, it organises for those with 'reason' an awareness of the 'mad' as the abject Other. If the 'mad' take on guilt, *inside them*, then through this guilt they punish themselves for being other than 'normal'. The power and pain of guilt operates in such a way that humans, even the 'mad', wish to escape the oppressiveness of guilt, take on an awareness of themselves as free and responsible subjects, and consequently return to the order of reason.

This operation of guilt and subjection as an individual is not reserved for the 'mad'. It is the way we all come to experience ourselves as individual subjects. The practices of normalisation are found in all schools. Students, through the processes of subjection, come to desire to 'get it right', to be accepted and recognised as 'normal', and to work at becoming the best possible human they can possibly become. "Modern forms of schooling are understood, in humanist terms, as not shaping through coercion, but through the subject taking up for herself the desire to be appropriate" (Davies *et al.*, 2001, p. 172). To this statement I add 'himself' as well as 'myself', as this process of subjectification applies to us all.

In their failure to take up for themselves the desire to be appropriate and perform as 'normal', the 'mad' are read as ill—their mind and body disordered, diseased. The 'mad' are understood, in the dominant discourses, as having the "imaginary stigma of disease" caused by the operations of the natural body (Foucault, 1988, p. 205). This reading of 'madness' as a disease of the body is particularly evident when problematic behaviour is read as being caused by chemical imbalance in the brain and in the consequent use of medication to restore that balance. Medication is the main mode of treatment for our students in the context of mental health and is often viewed by the teachers as another way of confining and restraining.

Sam has just gone onto medication. Six Ritalin a day. We are in the playground and he's pacing. One team member talks about medication as a 'chemical straightjacket'.

Cath:	*What's up?*
Sam:	*I hate the tablets.*
Cath:	*Why? How does it feel inside your head?*
Sam:	*I don't know. I just hate it. All fuzzy. I can't think.*
	[I don't know what to say. He seems so worried about it.]
Cath:	*(singing) In my head, in my head, they are fighting.*

[Sam joins in laughing and we both sing the song.]

Cath's Notes

The restraint of medication often silences me. It is the 'normal' way that the medical profession treats those with 'emotional/behavioural disorders'. While its use continues to be questioned (Graham, 2008) such questions do not seem to stem the use of prescription drugs to treat the behaviour of children. This remains one of the most *dis*abling things I have seen. On this occasion, I used humour by singing some words of a popular song. In the context of the special school, humour was the only way I could see to deal with Sam's worry about the physical effects of the medication. The impact of the practices surrounding 'madness' is often hidden by the power of psychiatry and the medication that is at its disposal.

Foucault (1988) talked of the awesome power of psychiatry and those who perform it not wanting to see themselves as miraculous, and so attributing cures to the nature of 'madness' itself. In psychiatric thinking it is a false madness that is being cured, as "madness was not what one believed or what it believed itself to be; it was infinitely less than itself" (Foucault, 1988, p. 276). 'Madness', as an illness, can be contained, described, quantified and qualified, particularly with the use of medication. Yet it is not medication alone that provides the cure. Even though, according to Foucault (1988), 'madness' is constructed as an illness, some behaviours cannot be totally controlled through medication. Consequently, a regime of firm behaviour management, order, and consequences accompanies the medication regime. 'Madness', according to Foucault (1988, p. 269), being classified in a medical context, is caught in a continual judgement that "never ceases to pursue it", medicate it and rule it.

In the asylum talked about by Foucault (1988), some mad managed to resist, but this meant that they would be confined even further: "disobedience by religious fanaticism, resistance to work, and theft, the three great transgressions against bourgeois society, the three major offences against its essential values, are not excusable, even by madness" (Foucault, 1988, p. 268). For our children, resistance to work, theft, and fanaticism (not so much religious but bizarre), are also not usually excusable in the dominant discourses.

Mark is eight years old and has moved here from a joint psychiatric and educational placement. He was quiet on the first day and on the second day spat on the ground. A team member told him that we don't do that here and that if he did we'd make him wipe it up. He then got down on his knees and wiped his spit up with his face. He also took Lee's hand as if to kiss it and bit her. By the third day Lee and I were talking about what to do with him. His has potential to do mad to the extreme. I asked Lee about what she felt when he did these things.

Lee:	*I have never seen such a disturbed kid—that thing with the spit was really disturbed. I'm not sure that I can handle this.*
Cath:	*Is that all you felt? What did you feel when he wiped the spit up with his face?*
Lee:	*Really?*
Cath:	*Yes. Really.*
Lee:	*There was a part of me that thought "Yes! That will show everyone".*
Cath:	*Then maybe that's what we need to go with. He knows that there is nothing that we can do to make him do anything so we need to give him choices all the time. His mad stuff we need to be impressed by. Like wow, that's really good. I haven't seen anyone that impressive for a long time. You're really good at the disturbed show.*

It took a matter of days for Mark to at first be surprised, continue a few things, then give up.

Cath's Notes

Mark's resistance in doing/being 'mad' to the extreme resulted in him being confined from one special place/school to this special school. I was concerned about this mostly because I knew that he could have been read as 'too difficult' and/or 'unfixable' and that this might have distressed and even angered some members of the school team. The team member who talked about wiping up the spit was disgusted by the act. In reading this doing/being 'mad' to the extreme as a possible resistance, I offered Lee another way of making sense of Mark's behaviour. It is one with which she connected; his resistance could be read as heroic. In positioning Mark as possibly heroic, perhaps Mark was able to read himself as respected and accepted in spite of the extremities of his behaviour. The issue for me is: could it be read that in giving up his 'mad' behaviour Mark also gave up his way of performing resistance? Can performing 'mad' be read as a form of resistance to the dominant discourses? Probably not, as resistance involves making the force of dominant discourses less inevitable. The forces of the dominant discourses around the 'mad' continued to position Mark as he moved on from us to yet another special place and then another. While resistance will be looked at in more detail in Chapter 6, *Counteracting dominant discourses: using poststructuralist theory to bring about change,* I raise this now as an example of the complexity of working in and between discourses, and the fragility of any certainty associated with working in this way.

CONCLUSION

In the rationalist/educational discourses that dominated our thinking and practices at the special school, the abundance of emotions and extremes of behaviour displayed by the students were rarely to be read as 'mad', in spite of the categories of 'disturbed' ascribed to them through psychological/humanist discourses. Madness is a category usually reserved for adults. What happens when those positioned as 'mad' are children? Then, in almost all cases, the 'madness' of the adult is not assigned to them. Since those adults who are confined as 'mad' are treated as 'children', children who display an over-abundance of emotions and extreme behaviour, paradoxically, are rarely read as 'mad' in the dominant educational discourses. Yet they do not escape the 'treatment'. Nearly all of the systems that we put in place for adults named as 'mad' are used with children: confinement to and in the margins, firm and systematic management of behaviour, close surveillance and observation, rewards and punishment, ordering of their lives, and medication. These were all part of the dominant discourses for us at the special school. Often it seems that the systematic monitoring of and intervention in children's behaviour and the application of rewards and punishments is even more rigorous, as if to banish any construction of 'madness' from the lives of innocent children. This positioning of children as not 'mad' but simply and complexly demonstrating learned misbehaviour which must be unlearned, may explain why the students at our school were generally excluded from, or did not have access to, the same therapeutic options open to adults, except medication. The purity of childhood, even when extreme and unreasoning, can never be blackened by the darkness, the very idea of 'madness'. Yet, as this chapter has shown, the dominant discourses in which the special school works prescribe the treatment practices around 'madness' that are to be implemented, in abundance, if teachers are to get it right as competent special educators. Thankfully, we did not always get it right.

In the next chapter, *The Bad: Being positioned as 'bad' and counteracting that positioning,* I use Foucault's work on discipline and punishment to make sense of the discipline practices that are at work in schools such that most students in mainstream/regular schools 'get it right' at being good students and come to desire getting it right. I then explore the workings of punishment for those students in mainstream schools who perform 'bad' behaviour yet remain in mainstream/regular schools. This exploration is used to gain insight into the ways students in the special school, by contrast, perform 'bad' behaviour in such ways that they are read as 'abnormally bad' and confined even to the margins in a special school.

REFERENCES

Burman, E. (1994). *Deconstructing developmental psychology.* New York: Routledge.

Council for Children with Behavioral Disorders (CCBD). (2009). Position summary on the use of physical restraint procedures in school settings. *Behavioral Disorders, 34*(4), 223-234.

Crisis Prevention Institute. (1987). *Nonviolent crisis intervention.* Brookfield, WI: Author.

Davies, B., Dormer, S., Gannon, S., Laws, C., Rocco, S., Lenz Taguchi, H., & McCann, H. (2001). Becoming schoolgirls: the ambivalent project of subjectification. *Gender and Education, 13*(2), 167-182.

Foucault, M. (1980). *Power/Knowledge: Selected interviews and other writings 1972-77.* Brighton: Harvester Press.

Foucault, M. (1988). *Madness and civilisation.* New York: Random House.

Foucault, M. (2000). So is it important to think? In J. D. Faubion (Ed.), *Michel Foucault. Power.* New York: The New York Press.

Graham, L. J. (2008). Drugs, labels and (p)ill-fitting boxes: ADHD and children who are hard to teach. *Discourse: Studies in the Cultural Politics of Education, 29*(1), 85-106.

Linnell, S. (2010). *Art therapy and narrative therapy: An account of practitioner research.* Online. Bentham Publishers.

Laing, R. D. (1969). *Self and others.* London: Penguin.

NSW Department of Education and Training. (1983). *Physical restraint of school pupils.* DET Memorandum. Sydney: Author.

NSW Government Committee on Children and Young People. (2002). *Issues paper 5: The use of prescription drugs as a mental health strategy for children and young people.* Sydney: Author.

CHAPTER 4

The Bad: Being Positioned as 'Bad' and Counteracting that Positioning

Abstract: As detailed in Chapter 1, *Researching special schools: a poststructuralist approach*, this work explores the capacity to apply poststructuralism, in theory and in practice, in a setting where other discourses are dominant. I focus on my own work as principal in the context of a special education school where I worked with students categorised as 'emotionally/behaviourally disordered'. I analyse the discourses that inform this kind of work, both from the position of one who inevitably took them up, even becoming expert in them, and from a Foucauldian position of critique which sets out to render these discourses less able to be taken up.

In this chapter I use Foucault's work on discipline and punishment to make sense of the discipline practices that are at work in schools such that most students in mainstream schools 'get it right' at being good students and come to desire getting it right. I then explore the workings of punishment for those students in mainstream schools who perform 'bad' behaviour yet remain in mainstream/regular schools. This exploration is used to gain insight into the ways students in the special school, by contrast, perform 'bad' behaviour in such ways that they are read as 'abnormally bad' and confined even to the margins in a special school.

Keywords: education, disability, emotional and behavioural disorders, behaviour management, discipline, binary/binaries, punishment, violence, Foucault, poststructuralist research, deconstruction.

We were sitting in Bob's office. Bob is the principal of the regular school that Shane attends for two days each week. Shane had been suspended for two days when he walked out of assembly and refused to take his hat off. Persistent disobedience. Wrong sort of hat. We were at the meeting to resolve the suspension so that Shane would be able to return to the school.

Bob: *You're a child and I am an adult. I have the power, and as you are a child you have no power. That is how it is. When I was a child I had no power, and I had to listen to the adults around me, my parents, teachers and other adults that were involved in my life. They knew what was best for me and the adults in your life know what is best for you. Do you understand, son?*

Shane was silent. I looked at Shane and noticed that he had a paper clip in his hands that he had bent so that it was a straight piece of wire. He was scratching his wrist with this wire. The scratches were deep enough to draw spots of blood. He had a face like a thundercloud, but remained silent.

Bob: *You must make sure that you wear your school uniform everyday of the week. We don't have school uniforms for fun you know. We have them for a reason. When you put on our school uniform, you are agreeing to obey the rules of this school. You are saying that you know that the teachers at this school have the power and that you will do whatever it is that they tell you to do. That uniform says that you are happy to be controlled by the teachers at this school whenever you wear it.*

Cath's Notes

In the story above, Bob, the principal, articulates some of the workings of discipline for Shane who has failed to follow the school rules. I read Bob's speech as one designed to instruct Shane in the workings of discipline at the regular school and in the way Bob saw power working—a kind of power that one is happy to have applied. In giving Shane the chance to return to the school after his suspension for 'bad' behaviour, I read Bob as hoping that the punishment of suspension would work to ensure that Shane would not perform 'bad' behaviour in the future because he would both want to avoid punishment and desire being a

Cath Laws

part of the school—a 'normal', happy student.

In the dominant rationalist/educational/psychological/humanist discourses, the ways we make sense of those who fail to get their performance as 'normal' students right by persistently doing/being 'bad' are complex and often difficult to theorise. This chapter explores discipline and punishment as it has come to be practised today, particularly with those students who are seen as undisciplined and lacking self-control—the 'bad'. The work of Michel Foucault (1977) is useful in exploring the ways power and discipline work in schools through normalisation and surveillance, through the specificity of space, place and time, and through the body, to produce the 'student' who desires to get it right, to be 'normal'. It is also important to examine the ways punishment works to produce, through individualisation, the construction of codes and consequences, and the ideas/feelings to be taken up as one's own and embodied, for the successful performance of 'normal' student. It is useful to tease out the workings of punishment on those students who apparently refuse to take up a performance as a 'normal' student and who are read as 'abnormally bad' students. This includes the management of their behaviour, the network of disciplines created around them, and sending them away, even from the margins. The dominant psychological/educational practices of searching for a cause and searching for a conscience in the 'abnormally bad' are also examined. I then turn my attention to the contradictions in the sympathy and admiration I observed, and experienced, for those who demonstrate a struggle against/with the norm, and the disgust/helplessness experienced in the face of some 'abnormally bad' behaviour. Finally, I reflect on the ways punishment, in working to categorise the 'abnormally bad', is not intended to rehabilitate, but to delineate the possibilities of behaviour.

While there was hardly any blood coming out, the puncture mark in six year old Steven's cheek was very deep. He was whimpering and his face was very pale. He was still in shock—physical/medical shock as well as shock at what had happened. He would probably need a stitch. Matty, twelve years old, had stabbed him with his pencil. Out of the blue. Just turned and stabbed him. Steven had not said anything to him. When his teacher pointed out to Matty how serious the wound was, he just said "Who cares?" I was trembling as I cleaned up the wound. Anger and hopelessness.

Cath's Notes

Before beginning this exploration, I tell the story above to illustrate how the violence of students read as 'bad' continues to immobilise and confound me. In the first story, of Bob and Shane, I demonstrated sympathy for Shane —to go through all he did because of a hat seemed to be beyond reason. In the second story, I see myself as feeling no such sympathy for Matty—rather I felt anger and hopelessness. Yet it could just as easily have been Shane who stabbed the little one, especially when he first came to the special school. The journey of this chapter is complex, as are the emotions around those who perform/do violence 'on purpose', seemingly rationally and without conscience.

As in earlier chapters, I point out that I write the stories of the special school in very ironic ways which readers might find puzzling. My use of irony is not intended to hurt or shock. Rather, I have come to use irony to pick at the threads of subjectivity and to raise the possibilities of reading taken-for-granted practices differently.

THE WORKINGS OF POWER

Power forms the subject and provides the very condition of the subject's existence. Power is not something that must always be resisted or opposed. Power is what we come to depend on for our existence. Foucault maintained that we need to stop describing the effects of power in negative ways such as: "it 'excludes', it 'represses', it 'censors', it 'abstracts', it 'masks', it 'conceals'" (Foucault, 1977, p. 194). Power is also productive—it produces our reality, the domains of objects and the rituals of truth that guide our everyday life. Power is not something that needs to be abandoned so that we are free of its restrictions and have access to the 'real truth and knowledge'. Power produces all knowledge, and power and knowledge directly imply one another. For Foucault (1977, p. 27) "there is no power relation without the correlative constitution of a field of knowledge, nor any knowledge that does not presuppose and constitute at the same time power relations". Without the workings of power, there would be no fields of knowledge and "it is power-knowledge, the process and struggles that traverse it and of which it is made up, that determines the forms and possible domains of knowledge" (Foucault, 1977, p. 28).

The workings of power-knowledge were evident at the special school in the particular ways we came to make sense of the behaviour of children: the ways that we came to manage their behaviour; the very idea that their behaviour is read as in need of management. Power-knowledge constitutes us as teachers who must manage the behaviour of children so that they come to manage their own. Ideas around prison and confinement of the 'bad' have come to provide a "universal pedagogy of work" for those who have proved resistant to the workings of the dominant discourses (Foucault, 1977, p. 121). For students in schools it is not only their school-work/learning, but also their work in performing as a 'student' that constitutes a particular power-knowledge around schooling and the management of students. The power-knowledge that operates around punishment for crimes and discipline in schools is similar. The similarity was even more striking at the special school. Many of the students came to the school because of their 'bad' behaviour, their inability/refusal to be disciplined in the 'normal' ways and their inability/refusal to become self-disciplined.

"Discipline is a political anatomy of detail" (Foucault, 1977, p. 139), and to carry out "a meticulous observation of detail" is important, as modern humanism is made possible from such details (Foucault, 1977, p. 141). All details are important in helping to see how we are held in our places as teachers and as students. In the context of school life it is "the meticulousness of the regulations and the supervision of the smallest fragment of life and of the body" that are important (Foucault, 1977, p. 139). This chapter offers glimpses of an examination of the detail of everyday life of students and teachers at a special school and of the workings therein of disciplinary power.

THE WORKINGS OF DISCIPLINE

At work in both special and mainstream schools is the "multiplicity of often minor processes, of different origin and scattered location, which overlap, repeat, or imitate one another, support one another, distinguish themselves from one another according to their domain of application, converge and gradually produce the blueprint of a general method" of discipline (Foucault, 1977, p. 138). Discipline enables the "confused, useless or dangerous multitudes to be transformed into ordered multiplicities" (Foucault, 1977, p. 148). To achieve this, practices of discipline that are subtle and widely spread in society have developed over the centuries. The practices around discipline involve mechanisms of power that structure the everyday lives of individuals.

In Term 4, things kept getting better for Phillip. He still whinged but soccer helped him to be more of a 'team player'. He was on the soccer team when we played a real world high school and he walked off the field when Mark scored an own goal. It seemed it wasn't that he scored it—it was that Mark wasn't mortified by this. Mark didn't seem to care. It was this that Phillip couldn't understand.

Cath's Notes

The machinery of discipline, adapted and refined, assumes responsibility for, and places under surveillance, everyday behaviour of students in schools: their identity, their activity, and their apparently unimportant gestures. In the dominant educational discourses, students in schools must be seen to work together, to be part of a team. They must want to achieve, reach goals, score goals. I read Phillip in the story above as knowing this; perhaps this is why he was so angry with Mark when he placed the ball in his own net and scored a goal for the other team. I read Mark as also knowing this but that, perhaps, he did not care. Perhaps he just wanted to put the ball in the net—experience the feeling of scoring. He might have been able to get away with it if he had then behaved as though he was ashamed and sorry that he had let the team down. But he did not do this—he acted as if he had scored a goal against the other team. He knew the rules and yet, in an *undisciplined and abnormal* way, flouted them and did not seem to be sorry. I read Phillip as being more disciplined, more 'normal', about the rules of soccer. The lessons to be learned, this ritual coding of rules and discipline, must be repeated again and again, even (or perhaps more especially) at play and sport. Through the practice of discipline the patterns of domination and submission are played out. Disciplinary power is indiscreet and discreet at the same time. It can be indiscreet since it is everywhere, always watching, even at a soccer game. It can be discreet "for it functions permanently and largely in silence" (Foucault, 1977, p. 177). Phillip, however, was not silent and he also behaved in an undisciplined, not 'normal', way. By walking off the field, he also got it wrong.

Phillip's new best friend Fred said that it was because Phillip played a certain position on the field that was really hard and that he could understand why Phillip got upset—but Fred knew that in terms of being a 'proper' soccer player, Phillip had lost it. But it didn't matter to Fred—he let it go for Phillip's sake. Fred will make it—why? Because he plays sport properly.

Cath's Notes

Fred, however, displayed a great deal of discipline. I read him as knowing that Mark and Phillip both got it wrong. While Fred knows the discipline of soccer and what needs to be done to get soccer right, it seems that the discipline practices around friendship were more important. He did not let Phillip know how wrong he had gotten it. Possibly Fred knew that Phillip already knew this. The rules around being a 'good mate' seemed to take precedence, and Fred, showing his understanding of how this discipline practice works, stayed silent. Fred's achievement of discipline, of normality, should not be seen as something where his natural exuberance had somehow been painfully suppressed. 'Getting it right', responding in appropriate and 'normal' ways to control and discipline, and following the rules, enabled Fred to be admired, respected and seen as someone who had what it takes to do/be a good friend.

Normalising

The practice of discipline permits "an internal, articulated and detailed control—to render visible those who are inside it" (Foucault, 1977, p. 172). The supervision of each individual and the simultaneous work of all students are made possible by the allocation of individual places and the use of space in schools. Surveillance of students helps to ensure that control is possible. The state control of the mechanisms of discipline, for example schooling, policing, imprisonment, is made possible partly by giving power a permanent and continuous surveillance, in which we all are made visible while power stays invisible. Such surveillance is detailed, hierarchised, continuous, and functional in that it permits the progressive objectification and the "ever more subtle partitioning of individual behaviour" (Foucault, 1977, p. 173). In this sense, ideas about watching to ensure the 'norm' are extremely powerful. The 'norm' imposes homogeneity in ways that mean those who stray from the 'norm' are made visible, branded. The 'norm' individualises and makes it possible to measure the gaps and to hold in the spotlight what it is to be 'normal'; it makes visible who are the 'normal' and who are the 'not-normal'. In the extract above, it seems that only Fred got his performance as 'normal' right.

> To fail to achieve an adequate 'fit' within an officially recognized position is to be de-authorized—to be denied recognition as an author of a text, and to have one's text dismissed from the start as incoherent, illegitimate, or unbelievable. (Smith, 1995, p. 169).

Continual surveillance, and the idea of continual surveillance, serve to make students adjust their behaviour, to act as though they are being observed and to take on for themselves the surveillance, observation and monitoring of their own behaviour so that they can be recognised as 'normal students'. In the dominant discourses, students need to be seen to conform so that they might all be subjected and be like one another, not stand out or be seen as getting it wrong as students. At the same time, they are asked to be an 'individual' displaying their individual talents, strengths and ideas and to develop "understanding of themselves" as individuals (NSW DET, 1997, p. 5). While being 'normal' is not something that I consider to be necessarily painful in itself, achieving 'normal' can be difficult and there can be confusing pressures. I observe 'pressures' in the sense of students needing to be like one another and, at the same time, an 'individual'. I observe pain for those who fail to achieve 'normal'.

Space and Place

Foucault articulates the importance of discipline in the modern, humanist society. Discipline creates an individuality that is "cellular (by the play of spatial distribution), it is organic (by the coding of activities), it is genetic (by the accumulation of time), it is combinatory (by the composition of forces)" (Foucault, 1977, p. 167). Discipline, as it works in schools, draws up specific tables that specify time and activity, prescribes the movements of students from one place to another, and specifies how this movement must be performed. Foucault saw discipline as "an art of rank, a technique for the transformation of arrangements. It individualises bodies by a location that does not give them a fixed position, but distributes them and circulates them in a network of relations" (1977, p. 146). In this organisation of 'classrooms', 'classes' and 'years', complex spaces are created that are at the same time architectural, functional and hierarchical. Students are allocated spaces and classes and a hierarchy is established based on age: 'littlies', primary, high school, seniors, juniors. The older the student the more privileges and responsibilities are attached to the rank. In having a 'class' of students, the class becomes homogenous—it is no longer made up of individual elements arranged side by side and row by row. Through homogenisation as a 'class', a 'school', and a 'student population', a whole series of codes of disciplinary practices position the 'normal, individual' student within power relations.

Lee has done this amazing thing with some of the kids in her class—the invention of a 'senior/junior' thing. She has always had the 'seniors', but now she's named a couple of the seven year olds 'junior seniors'. They are really happy with this and behave accordingly. The youngest kid is the 'senior junior'. There are no 'junior juniors'.

Cath's Notes

Students in schools come to believe that the older they are the more rights/privileges they will be able to access. Being 'mature' gets it right as a student but it is also advantageous to students as they are positioned as worthwhile and valuable. Age is used as a disciplinary technique that marks and distributes power in schools, and the students willingly take up getting age right as responsible, mature students. Lee tapped into this with naming their appropriate behaviour as moving towards 'senior', allowing them to take up the position of student. 'Junior junior' is not desired. It is being a baby and being a baby is read by the students as being powerless and needing to be looked after. It is interesting to see how, while homogenisation and sameness are desired in Australian schools, being an 'individual', different to others, is also desired. In Lee's class no two students wanted the same category, so she had to continue to invent—the 'oldest senior junior' and the 'new senior junior'. Each student seemed happy to be seen to be growing-up and growing-into being a 'normal individual' within the group.

Discipline requires enclosure, specified space and specified place. In this enclosure the daily practices are confined and repeated. Buildings and classrooms in schools are partitioned and each individual comes to know which space is their space. Each space is also functional: the classroom, the toilet block, the canteen, the upper playground, the lower playground, the grassed area, the asphalt. Within this space each individual also has a place—a desk and chair that become 'their desk', 'their chair'; their 'hook/peg'. To come to know their place within the confined space, young children often have their name written on their desk by the teacher and their name written on the hook for their bag: 'a place for everything and everything in its place'. High school classrooms are even more functional and, possibly because they relate to subject areas and because there are so many more rooms/subjects, it is much more difficult for older students to find their right places.

Educational space functions like a learning machine but also a machine for hierarchising, rewarding, supervising and surveilling. In the spaces and places of schools, students' presence and absence is closely monitored and surveilled. Schools establish mechanisms for monitoring presences and absences, to know where and how to locate individuals and to be able, at each moment, to supervise the conduct of each individual, to assess it and judge it. In the dominant discourses disciplinary power is exercised in ways that are almost invisible. Yet those who are subjected must be visible. In discipline it is the subjects who have to be seen, continually. One way this is done is through students wearing a 'uniform' that marks them visibly as a student.

Sam was sitting on a chair in the administration area of the high school. We had gone there for a meeting about his progress but we were surprised to find him sitting there, waiting, in trouble.

Cath:	*Sam, what have you done?*
Sam:	*Uniform.*
Cath:	*You're not in uniform? But you've got your uniform on. What have you got wrong? Is it the shoes?*
Sam:	*Summer.*
Cath:	*You've got on your summer uniform and you should have your winter one on?*
Sam:	*I don't know. No. It's a mufti day.*
Cath:	*Mufti day? Oh, it's a day you are not supposed to wear uniform?*
Sam:	*No. It's a mufti day.*

Sam was sort of in shock and so was I. We had spent so long talking to him about making sure that he was in uniform as it really matters in high school. We hadn't taught him about when getting it right means not getting it right.

Cath's Notes

The details of schooling are so complex that, even with the best of intentions, students can very easily get it wrong. Sam had got it so wrong that he was sent to the 'in trouble' area of the school to wait and reflect on what he had done wrong. He was confused and so was I. I thought that for him to be sent to the 'office' area, the space of the school's adult hierarchy, separate from the students, meant that he must have gotten something very wrong. For the school he had. Not joining in and wearing non-school clothes on a 'mufti' day would have indicated to them that he was not wanting to get it right as a student at that school and standing apart, not complying, not being a contributing member of the student body. Not being 'normal'. How students clothe their bodies is extremely important in schools. It is the 'inside' that must get it right as an individual; the outside of the body must get it right as being part of a group, the team, the school.

Space and Time

Movements of bodies and the timing of movements around schools are also controlled. School days are segmented into 'periods' of time in which specific activities are timetabled with rules detailing what is supposed to be done in this time and the quality of what is supposed to be done. Time is used to chart the development and behaviour of each student in school and time almost provides a map of the minute behaviours required to get it right as a student. Even in 'free' time students are required to engage only in those activities specified for free time. Students cannot ever be idle. Techniques are established "for taking charge of the time of individual existences; for regulating the relations of time, bodies and forces" (Foucault, 1977, p. 157). Not only is daily time segmented, but longer periods of time are also marked including terms and holidays, half-yearly and yearly reports, junior years, senior years. Disciplinary time has gradually imposed itself on pedagogical practice. A whole analytical pedagogy has been formed and it is meticulous in its detail. "Power is articulated directly onto time; it assures its control and guarantees its use" (Foucault, 1977, p. 160). School assemblies are examples of the use of time where control is exercised in a space in which activity is controlled, the body is confined and time is extended to elaborate the act of control.

Bodies in Space and Time

Control of the body is an important tactic of discipline. Through individual bodies and control of them, a subtle coercion is exercised. Discipline is able to obtain "a hold on the body at the level of the mechanism itself" through the control of movements, gestures, postures and speed (Foucault, 1977, p. 137). The tactics of discipline include rules about how the body is to be clothed, and the type of school uniform required can restrict and define movement of students. There are also rules about how students are to move about the school, how quickly they can move and where, how they are to sit, where they are to put their hands, how they are to hold their writing implements. The human body is taken over by the "machinery of power that explores it, breaks it down and rearranges it" (Foucault, 1977, p. 138). Control of the body indicates control of the self and therefore control of individual behaviour. Ideas around self-discipline, control of the body and behaviour allow "a more finely tuned justice" (Foucault, 1977, p. 78) and mapping of the social body. While the mechanisms of power operate on the bodies of students, this cannot be automatically read as oppressive. Students come to desire demonstrating self-control and displaying fine control of their bodies (Davies *et al.*, 2001). Discipline, in acting on and through individual desire, produces subjected and practised bodies, the body of a student, the student body.

PUNISHMENT

The workings of disciplinary power involve a normalising judgement in such a way that we come to desire such normalcy. I do not read 'discipline' as something inhumane or damaging to us; it is the way we come to get it right in negotiating the social world. For those, however, who fail to take up *appropriate* behaviour, punishment catches the "slightest departure from correct behaviour" (Foucault, 1977, p. 178). The workings of punishment have been refined over the years. In times when cities were small, rural populations large and standards of living low, criminals were seen as "harassed", "ill-fed" and the poor of our society (Foucault, 1977, p. 75). There was some sympathy for the crimes the poor had to commit to stay alive. Aspects of this view are still with us, particularly in Australia. As a penal colony, there is a sense that those who colonised the land were victims of social ills. This admiration for the poor who rebel, who stand up against unfair conditions and fight for their rights, is historically produced in us. While this is not always the way that crime and 'bad' behaviour are viewed by teachers and the wider society, traces of admiration could be seen in our work at the special school.

Greg's regular school principal rang to say that they had had a phone call from a neighbour about the school raffle. Apparently Greg had bought a book of raffle tickets and was selling them in his neighbourhood as a school raffle and was pocketing the profits. We were both impressed.

Cath's Notes

Both Greg's principal and I expressed some admiration for Greg's initiative, even a celebration of the creativity and courage of the 'bad' behaviour. Yet if Greg's act had been performed on a large scale, his behaviour would probably have been read as criminal, and society would need protecting from him. Foucault proposed that with the general rise in standard of living and increase of wealth there was a need for the security and protection of society. Consequently, the 'bad' are seen as "cunning, sly, calculating" (Foucault, 1977, p. 75) as well as dangerous, and deliberately greedy—stealing more than their share with no consideration for others. Penal codes detailing punishments were implemented as a spectacle to let others know what happens to the 'bad'. There are still traces of this punishment as spectacle in the work of schools.

Shane was suspended from his regular school today. In assembly he was wearing his baseball cap. When he was asked to take it off, he refused—got up, turned his back on the principal, said nothing and walked out of the hall past a couple of hundred students.

Cath's Notes

Gathering the school together as a whole for assembly is one of the marks of mass discipline. One of the ways to control such a mass is to target an individual. Shane was targetted. He looked different to the others by wearing his hat. In front of two hundred others, he was named and told to take off his hat. 'Normally', to get it right as a student, Shane should have taken off his hat immediately. The spectacle of being named, pinned in assembly, would usually elicit enough fear and shame from students to result in immediate compliance. Yet such public punishment must not go so far that it has the effects of terror; "it must open up a book to be read, a lesson to be learned" (Foucault, 1977, p. 111). Punishment must not frighten people or be performed so intensely that it leads to anger and revolt either by the 'bad' or by those observing the punishment. Observers must see the punishment as just, deserved, and containing within it the possibility that the wrongdoer will be changed for the better. Everyone must see punishment not only as natural, but also as in her or his own interests. Shane did not do the right thing when the principal had told him to take off his hat. Worse yet, he walked out of the assembly. Shane's behaviour could not be read as 'normal' and the punishment of suspension, being sent from the school, was probably seen by the principal as equal to Shane's misbehaviour. The principal said nothing more to or about him in the assembly—perhaps he did not have to. The other students probably knew that suspension would be the consequence for such a blatant act of 'badness'. In the dominant discourses, the punishment of suspension could be the only response to such public disobedience, such abnormality.

THE WORKINGS OF PUNISHMENT

Through the Individual

The management of those students who do not keep the rules of schools is achieved through the treatment of each child as an individual. The "control and transformation of behaviour is accompanied—both as a condition and as a consequence—by the development of a knowledge of the individuals" (Foucault, 1977, p. 125). Students, as individual subjects, are subjected to habits, rules, orders and an authority that is exercised continually around them and upon them. For students to get it right, in according to the dominant discourses, these must function inside the *individual* automatically, and be internalised.

As part of this technology of individualising, the motivation of the wrongdoer is explored. Was the act carried out on purpose? Was it performed deliberately or was there any extenuating circumstance? It was once the case that these issues of 'intent' were not considered and it was enough to find out who committed the act and to apply the related consequences. Foucault proposed that this concern with intent enables us to ask, "how can we assign the causal process that produced it[?]" (1977, p. 17); we can ask whether the act originated in the person through instinct, heredity, the unconscious, or whether the cause can be attributed to the environment. A whole set of assessing, diagnostic, prognostic and normative judgements surround the wrongdoer, and this has turned the "assertion of guilt into a strange scientifico-juridical complex" (Foucault, 1977, p. 19).

In this same way, teachers ask questions about the individual whose acts of non-compliance fail to respond to the usual discipline and punishment practices in schools. For those who consistently get their behaviour wrong, teachers examine their nature, their circumstances at home, and events in their lives that could explain, in a psychological sense, their misbehaviour. In looking at the circumstances of the wrongdoer, teachers focus on individuality in a way that attempts to elicit causal explanations that might mitigate the intention to do the wrong thing. If teachers can explain the behaviour of wrongdoers in such a way that the wrongdoer's behaviour is 'reasonable', given the circumstances of their lives, then teachers can see themselves as gaining understanding and insight into the behaviour of the 'bad'. Working within the dominant discourses, teachers can choose to see individual students as not being beyond help; they can look for ways to explain persistent misbehaviour; they can keep trying, looking for a cure and giving wrongdoers chances to get it right.

Codes and Consequences

Continual surveillance of students and students' surveillance of themselves is done through a "normalising gaze" (Foucault, 1977, p. 184) that makes clear when, where and whom to punish. The principles that have been developed for regularising, refining and universalising punishment involve a multiplication of the ways punishment works. There are similarities in the workings of power and punishment in prisons and schools. The workings of this power involves mechanisms that "reduce the desire that makes the crime attractive; increase the interest that makes the penalty be feared; reverse the relation of the intensities, so that the representation of the penalty and its disadvantages is more lively than that of the crime and its pleasures" (Foucault, 1977, p. 106). In the same way that governments have a penal code that outlines crimes and their punishments, schools outline in their discipline codes the rules to be kept and the consequences that can be imposed (NSW DET, 2006).

In the dominant discourses, rules and codes of behaviour appear as the *natural* order of things, and punishment as a *natural* consequence of breaking rules. A system of rewards/punishment, or positive/negative consequences, is established where students "are more encouraged by the desire to be rewarded" than motivated by the fear of punishment (Foucault, 1977, p. 180). It is likely that no other student in assembly would have wanted to be Shane when his named was called or when he was outside of the assembly, alone. Consequences, both negative and positive, are intended to transform and modify behaviour. In everyday discipline there are "direct examples of virtue" (Foucault, 1977, p. 113) and rewards for that virtue, just as there are examples of 'bad' behaviour and punishment for the 'bad' behaviour. There is an interesting way that consequences are made sense of in the dominant discourse exemplified by the advice of experts on behaviour management such as Dreikurs, Grunwald and Pepper (1982). They talk of two types of consequences—'logical' and 'natural'.

In this behaviour management discourse, natural consequences are seen as a very effective way for children to learn about natural rules—if children put their hands in a fire they will get burned. Some natural consequences can be used at school—if one child hurt another child, that child might retaliate. It is acknowledged in this approach that natural consequences cannot generally be used at school. Now that corporal punishment is no longer used, if a student hurts a team member, teachers cannot hurt them in return through hurting their body. Since punishment must be seen as humane in the dominant discourses, schools are advised to use logical consequences as these are seen to express the reality of the social order—if students break rules then there will be consequences, such as limits on their freedom through detention. Logical consequences are seen as rational in that they are related to the misbehaviour—if students do not do their work then they must do additional work to make up for it. Logical consequences are also seen as non-judgmental in that they are seen not to imply an element of personal moral judgement on behalf of the person applying the consequences (Dreikurs et al., 1982). Yet there is much moralism in the idea of consequences, just as there is much rationalism.

We were sitting in a suspension resolution meeting. Bob, the principal, was talking to Shane, the student.

Bob: *Son, do you know why I don't speed when I drive my car?*

Shane: *Because it's dangerous?*

Bob: *Well yes, but that's not the answer I wanted, try again.*

Shane: *Because you will get booked?*

I thought both these answers were reasonable, and had no idea where this was heading.

Bob: *It doesn't matter if I get booked; I have a lot of money. I will pay the fine. No, the reason that I don't speed is because when I get in the car I am agreeing to obey the rules of the road. I know that the police have the power of the road and when I drive I have to obey their rules. It is the same as when you put on our uniform and come to our school. So, I don't want to see you near my office again. You shouldn't need time-out if you are really ready to come back to our school.*

Bob rose from his chair and stood over Shane and continued.

Bob: *So if you agree to follow our rules we will see you back here on Monday, but I warn you, I do not want to see you in here again, because I may not be so lenient next time.*

Cath's Notes

Bob's story of why he, as an adult, follows the rules, delivers an interesting 'moral' to children about why they should keep the rules. It is not about safety or fear of consequences but an agreement to be subjected to those who administer power and, in that subjection, an acceptance of the consequences of breaking the moral code.

'Positive consequences' used in schools are tied to the teacher's approval—stars in books, stamps on hands, award cards, smiles, comments about the goodness of children's behaviour in getting it right as students. In the dominant discourses the approval of the teacher becomes the path of desiring to get it right as a student, and the teacher's disapproval provides the border delineating the abyss of what might happen if students get it wrong. The 'negative consequences' used by teachers often involve firm, disapproving looks, statements about the inappropriateness of behaviour, comments about lack of effort, firm statements about what is expected to get it right and about doing better.

Pat, a teacher, was really upset at school today. His daughter has just started school and brought home a pre-writing activity sheet. She hadn't kept her squiggles in the lines. On the third day of Kindergarten her teacher had written on it, in red pen, "You can do better". Pat's daughter could not have even read the comment. A supposedly motivational comment. But it was not only meant for her, it was meant for her parent. A warning that she had better learn to get it right in school and stay in the lines. Pat said that his daughter was a bit sad that she didn't get a star like the other kids but he was both mortified and furious—he said he wondered what he was doing to her by sending her to school.

Cath's Notes

Students desire to perform the acts that result in positive consequences for them. A child who has just started school cannot possibly know exactly how to get the scribbles on paper just right or read the comment of the teacher. But perhaps this is not what was being taught. Perhaps one of the things being taught in this story is the power of the teacher's approval/disapproval, and the importance of classroom scribbles in gaining/not gaining that approval. Both father and daughter felt the shame. In this way, punishment works on emotions and desires. Punishment relates to laziness and lack of effort in the world of schools. In this case, Pat's daughter wrote in such a way that it was read by the teacher as a lack of effort and this was communicated to Pat, possibly so that he could also join in helping his daughter to get it right in future. Shameful punishments are effective because they are based on the emotions that are at the root of the 'bad' act (Foucault, 1977, p. 107). Possibly, Pat felt the shame all the more because, as a teacher, he felt that he should have informed his daughter about staying in the lines and demonstrating effort. In the dominant discourses, getting it right in schools and avoiding punishment involves staying in the lines, putting up our hand, using our best manners, doing our best work, trying our hardest.

Feelings, Ideas and Punishment

To be most effective, as immediate a link as possible must be made between the idea of a wrongdoing and the punishment that could be implemented for that wrongdoing. The idea of the offence must be "enough to arouse the sign of the punishment" (Foucault, 1977, p. 105). To help this to happen, punishment is directed at others, at all the potentially guilty. Students come to see that rewards proceed from doing the right thing and punishment proceeds from doing the wrong thing, and all students must see that this happens. Students are rewarded individually as a way of "reinserting them morally and materially" into the world of school (Foucault, 1977, p. 124). Often the 'bad' behaviour of one individual can result in punishment of a whole class. For example, when someone does not 'own up' and admit guilt for a wrongdoing, the whole class might be placed on detention. Students who do the wrong thing come to see that 'bad' behaviour is morally wrong because its effects can be dispersed onto the 'innocent'.

In the dominant discourses, "punishment can only generally function if it comes to an end" (Foucault, 1977, p. 107). It seems that the duration of a consequence must be long enough for students to understand how serious the breach of rules was for a particular purpose, time and setting. It cannot, however, be so long that other students see it as unreasonable or the one being punished begins to rebel.

For the condemned in prison, the law requires "that its victim should authenticate in some sense the torture" that she/he has undergone (Foucault, 1977, p. 66). In schools the authentication and reparation required from wrongdoers is an apology.

Bob, the principal, began the meeting to resolve Shane's suspension by going over the incident that had resulted in Shane's suspension. Bob told Shane that if Shane did not resolve the suspension by apologising for his actions and admitting that he had acted inappropriately, then he would not be allowed to return to the school. Shane said quietly, "I'm sorry. It was wrong".

Cath's Notes

Just as criminals "must if possible judge and condemn themselves" (Foucault, 1977, p. 38), wrongdoers in schools must come to see that they are getting it wrong and move to condemn themselves and admit their 'bad' behaviour. This is more than an admission of guilt for acting against the rules. Acknowledging a wrongdoing through apologising is an act required to show that wrongdoers can get it right and be 'normal', at least morally, through being sorry. It is this ritual that began the meeting with Shane and the principal of the regular school that Shane attended part-time. Shane got it right in apologising, demonstrating his capacity for rehabilitation, giving himself the possibility of returning to the world of students. In the dominant discourses, students' acknowledgment that they have done wrong becomes more important than fixing up the wrong that has been done. Through the workings of punishment, it is the *nature* of the wrongness of the act that must be recognised.

The Body

Foucault maintained that, in relation to punishment, "it is always the body that is at issue" (Foucault, 1977, p. 25). There may be a 'knowledge' of the body that is not about the physiology of its functioning and mastery of its forces, that is more than the ability to control them: "this knowledge and this mastery constitutes what might be called the political technology of the body" (Foucault, 1977, p. 26). The technology of the body can be seen at work in many ways including restrictions on ways those who are in trouble at school can sit, stand, and move: Stand up straight! Keep your hands by your sides! Sit there and don't move! Stand perfectly still! Look at me! Don't fiddle! In the application of punishment the physical position of the bodies of those who are not getting it right in schools is corrected, supervised, and tightly controlled.

The body can also be restricted, deprived of liberty or made to work. Punishment is no longer about the application of pain. "From being a part of unbearable sensations punishment has become an economy of suspended rights" where the submission of the body and its forces is paramount (Foucault, 1977, p. 11). Standing in the corner, sitting outside the principal's office, and being sent to stand at the back of the room are all ways that teachers tighten and confine the bodies of the 'bad' in schools.

THE WORKINGS OF PUNISHMENT FOR THE 'ABNORMALLY BAD'

Foucault maintains that we must "rid ourselves of the illusion that penalty is above all (if not exclusively) a means of reducing crime" (1977, p. 24). Penalty and punishment are instruments of a power that is more about a "network of relations, constantly in tension" rather than power seen as a quality, property, or possession held by particular individuals (Foucault, 1977, p. 26). The network of relations operating to ensure order in schools results in the great majority of students taking up appropriate behaviours for the great majority of time. While there are students who maintain inappropriate behaviours in spite of the workings of discipline and punishment, most of these students remain in the regular school setting, persistently annoying, consistently in need of correction, and subjected to ever more techniques of punishment.

It seems that getting it right as a 'normal' student does not mean that 'good' behaviour is always performed. In fact, getting it right at being a student may mean that some 'bad' behaviour is permitted, even expected, to be performed. It is expected, because the 'normal' student must also be read as an individual with an independent and strong personality. Along with the permission/expectation that students will perform 'bad' behaviour some of the time, there are also times when teachers are not 'too hard' on the 'bad' because these students can cause moments of fear. Teachers come to be "'passive' in relation to the child's 'active'" (Walkerdine, 1989, p. 31). Many teachers come to know that pushing too hard on some students can lead to revolt and this caution can turn to fear/loathing as power can be turned back on teachers by the actions of the 'bad'. Many teachers talk of the humiliation they feel at the hands of 'bad' students.

I went to a lesson with Mark at his regular school. The class was really awful—many treated the teacher with such disdain, it was humiliating. Mark was really well behaved and said later that he was shocked at the behaviour—that they were 'full-on'. The teacher later said that he hated working with the class but where could they go?—there weren't enough special places to take all the awful kids. But "that's the job".

Cath's Notes

It seems that sometimes the job of teachers is to suffer the 'bad' behaviour of students. As well as seeing it as 'the job', the dominant discourses involve a search for the reasons, even justifications, for students' 'bad' behaviour. This search can individualise students' background, family, motivation and/or emotional state, and often conclusions are drawn that, in spite of 'bad' behaviour, they are basically 'good kids'. Many can be seen as good kids because they can sometimes take up the appropriate position, demonstrate a desire to get it right at being a 'normal' student, and be reformed.

We were at a meeting at Fred's regular school. He had been in a lot of trouble—especially with another student, Bill, who had befriended him. The principal said that he didn't think Fred would make it at the school as he was getting into a lot of trouble with Bill. The principal spoke of an incident, saying, "Fred just told me to get lost and walked off—at least Bill did apologise. I know Bill's behaviour is probably worse than Fred's but at least Bill plays the game".

Cath's Notes

Bill, in spite of his 'bad' behaviour, had given sufficient indication that he was sorry for his 'bad' act. Bill would stay at the regular school as he was able to get it right by apologising, 'playing the game', even though the principal indicated his belief that Bill's 'bad' behaviour would continue. Bill could be read as being conscious of what it takes to get it right as a 'normal' (if difficult) student and, by apologising, possibly demonstrated that he also has a conscience. Yet for Fred, it was another story. The teachers at the regular school decided that they could not see themselves ever managing Fred's behaviour, or Fred ever getting it right enough for him to be successfully integrated there. Consequently, Fred would need to leave the regular school.

I was sitting with Paul, talking about how he was going at his regular school.

Cath: *So how do you think you will go there full-time next year?*

Paul: *OK, I guess.*

Cath: *How are the kids?*

Paul: *They're all right—they muck up a lot.*

Cath: *In the class?*

Paul: *Yeah. They don't listen and muck up. It's funny. Some of them should be here.*

Cath: *Why do you think they're not?*

Paul: *Don't know. They're all right.*

Cath: *I have a theory that what gets a kid to a place like this is hurting teachers. What do you think?*

Paul: *Probably.*

Cath: *Have you ever hit a teacher?*

Paul: *Mmmm. When I was in Year 3, I pushed the principal and he fell over. (laughs)*

Cath: *Really? Do you think any of the kids in your class at regular school have done that?*

Paul: *Probably not.*

Cath: *Most of the kids at our school have hurt teachers—Chris spat at his principal. Would you push a teacher now?*

Paul: *No!*

Cath: *So you think you might go OK at school?*

Paul: *Yeah. Sort of. But I don't think Sandy will.*

Cath: *How come?*

Paul: *He's just not normal Miss.*

Cath: *Mmmm. He really gets upset—like he can't control it—and then he hates himself afterwards.*

Paul: *He can't control it Miss.*

Cath's Notes

In this discussion, Paul identified that there were students who were 'bad' at his regular school. To get it right as a student making his way back to a regular school, Paul was supposed to find the 'bad' behaviour of some students amusing, funny. Being a little bit 'bad' is appropriate, 'normal'. In my thinking about why some students came to the special place and some did not, I speculated that one of the practices operating is that 'special' students take *extreme* action, such as hurting teachers, and Paul confirmed this as a possibility. Almost all of our students at the special school had hurt teachers in regular schools in a deliberate way. And those few students who had not? Sandy was one of them. His behaviour at his regular school (sitting and banging his head against a wall for almost an hour) was seen as mostly 'mad'. Perhaps Paul also believed this of Sandy: "he's just not normal Miss". Perhaps Sandy, in the dominant discourses, performed 'bad' abnormally. Perhaps because the 'abnormally bad' turn on teachers, they must be sent away, like the 'mad'. Even with close supervision and attempts to localise and limit the perpetrators' power to do damage, acts of 'abnormality', particularly those that involve violence towards teachers, cannot be tolerated. The 'abnormally bad' must be further differentiated.

Students read as 'abnormally bad' seem to be those for/with whom the intensive individualisation and practices around punishment do not seem to work. They seem to be those who hurt others, deliberately and consistently. But more than this, they do not seem to display remorse for their actions—do not seem to display that they have a conscience. These students go beyond the normally 'bad' and come to be read as 'abnormally bad'. Even within the category of 'bad' there is a binary of normal/abnormal. The 'abnormally bad' are not those who are read as 'mad' in the sense discussed in Chapter 3, *The Mad: being positioned as 'mad' and counteracting that positioning.* Some students are read as performing 'bad' and doing it in such seemingly extreme, and possibly non-emotional, ways that their 'badness' is 'abnormal'. They must go to the special school. They are sent away. This serves as a message to the 'bad' who remain in regular schools, and it limits the effects of the 'abnormally bad' on the 'normal' students in the regular school.

Managing the Behaviour

Foucault (1977, p. 182) saw the "art of punishing" to involve the referral of "individual actions to a whole that is at once a field of comparison". Students who are read as 'abnormally bad' can only be seen, in the dominant discourses, as dis-ordered, delinquent, disturbed—different from the ordered, the compliant, the 'normal'. The distance their behaviour places them from the norm is quantified in terms of "frequency, duration and intensity" (NSW DET, 1999, p. 27). The mechanisms of power disposed around the 'abnormal' are designed to brand them and, through this branding, alter their behaviour. The workings of discipline and punishment provide an example for all that is "based on the lesson, the discourse, the decipherable sign, the representation of public morality" (Foucault, 1977, p. 110). "Indiscipline" causes a "rupture" in the working of society and, through their 'wild' behaviour, the 'abnormally bad' are seen as rejecting civilisation itself (Foucault, 1977, p. 291).

Today, Peter was on the roof with Chris and some little kids were climbing up after him, as he's the leader. I walked out and thought about my usual 'get off the roof' stuff but reconsidered. He wouldn't have come off anyway. Instead, I looked and said, "Oh, good one Peter". He looked behind him, saw the little kids, and said, "Oh shit—get off you'll hurt yourself". I let him deal with it. Rewards and things help him to see himself as OK, but am I legitimising his behaviour?

Cath's Notes

In schools climbing on a roof is not usual, not 'normal'. It can be read as 'abnormally bad' and as a sign of one who cannot be controlled. In the dominant discourses, it is seen as best to administer consequences to students while they are in the act of being 'bad'. The students in this story were up high, out of reach of adults, seemingly powerful, and, for that moment, out of reach of consequences. In the dominant behaviourist discourse, negative consequences are the withdrawal of positive consequences. In order to be able to administer negative consequences, positive consequences must first exist. There must be rewards that can be taken away. Rewards, for Peter and all the other students, were in place at our special school: visual and verbal reinforcement for academic work (stamps, stars, stickers); concrete rewards for positive, appropriate, compliant behaviour (vouchers which can be traded in for drinks and food); and a positive, supportive relationship with teachers. Through receiving these rewards it was thought that students would come to view themselves positively: "I must be an okay individual if I am getting these things". Taking these reinforcements away forms the basis of negative reinforcement in the dominant special education discourse. In the story above I thought about 'talking firmly' but feared that this would have positioned me as one without power if he failed to get off. To get it right as a principal, I must be seen to have control. Because I recognised Peter as one who had influence and was misusing it by putting the younger students in an unsafe situation, he took up the position as a responsible senior and told them to get off. Win–win. Yet I was also concerned that in handing him this authority I might be seen to be getting it wrong as a principal by making it legitimate for him to have some authority in the school. In the dominant discourses, students are not supposed to have authority. After all, the 'abnormally bad' were sent to the special school to make sure that they came to know the limits of their power. So I was held between wanting to be seen to get it right in my profession and knowing that I must act. I acted to make sure the students came down from the roof, but I worried, in not administering any negative consequences, that I might have been getting it wrong as a principal.

A thorough, constant and consistent supervision is what the dominant discourses told me should be used with the 'abnormally bad'. This "supervision—both knowledge and power—over individuals who resisted disciplinary normalization" is used in prisons (Foucault, 1977, p. 296) and also in the special school. Plans to change the behaviour of the 'bad' identify "what needs to be taught, how it is going to be taught, who is going to teach it, when it will be taught and where it will be taught" (NSW DET, 1999, p. 14). Foucault (1977, p. 193) proposed that psychology has its origins in the "procedures of individualisation" and that through a psychology of learning and behaviour change, 'abnormally bad' individuals are scrutinised to discover the specific stimuli that precipitate their 'badness' and the type and intensity of consequences that are likely to decrease 'bad' behaviours. Each 'abnormally bad' individual has an "individualised learning program" (NSW DET, 1999, p. 14) describing the fine detail of their behaviour and specific consequences to be applied to help eliminate the 'abnormally bad' behaviour. Through such specificity and tight control applied to the 'abnormally bad' individual, behaviour is supposed to be contained, controlled and possibly changed.

The limits on the types and extent of behaviour codes and consequences used with the 'abnormally bad' are delineated by theories of behaviour change. Suspension and isolation are suggested as strategies (NSW DET, 1997), but their use is contained by the available knowledge about effective management practices and moral limits about the practices that seem to go 'too far'. Knowledge and morality are intertwined in this. For example, it is no longer considered appropriate to use corporal punishment with children. This is based on information that causing pain is not an effective way to bring about change (Bandura, 1977) and, at the same time, on ideas that harming children through physical punishment is an immoral act. Using physical punishment with children can be seen to have harmful psychological effects; it demeans the humanity of the child; and it demeans the humanity of the adult. At the same time we have psychological knowledge that physical punishment is not an effective strategy anyway. Educational psychology "is supposed to correct the rigours of school" (Foucault, 1977, p. 226). Psychology, both individual and educational, provides the knowledge that details the techniques for the punishment of children and, at the same time, places limits on the use of those techniques.

Yet these limits seem to be more elastic when applied to the 'abnormally bad'. There is some autonomy in the practices for the 'abnormally bad'. Punishment in this context often seems to have its own rules and its own knowledge. Often a school for the 'abnormally bad' is allowed to "fix its own norms, decide its own results" (Foucault, 1977, p. 129). Consequently, 'special' practices have been enabled for the 'abnormally bad', including isolation in 'time-out' and physical restraint. Practices of isolation and the deprivation of liberty as a behaviour management technique are allowed for in policy statements designed to guide general school practice: "Consideration can be given by schools to establishing isolation or time-out rooms" (NSW DET, 1997, p. 8). Such an isolation room in a regular school, operating as the ultimate in-school isolation, is thought to be in line with William Glasser's (1986) recommendations. (These are discussed in Chapter 2, *Discourses at work: examining dominant discourses in the special education of students positioned as emotionally/behaviourally disordered.)* In some special schools, there are also ideas about physical control and isolation leading to cathartic expression of rage, which in turn leads to capitulation and gradual establishment of trust that finally allows control by caring adults (Cline, 1992). Foucault spoke of how, through the workings of discipline, "punishment will be able to function openly as treatment" (1977, p. 256). This clarifies for me how it is that isolation in the regular school is a consequence, yet, in the special school, such a consequence is also meant to function as a treatment.

Through a Network of Disciplines

Just as the overall aim of an institution like a prison is "the constitution of a body of knowledge" that regulates practice (Foucault, 1977, p. 250), the special school's aim in the dominant discourses is to regulate the behaviour of the 'abnormally bad'. Consequently, it is supposed to be a place of observation through surveillance and the psychological/educational knowledge that must be acquired about the student. It is not so much the behaviour of the 'abnormally bad' that comes to characterise them, but the stories of their lives seen "from the triple point of view of psychology, social position and upbringing" (Foucault, 1977, p. 252). In such places as the special school the networks of support services are marshalled so that the 'abnormally bad' are engaged in a network of disciplines enabling them to be "medicalized, psychologized, educationalized" (Foucault, 1977, p. 306). This multi-disciplinary approach results in the movement of individuals from one disciplinary authority to another. These disciplines, particularly psychology, are given ever more important powers in the lives of the 'abnormally bad'. This allows a multiplying of the individualising technology as each discipline reproduces "in a more concentrated or formalised form, the schema of the power-knowledge proper to each discipline" (Foucault, 1977, p. 227).

Sending From the Margins

If the 'abnormally bad' still do not get it right, even in the special school, then the strategy used most often to punish them is suspension. Being given time away from the school, the deprivation of schooling, is seen as the most extreme strategy that can be offered (NSW DET, 1997). A punishment apparatus such as suspension is not a strategy that gets results once and for all, but forms part of a range of tactics. In placing suspension as the ultimate punishment and building administrative rituals around it, several things are achieved: schooling is read as more valuable if the ultimate punishment is to be deprived of it; the ultimate responsibility for discipline of students is firmly returned to the family; and the example is set for other students to learn to increase their valuing of being the good students and avoid the humiliation of being 'the bad'.

On Monday I paid over two hundred and fifty dollars to get all the alarms to the classroom fixed up. Chris got up on the roof and pulled them out when I was away from school. Kids said that Chris had done it. I went over to the room where he was playing with a Game Boy and asked him if he had pulled the wiring out. He kept playing the game and said he had. I asked him what got into him to do that—he ignored me and kept playing the game. I was so furious I said, "Right—that's it, you're suspended". He came rushing out after me. I sat on the verandah and he sat beside me. I was still furious.

Chris: *Please don't suspend me.*

Cath: *I'm really angry about the damage. The money I spent in getting that repaired I could spend on other things for the school.*

Chris: *I know—I am really sorry. Please don't suspend me!*

[He has tears welling up in his eyes.]

Cath: *What can you do to fix it up?*

Chris: *I can't fix the wiring.*

Cath: *No. I know that—but you could help clean the place up—clean up the playground.*

[Chris bursts into tears and runs out of the school. Peter, another student, sees him crying and runs up to him.]

Peter: *What's up mate?*

Chris: *(sobbing) She's not going to suspend me!*

[Peter looks at me and shrugs. Chris grabs the bin—still sobbing—and starts to pick up papers in the street.]

Cath's Notes

This story shows a mixture of consequences used in schools (both natural and logical), a clear indication that suspension is being used to punish, and the expectation that students should demonstrate sufficient contrition for doing the wrong thing. The story indicates that some students take on seeing suspension as a devastating consequence. Those who are suspended are deprived of their friends, and this is possibly the most effective aspect of suspension.

Other readings of this story can demonstrate the multiple ways that I was positioned as I felt my way through the complexity of getting it wrong/right as a principal. If I read this story in the light of the dominant discourses, then I got it wrong. By letting Chris 'off the hook', I was reinforcing inappropriate behaviour that would be performed again so that he could achieve what he wanted. I *should* have suspended him so that he would learn that he must accept reasonable consequences for his behaviour.

If I read this story in the light of getting it right as a caring, humane, woman then I also got it wrong. I should have been calm about the damage and not displayed my anger. I could be read as modelling for Chris a temper tantrum similar to the ones he displayed. I should have asked myself how I expected him to learn to do the right thing if I did not model it for him. But most importantly I should not have caused Chris to become as upset as he did. It is this reading in which I often catch myself, and even now, tears well in my own eyes at the memory of Chris's distress.

If I read this story in a poststructuralist light, I can better see the positions of one who is both immersed in and yet attempting to deconstruct dominant discursive practices. The teacher/principal has to keep order, while at the same time be humane. The teacher/principal has to be responsible for the school resources and, at the same time, be responsible for the welfare of children. The teacher/principal has to be consistent in the implementation of consequences and, at the same time, consider individual needs. Perhaps, caught in these binaries, I can read myself as trying to find a way through my anger and Chris's pain and offer him a way to fix things. Yet I feel/felt no satisfaction in finding this way through; even though Chris had found a way to get it right, watching him sob as he picked up the papers still resonates. The binaries and limits of the dominant discourses can be desirable and satisfying. At the same time, they can be sickening and painful.

For students, the emotions and feelings being constructed around the ultimate punishment of suspension involve the students being pointed to as different and in need of correction. But beyond that, their behaviour can be read as so 'over the edge', so abnormal, that they can no longer be considered as school students, even special school students. They need to get it right, and be seen to get it right, for them to take up the position of students again.

Searching for a Cause

Any determining cause that can explain 'abnormally bad' behaviour is sought out. Causes such as single-parent family, chemical imbalance, abuse, deficient social skills, or learned aggression gain prominence at different times to explain 'abnormally bad' behaviour. A behaviourist psychology, prominent in special education practice, might argue that its theories do not search for causes as such (Baer, Wolf and Risley, 1968). Rather, things that are external to the individual are the focus—the stimulus and antecedents to the inappropriate behaviour and the reinforcement and consequences that follow the behaviour. Still, in the manipulation of the stimuli/responses the total focus is on *individual* behaviour change.

The individual is the focus of such a psychology, as are the ideas around finding causes. Foucault (1977, p. 252) proposed that establishing a "determining cause" became important, as some kind of 'extenuating circumstances' needed to be found to explain why some individuals fail to become recognisably 'normal'. Rather than the social system being seen as responsible for creating the circumstances that produce the categories of normal/abnormal and bad/good, a merging of educational, corrective and psychological discourses takes place to (re)form those who are seen as 'bad individuals'. A network of causality is drawn up that enables the life stories of the 'abnormally bad' to explain how they came to be 'abnormally bad', and they are then categorised/read as disturbed/abnormal individuals. Once we have such an object as the 'abnormally bad', special education teachers can assess, measure, diagnose and treat/intervene. Causes/antecedents are needed so that, within the dominant discourses, special education teachers can resist seeing the power structures operating and instead see the treatments/interventions/consequences to be implemented in relation to the causes/antecedents, in order to change the behaviour of the 'abnormally bad' individual.

Searching for a Conscience

While the causes, treatments and follow-up procedures are laid out for the special educator to implement, there are significant feelings of confusion and anger surrounding the 'bad'.

My anger with Charlie's aggression finally came to a head for me when, as the students were about to get into their transport to go home, he calmly went to stomp on the head of a much younger and smaller student whom he had knocked to the ground. Charlie had already punched him in the nose and it was bleeding. The younger student tried to curl up into a ball to protect himself. Charlie was just about to stomp his boot directly onto his face when I grabbed Charlie and pulled him back—with a great deal of strength. I felt awful—I knew how I felt about Charlie. I hated the way he decided who should live and who should die—and that my grabbing him was the way I had dealt with this. I knew I couldn't let him hurt the little one but I still felt like I was at his level. He was suspended, of course, but what will it take to change him?

Cath's Notes

While I had done my 'duty of care' in protecting the younger student, there was anger and confusion about Charlie's 'pure' aggression. Perhaps, in addition to the aggression, it is also his beliefs and 'nature' that are seen to be less civilised than those of the teacher/principal. I could not contemplate, as a humanist subject, such acts of aggression performed 'calmly'. In the humanist discourse, acts of aggression are almost forgivable if they are performed through an excess of emotions, temporary loss of control, temporary insanity. Charlie's aggression was performed calmly with no outward sign of emotion. It is this type of violence, read as deliberate and uncaring, that caused me confusion and pain—children are not supposed to cause pain to others in such a deliberate and callous way. My reading of Charlie left him no space to be read as 'mad' as he performed his act without an excess of emotion. Consequently, he could only be read as 'abnormally bad' as he showed no signs of contrition or remorse, no moral conscience.

It seems that to take up the position of, and to be positioned as, 'abnormally bad' means that contrition or caring has not/cannot be displayed. Perhaps the category of 'abnormally bad' is a space where violence, toughness and remorselessness are the 'norm'. Perhaps in the lives of these students the abnormal is the norm (Ewald, 1992). Perhaps in demonstrating contrition Charlie would have been getting it wrong in his version of 'normal'. To display contrition, in the dominant discourses, is read as being on the way to 'recovery'. In Charlie's world, perhaps such recovery/healing is read as a weakness—getting it wrong for him. Perhaps to display such weakness would only make Charlie more vulnerable to the pain in his world. Perhaps to get it right in performing 'abnormally bad' Charlie could not possibly have done anything else than to show no remorse.

Disciplinary power constantly "supervises the very individuals who are entrusted with the task of supervising" (Foucault, 1977, p. 177). As a teacher, a principal, I was also subjected to the workings of discipline and recognised that the 'normal' way of dealing with aggression is often through some type of institutionalised aggression. In this story, I reacted physically and, in being physical, saw my actions as similar to the actions of Charlie. While this causes me some pain in reading/writing this, I see myself as immersed in the dominant teacher discourse of protecting the younger student while at the same time feeling remorse for possibly hurting Charlie through perhaps too vigorous protection. Doubly damned.

Admiring the Struggle

Power in schools works through the complex relationships of all those in schools. Power is not simply a teacher's power exercised over the powerless students; power invests students, "is transmitted by them and through them; it exerts pressure upon them, just as they themselves, in their struggles against it, resist the grip it has on them" (Foucault, 1977, p. 27). In this sense, 'bad' behaviour can be read as a struggle and there are sometimes traces of admiration for those who struggle. They can be read as brave and amusing by other students—and even teachers.

Peter's mother had died. He was back full-time at a new regular school but when his teacher at the regular school heard the news, she organised for him to visit us. Although Peter had not lived with his mother for some time, his new teacher thought that it would be better for him to spend time with us in case the death of his mother sent him over the edge. She didn't want that to happen as he had been going really well there—he was a problem, but one the school was dealing with.

Cath:	*When is the funeral?*
Peter:	*On Friday.*
Cath:	*Where?*
Peter:	*At Liverpool.*
Cath:	*Your teacher would like to go and I'll go if I can. Is there anyone else you'd like to be there?*
Sandy:	*Yes I'd like to go Miss—Peter?*
Mark:	*Yes can I come?*
Peter:	*What is this—a fucking school excursion?*

Everyone laughed.

Cath's Notes

Peter's ironic humour in the face of a very bleak time was found amusing by the students and myself. While Peter was attending a regular school full-time, his behaviour was still regarded as problematic, and, while he was exhibiting 'bad' behaviour, he was being maintained there. He had managed to engage with his teacher, get it right enough, for his teacher to want to persist with him. Many teachers, in the dominant discourses, take up the idea of teaching as a calling and they desire to make a difference in the lives of children. This can be even more rewarding if very difficult children are 'turned around'. I read Peter's teacher, in her arranging for him to visit the special school in a time of pain, as demonstrating her concern for, commitment to and connection with him and, at the same time, as being wary that such a crisis might precipitate the sort of behaviour that could not be managed in the regular school, and possibly sever the connection she had established with him.

Like those who work with the 'bad' in prisons, teachers are "technicians of behaviour: engineers of conduct, orthopaedists of individuality with the task of producing bodies that are both docile and capable" (Foucault, 1977, p. 294). In the special school this production of docile bodies is very often successful.

I ponder on the way that most of the kids don't want the chaos. The kids leaving in the taxis were very settled on Thursday and Friday so I didn't do any orderly leaving by classes. I find it so interesting that the kids come together to rescue situations much of the time. Like at high jump—lining up and playing the game. Why do they bother?

Cath's Notes

This success is not achieved simply through the application of punishment, but in a complex way with many students desiring to get it right as students—even, or especially, students who live the category of 'abnormally bad'. I observed such a desire in Charlie at different times. Yet many of our 'special' students were 'tough' boys who must control their bodies and their position as tough boys even in the face of pain.

At camp, I was in the bathroom and watched Fred walking across from the dam by himself. He's got no shoes on and is stepping on all these burrs. They must be hurting as he's crying. He starts saying to himself, "Stay cool, stay cool". He repeats this over and over while he finds a patch of dirt to sit on and pull them out. He's still got tears rolling down his face but is saying his mantra. I walk out to the front door to see him coming around the corner—not a tear in sight and his typical swagger.

Cath's Notes

In performing as 'abnormally bad', it seems that the body must be controlled by the mind. The bodies of the 'mad' are permitted, in the dominant discourses, to break down and be emotional, as 'madness' is constructed as an illness within the body. Yet the bodies of those performing as 'abnormally bad' are read as being controlled by the mind. It seems that it is the individual conscious mind that is constructed as being responsible for an individual's 'bad', and even 'abnormally bad', behaviour.

SO WHY DOESN'T IT WORK?

In the dominant discourses a teacher's job is to build responsibility in students and to give them the idea that they have freedom to choose their path in life. This 'freedom' can be seen as the idea of "bourgeois individuality. It is the fear of mass revolution which necessitates an apparently non-coercive form of government" (Walkerdine, 1989 p. 75). Through a system of discipline, as responsible teachers we try to ensure that students take up ways of using their freedom in responsible ways. If they do not do this then a system of punishment is implemented and intensified. Given such complex and intensive systems of discipline and punishment, it might be expected that the practices of the special school could 'repair the problem' and produce compliant students able to get it right in regular school. Certainly, the idea of 'fixing' problems is embedded in the thinking of teachers at the school and in my own.

Interesting to think about blame—someone had to be blamed that Chris wasn't getting better/doing as he was told/compliant. The idea that we must fix them up—I am also caught in this 'professionalism'—what else do I get my money for if I can't make him fit in?

Cath's Notes

Foucault saw that punishment is not intended to eliminate offences and bad behaviour "but rather to distinguish them, to distribute them, to use them" (1977, p. 272). He analysed the shift from a criminality that was mainly about crimes such as murder to one where crimes are mainly about property as a shift that

> forms part of a whole complex mechanism, embracing the development of production, the increase of wealth, a higher juridical and moral value placed on property relations, stricter methods of surveillance, a tighter partitioning of the population, more efficient techniques of locating and obtaining information: the shift in illegal practices is correlative with an extension and a refinement of punitive practices. (Foucault, 1977, p. 77).

Perhaps special schools for the 'abnormally bad', just as prisons, are not intended to cure and rehabilitate. Foucault (1977, p. 276) proposed that prisons are not intended to reform criminals but to produce delinquency. In differentiating this form of criminal activity so that it becomes dominant, other forms of criminal activity are able to be colonised and cease to be so devastating. Such differentiation "helps to establish an open illegality, irreducible to a certain level and secretly useful" (Foucault, 1977, p. 277). Foucault's idea was that by the production of the delinquent, society is mainly confronted by "localized criminality, limited in its power to attract popular support, politically harmless, and economically negligible" (1977, p. 278). This enables society to maintain a low level of everyday illegal practices and prevent broader, more socially dangerous forms of crime—even revolution. This political use of delinquency ensures that the types of crime committed are relatively minor, such as car theft or drug use. Yet they are made out to be of such critical importance to the rest of the community that more rigorous consequences are demanded by the community to keep them safe. Through constructing petty crime as serious, those who commit such crimes are branded, their lives scrutinised and surveilled and their crimes localised. While Foucault's ideas may at first be counterintuitive, perhaps the focus and surveillance of low level crime may serve the purpose of containing more radical forms of crime. For if we are so concerned with low level crimes and installing the apparatus to prevent and deal with these, then most criminals perform crimes that are already labelled as very serious in society and are less likely to move to more extreme activities as the less serious activities result in more serious consequences.

Perhaps the category of 'abnormally bad' functions in similar ways in that the same patterns of violence are reproduced and, in being predictable, are better able to be controlled. Perhaps more extreme behaviour is better contained, or not even entertained. Perhaps other forms of violence, for example emotional violence, are made less visible. Certainly, like Foucault's delinquent, the 'abnormally bad' student has been "invested, segmented, isolated, penetrated, organized, enclosed in a definite milieu" and produced as a pathologised subject (Foucault, 1977, p. 277). Perhaps, for both the criminal/delinquent and the 'abnormally bad' it is not accidental that the processes of discipline and punishment mostly catch and confine the poor and the marginalised in our society.

CONCLUSION

The practices of discipline and punishment that Foucault observed in prisons have some resonance with current available practices for those in regular schools who perform 'bad' behaviours and for the 'abnormally bad' who are sent from the regular school to the special school. With students who remain at the regular school, the normalising, surveilling and individualising practices of discipline work to subject them as students who, while/as well as being 'bad' some of the time, come to get the performance of student right. Technologies of punishment work to lay down the limits of what is tolerable, allow some types and extremes of 'bad' behaviour and not others, and make it clear what can be tolerated and what cannot at a particular time and place.

What cannot be tolerated in the regular school is the extreme, unpredictable, unreasoning and unreasonable behaviour of the 'abnormally bad'. These students are sent from the regular school to the special school where, just as in the prisons discussed by Foucault, the dominant discourses ensure that the 'abnormally bad' are subjected to the principles of extreme classification, intense correction, detailed modulation of consequences, special education, and close supervision. They are scrutinised for signs of 'cause' for their behaviour and for signs of a conscience and an emotionality that might indicate that they are on the way to recovery. Yet, perhaps, to move to be read as on the way to recovery is a position that is almost too difficult for them to take up. By failing to give signs of recovery they are rarely able to read as anything other than 'abnormally bad'. Perhaps in the dominant discourses they can do nothing else but fail, and so they are forever in the spotlight, handled with care, treated with caution. Ever vigilant, we wait for the 'abnormality' to surface and resurface.

In the next chapter, Chapter 5, *The Sad: Being positioned as 'sad' and counteracting that positioning,* I further examine the discourses that inform the ways we think about children and young people at the margins, specifically those who are living in state care and also branded as 'behaviourally/emotionally disordered'. I discuss the ways the dominant discourses seem to double back on children in out-of-home care and the ways they come to be positioned as somehow getting it wrong as appropriate children and not 'getting over' trauma quickly so that they can be placed in a new family. The practices involved in the dominant discourse around teaching children to get it right, not only as appropriate students but as appropriately lovable children, are explored.

REFERENCES

Baer, D. M., Wolf, M. M., & Risley, T. R. (1968). Some current dimensions of applied behavior analysis. *Journal of Applied Behavior Analysis, 1*(1), 91-97.

Bandura, A. (1977). *Social learning theory.* Englewood Cliffs, NJ: Prentice-Hall.

Cline, F. W. (1992). *Hope for high risk and rage filled children.* Evergreen: Evergreen Consultants Publications.

Davies, B., Dormer, S., Gannon, S., Laws, C., Rocco, S., Lenz Taguchi, H., & McCann, H. (2001). Becoming schoolgirls: the ambivalent project of subjectification. *Gender and Education, 13*(2), 167-182.

Dreikurs, R., Grunwald, B. B., & Pepper, F. C. (1982). *Maintaining sanity in the classroom.* New York: Harper & Row.

Ewald, F. (1992). A power without exterior. In T. J. Armstrong (Ed.), *Michel Foucault philosopher.* New York: Harvester Wheatsheaf.

Foucault, M. (1977). *Discipline and punish.* London: Penguin.

Glasser, W. (1986). *Control theory in the classroom.* New York: Harper & Row.

NSW Department of Education and Training. (1997). *Student welfare, good discipline and effective learning.* Sydney: Author.

NSW Department of Education and Training. (1999). *Who's going to teach my child?* Sydney: Author.

NSW Department of Education and Training. (2006). *Student discipline in government schools support materials.* Sydney: Author.

Smith, A. M. (1995). The regulation of lesbian sexuality through erasure: the case of Jennifer Saunders. In K. Jay (Ed.), *Lesbian Erotics.* New York: New York University Press.

Walkerdine, V., & The Girls and Mathematics Unit, Institute of Education. (1989). *Counting girls out.* London: Virago Press.

CHAPTER 5

The Sad: Being Positioned as 'Sad' and Counteracting that Positioning

Abstract: As detailed in Chapter 1, *Researching special schools: a poststructuralist approach*, this work explores the capacity to apply poststructuralism, in theory and in practice, in a setting where other discourses are dominant. I focus on my own work as principal in the context of a special education school where I worked with students categorised as 'emotionally/behaviourally disordered'. I analyse the discourses that inform this kind of work, both from the position of one who inevitably took them up, even becoming expert in them, and from a Foucauldian position of critique which sets out to render these discourses less able to be taken up.

In this chapter I examine the discourses that have informed the way we think about children living in out-of-home care who do not fit into the normal school system. I explore my own embeddedness in those discourses when I work with these children, and I subject the discourses to critique—to make them visible and analysable, showing the (often negative) effects they have on the children's lives. These are powerful discourses with powerful effects, and what I set out to do here is show how we are inevitably constituted by them and constitute the children with them, even while learning to distance ourselves from them and no longer hold them as revealing 'the truth' about the individual children we work with.

Keywords: Education, disability, emotional and behavioural disorders, out-of-home care, wards of state, binary/binaries, psychology, Foucault, poststructuralist research, deconstruction.

Samantha ran away with Peter today and found a dog that was lost. She clung to the dog and said she had to find its home. I made inquiries with neighbours and located the dog's home. Samantha didn't want to leave it—she wanted to wait until the owners came back to make sure that it was all right. I left her to it. She has been through too much and I don't want to fight with her any more—tame her. She has a right to be angry. I am immobilised by the pain she has been through, is still going through. She came back to school about twenty minutes later. At least someone has been found a home.

Cath's Notes

This chapter explores issues around state care for children, the development of a focus on the protection of the child, the positioning of the parent/mother as one who is responsible for the continuous care of the child, and the placement of children in situations most like the fiction of a 'real' family. I examine the positionings of these children as 'other than normal' in dominant psychological discourses, that happen through close observation, normalising practices, and 'treatment' involving care/control. I also examine the silences around pain, sadness, sexuality and poverty and the implications of these silences for the 'sad', for the teaching and support team at the school and for myself.

As in earlier chapters, I point out to the reader that the following stories of the teachers and students at the school are full of irony. I use irony as a way of 'checking up' on myself to catch myself out when I am reiterating dominant discourses. My use of irony also reflects my deep involvement in my positionings, particularly in this chapter when I reflect on the deep sadness around those students living in out-of-home care.

There was great complexity in the discursive construction of the students who we came to see as the 'sad' at our school. Predominantly, the students seen as the 'sad' were those, like Samantha, who were positioned in the category of 'emotionally/behaviourally disordered', and no longer lived with their families. The 'sad' are named, at first, in terms of their living arrangements, rather than branded by their behaviour/disability. This naming seems to evoke a status of 'other' than 'proper' living arrangements with one's biological family, particularly one's mother. These children live in arrangements that are the 'substitute' for, or 'alternate' to, care in the family home. They have been called 'wards of state' in NSW; once they were in 'alternative care', then in 'substitute care', now they are in 'out-of-home' care; in England they are 'looked

Cath Laws

after' children. Their naming is always in terms of their residence; they are tied to, yet always separated from, their one, true 'biological' home. At least one third of the students at the school lived away from their families of birth and were in the care of the state.

BEING IN STATE CARE

In 2009 in Australia there were over 31,000 children and young people living in out-of-home care (Australian Institute of Health and Welfare, 2009). In NSW, where our school is situated, there were 14,667 children and young people in out-of-home care in June, 2008, compared with 9,273 in June, 2002 (Wood, 2008). The main reason generally given for children coming into care is a parent acknowledging an inability to care for the child without relief/support, and the second most common reason (30%) is the child being at risk of abuse (NSW Community Services Commission, 2000). Children who enter a state care/protection system are seen as being among the most vulnerable children in Australia. They are victims of abuse, neglect or family breakdowns. They may not have support from their extended family, and are often educationally and socioeconomically disadvantaged (Osborn and Delfabbro, 2006; Law Reform Society, 1997).

Yet these children have not always been constituted, in the dominant discourses, as the most vulnerable in our society. Societies have always had to deal with children whose parents have died or whose parents cannot care for them. Large institutions and orphanages usually provided homes for these children, as did transportation to new colonies or territories (Hacsi, 1995). In Australia, early approaches to child welfare intervention were aimed at rescuing/reforming the children of deficient (often convict) parents (NSW Community Services Commission, 2000). These children were placed with 'good' families so that they could come to behave in socially acceptable ways. In the early nineteenth century adoption ceased to be seen as a viable option, as it was thought to enable irresponsible parents to abandon their children more willingly (NSW Standing Committee on Social Issues, 1989). In the late 1880s foster care came to be seen as a more viable option than orphanages. Children, usually those who were older, were placed with families who needed extra help in settling and expanding the colony. Large groups of children were imported from Britain for this purpose (NSW Department of Community Services, 1998). The removal of children from Indigenous Australian families was "to literally try and breed out the Aboriginal race" (NSW Community Services Commission, 2000, p. 25). It seems that children were placed in the care of the state system as a way of ensuring care in the context of the survival of a prevailing social order.

'BAD' PARENTING/MOTHERING

The idea that children were taken into care for their safety and protection became dominant in the middle of the twentieth century. The removal of children from their live and present parents arose from the focus on child abuse and its effects brought to public attention with the publication of the 'battered child syndrome' (Kempe, Silverman and Steele, 1962). Removal of children from their parents became a largely involuntary system for the families (Rosenfeld, Altman, Alfaro and Pilowsky, 1994). This post-war focus on the abuse of children and the need for them to be protected from abusive parents was accompanied by an emphasis on adoption—a clean break from the family to overcome any genetic influences or bad beginnings. Ideas of giving children a new life were reinforced by the ideology of motherhood, where care of children is not only a duty but also a source of fulfillment. This provided fertile ground for Bowlby's (1951) ideas about the disastrous consequences of maternal deprivation. 'Bad' mothers did not give their children enough love and attention. It was seen that if children persistently received 'bad mothering' then they should be removed from the 'bad' mothers and adopted by 'good' mothers. The number of adoptions in Australia peaked in 1971/1972 (NSW Community Services Commission, 2000).

After the second world war, there was a need to ensure that women relinquished the 'men's jobs' in which they had been employed (Game and Pringle, 1983). Not only did many women return to domestic labour but increasing proportions took up 'female jobs' in the paid workforce. To get it right as a woman, one could work in 'female' work or be married and have children. In 1947 less than one fifth of the female labour force was married (Game and Pringle, 1983). The work of Bowlby (1951) held woman with children totally responsible not only for the physical, but also the emotional and intellectual wellbeing of their children. If mothers failed to give children constant care, then in terms of the now dominant discourses on mothering, there would be disastrous effects on the child. Through the modern discourses on mothering, 'confirmed' by the work of Bowlby, women were compelled to attend continuously to their children's needs if they were to be read as 'good mothers'.

By 1975/1976 the number of adoptions in Australia had halved (NSW Community Services Commission, 2000). Factors that are seen to have caused this are the availability of effective birth control, provision of income support for single parents, changing community attitudes and women's increased economic independence (Healey, 1999). Married women had their own children who required constant care, and birth control helped to limit the number of children who were unplanned and made available for adoption.

The changing community attitudes, which resulted in less children being adopted, also included ideas about children's needs from their 'natural' family (NCOSS, 1987). The gaze of dominant psychological discourses includes the child and the family but does not hold up for scrutiny "the social-historical influences that construct the family unit" (Burman, 1994, p. 75). Issues of poverty or even the social construction of 'childhood' and 'family' do not seem to be the domain of the dominant psychological discourses. "The mother is glued to the family through discourses of family structure, and within that structure the child is glued to the mother through discourses of attachment" (Burman, 1994, pp. 75-76). Through ideas about attachment and a biological model of mothering, psychology "naturalises class and cultural privilege" (Burman, 1994, p. 85). The intense gaze on mothers, organised through dominant psychological discourses, reflects the broader social regulation of women's lives. In the 1980s the costs of large residential care facilities, and the prevailing economic ideologies of the 'family' as the basic economic/social unit, saw a move toward foster care as the most desirable option for children seen to be in need of care and protection. Ainsworth and Hansen (2005, p. 195) report that almost 94% of the Australian children in out-of-home care are in home-based care that is generally regular foster care or minimally monitored kinship care.

The removal of children from parents who are read as abusive involves a double movement in the dominant child protection discourse comprising the rescue of children and, at the same time, subjection of them to the pain of 'separation'. Such a separation is seen to result in emotional difficulties and damage to the child (Rosenfeld, Pilowsky, Fine, Thorpe, Fein, Saletsky and Nickman, 1997). The idea that separation involves pain and emotional damage is informed by a rhetoric that constitutes children as naturally bonded, through genetics, to their parents/mother. Being with one's birth parents has now become naturalised and is constituted as the morally right way to be. Consequently, families and children 'at-risk' have come to be supported as much as possible in state child welfare practices. In current practices, if children are to be placed away from, or 'taken' from the family, close connections must be maintained with families and the children returned to their natural family as soon as possible. Rutter's (1974) criticism of Bowlby proposed that the negative developmental outcomes observed in institutionalised infants were caused by the disruption of the child's entire life circumstances, not just the separation from mother. Yet, in the current dominant discourses, while children are removed for their protection, this is usually only on a short-term basis. In order to meet the needs of children, they are seen as needing to be with the family/mother, as separation is considered to be damaging. Such an individualised and familial focus happens with little awareness that such practices are informed by the dominant social and economic ideologies. Earlier practices that now seem unthinkable, such as removing Aboriginal children from their parents because of their race, and the forced child migration to Australia of primarily poor white children from Britain and Ireland, were similarly informed by social and economic ideologies.

I observed this dilemma of whether to leave abused children with their families or whether to remove them being played out by state authorities over twenty years. At those times when the dominant state welfare practices are to leave/support children in the home, a monitoring practice develops with the stated goal of protecting children. A kind of surveillance of families/mothers is enacted to ensure that children are receiving the 'right' kind of mothering. Mandatory notification of child abuse appears to be a major mechanism of this surveillance. With the mandatory reporting of child abuse introduced in the 1980s, reports of suspected child abuse to the statutory body in NSW increased at a phenomenal rate, for example a 90% increase between 2001/2002 and 2007/2008 (Wood, 2008, p. 119).

With the current focus on the family as the responsible unit, 'bad parenting' results in children being taken into state care. Between June, 1996 and June, 2005 the number of children in formal out-of-home care in Australia increased by 70% (Smyth and Eardley, 2008). There is a clear contradiction between the public desire to maintain the family unit while dramatically increasing the numbers of children taken into state care. This contradiction will be discussed later in this chapter, particularly in terms of the targetting of the 'poor'. Carter (2002, p. 15), for example, found that most parents with children in care were receiving a pension or benefit.

Children who are seen to be not safe in their families are to live in places as close as possible to a 'normal' family home, and returned as soon as possible to the family/mother. The underlying priority in most jurisdictions is to keep children with their original family wherever possible. If children are placed in care, the goal is ultimately to reunite them with their families where appropriate (Smyth and Eardley, 2008, p. 3). Again, this is the rhetoric. However, as children coming into care most often come from poor families, they are becoming less likely to return to their families. Wood (2008, p. 613) reports that there has been a significant increase in the numbers of children and young persons in out-of-home care remaining in care longer.

FINDING ANOTHER HOME

The contradictions lying at the heart of official discourses started to become more evident in the 1990s. Ainsworth (1999) argued that approaches to the care of children by the state are dominated by ideas about de-institutionalisation, normalisation, mainstreaming, least restrictive environments, minimal intrusion, and diversion. While children are removed from their family home because of abuse and/or the inability of the family to provide appropriate care for their children, once they are in care, the state is then scrutinised to ensure that children are, wherever possible, returned to their family home. If this is not possible then the next most desired placement is in another family home. 'Family' is seen, in dominant discourses, as the basic unit of social life. But while the nuclear family has emerged as the privileged form of family, it has never been a reality (Burman, 1994, p. 65). Perhaps, as Burman suggests, the focus on the 'family' providing the resources for the care of children has been produced "in a climate of increasing privatisation and reduction of welfare services and benefits, [and] the rhetoric of celebration of family support clearly works to exonerate the State from its responsibilities" (Burman, 1994, p. 71).

When a child is removed from an abusive situation, the most desirable type of placement is seen as either with family members or a placement that is like a family—a foster family. Placing a child in another 'family home' is constructed as least intrusive in a continuum of services (Clarke, 1997b). The types of services currently available for children in NSW includes foster placements, small residential homes run by community/church organisations, and units/houses rented for a child and carers who work to specific rosters. Delfabbro, Osborn and Barber (2005) discuss a 'continuum' of placements for children and young people in out-of-home care. This continuum has secure, more restrictive residential care towards one end and less restrictive family-like arrangements towards the other end. They propose that it is time to move away from this continuum and provide services that meet the specific needs of children and young people. It is interesting that ideas of 'restrictiveness' inform the types of living arrangements provided for those in out-of-home care. "Restrictiveness generally refers to the extent to which children are free to make choices concerning their own actions and experiences, and is usually compared with the typical environment experienced by children living at home with their biological parents" (Delfabbro *et al.,* 2005, p. 11). Ideas of 'choice' are dominant for those living in out-of-home care—they choose to behave badly, they choose to run away, and they choose not to connect with others. Those that choose family-like arrangements are entitled to more choices, while those that do not must have their choices restricted.

A major concern in the dominant child protection/welfare discourses is the movement of children in and out of the child abuse/welfare system (Delfabbro and Barber, 2003). 'Placement movement' is seen as an important indicator of the quality of state care. As children experience more placements, the probability of reunification with their family is thought to decrease and multiple placements are seen to produce unstable relationships that can negatively affect the ability of children to attach to significant others (Proch and Taber, 1985). Such instability is seen to foster personality disturbance for some children, and the consequences are thought to be long lasting (Festinger, 1983). That many children drift from home to home without permanency is often considered 'worse' than the abuse itself (Rosenfeld *et al.*, 1997).

Yet many children in care are provided with consistent carers and do not move on from placement to placement. Usher, Randolph and Gogan (1999) found that, similar to children placed with relatives, 75% of the children in their study soon left the care of the state. Of these, 80% experienced only one or two placements. Even for the children who remained in care, nearly 50% had no more than two placements. Among all children whose experience began in foster homes, fewer than 3% had more than six placements. The picture of children who are removed from home facing a life involving multiple placements does not seem to be an accurate one for the great number of children in state care. Delfabbro and Barber (2003, p.16) found less than 6% probability of a placement breakdown if a child was less than ten years old and if they scored at the lower end of a conduct disorder scale. These are the "easier to care for" children (Smyth and Eardley, 2008, p. 4). The young, the 'good', and the easy to care for seem to fare better in taking on a new family.

Delfabbro and Barber (2003) report that about 20% of children and young people who come into out-of-home care do not fit into foster care situations. The children in out-of-home care who came to our school were generally children whom foster care did not 'fit'. They had had multiple placements, multiple breakdowns, and were mostly living in houses/flats rented by welfare organisations, where care was provided by carers who worked to specific rosters. They were the children for whom the system was seen as failing (NSW Community Services Commission, 2000; Wood, 2008). The critique of the current practices suggests the system is failing some children, yet it is those children themselves, rather than the system, who are targeted for repair. They are read as 'high needs kids' (Wood, 2008) whose needs are thought to be complex, multiple and challenging (Delfabbro and Barber, 2003). They become the target for change in order to enable them to fit into the services that can be provided, with the most desired service being the one that is most like a family home.

THROUGH PSYCHOLOGY

Dominant psychological discourses inform child development and parenting practices and emphasise the importance of nurturing children. Foucault proposed that psychology "appropriates most of the domains of human sciences" (1994, p. 252). Education has been appropriated by psychology and this is particularly so in the field of special education. Dominant psychological discourses create the category of 'emotionally/behaviourally disordered'. While there are psychological approaches that embrace poststructuralist and critical theories, the dominant psychological discourse, through which teachers' work in special education is constituted, is developmental/categorising/behavioural. As Flax points out, psychology, like any other discourse or set of discourses, "is a product and reflection of human wishes and practices, including the will to power. The availability of certain kinds of knowledge is as much a matter of contingency, the available struggles of power, and the history of past and present practices as it is the triumph of truth over error" (1993, p. 31). In this context, the psychological practices in which teachers are immersed involve ideas about development, learning, emotions and their disturbance/regulation, and behaviour change, as well as ideas about attachment, loss and grieving.

Burman proposes that psychology, rather than telling us the truth of individual being, became dominant in order to meet demands generated by prevailing social anxieties. In particular, "modern psychology came of age with the political utility of mental testing" (1994, p. 18). Psychology, through mental testing, was able to "classify, measure and regulate, in particular, those populations deemed a social threat to the prevailing order" (Burman, 1994, p. 18). Psychology emerged as the science of the mental and was naturalised through the practices of measurement and categorising, particularly "the notion of mental age underlying IQ tests" (Burman, 1994, p. 14). The IQ of the students at our school was measured, and needed to be at least 'average' so that their behaviour could then be defined, in contrast, as aberrant and disturbed. None of the children at our special school fell into the 'intellectually disabled' category, since for children so classified, aberrant behaviour can be seen as part of the intellectual disability, and hence they must be sent to a different special place. By meeting the criterion of at least 'average' intelligence our students were positioned, through the dominant discourse, as children who knew what they were doing—doing/being 'mad/bad/sad' on purpose and with a purpose.

But the tools of measurement that are used by psychology do not merely describe what is already there, they *produce* "objects" and "subjects" (Burman, 1994, p. 3). Psychology demands that "technologies of measurement" (objects) be produced (Burman, 1994, p. 3) so that students like the students at this special school can be measured in terms of their disturbance (and thus produced as particular kinds of subjects). This production is usually achieved through the category of the psychiatric disorder they are given under the DSM-IV (American Psychiatric Association, 1994) and the Child Behaviour Checklist (Achenbach, 1991). The latter instrument indicates whether students are turning their 'mad/bad/sad' behaviour in on themselves (internalising), or on others (externalising). Psychological discourses that seek to measure and categorise the normalcy/abnormalcy of children and adults produce not only subjects, but also the obviousness, even inevitability, of the subjects' 'condition' (Laws and Davies, 2000). The inevitability of the 'sad' being read as 'bad' and 'mad' is produced through a psychological categorising that holds them in a place of damage/abuse where they not only get their behaviour wrong, but their very existence is tainted by being a child without a family.

THROUGH 'FIXING' THE CHILD

In helping the child in state care to 'fit' into a new family or return to their old family, psychological discourses are called on to provide both the category and the remedy. Foucault (1994, p. 256) talked of psychology always having its eye on "what can be known" about humans and their behaviour. In the dominant special education discourse, when we observe children it is also with a view to how we can change their behaviour. As special educators, we are immersed in a discourse that tells us that our primary focus must be to directly intervene to change behaviour and to discover the key to what makes a particular child 'tick'. As teachers we seem to be compelled to order what is disordered, calm what is disturbed, socialise what is delinquent, and fix what is broken. Psychology often hides the "chaos and complexity" of the lives of those under scrutiny (Burman, 1994, p. 19). Discourses of intervention rely on apparently 'objective' observations of behaviour from which teachers are required to develop a program to intervene—to make the child less 'bad' or 'mad' and even less 'sad'.

I took him into the office—his tiny little hand in mine—and cradled him, watching him watching his tiny little fingers touching tips, picking his nails. He said nothing. It was more what he didn't say. He could not be brave now and yet he could not cry either. I sat with him and his teacher for at least an hour—just holding—feeling pain all around me. He had no idea why he wasn't going to live with the new family—why they didn't want him.

Cath's Notes

In the dominant educational discourse, teachers use covert regulation to ensure the production of "self-regulating, rational individuals" (Walkerdine, 1990, p. 29). This regulation can become more overt with those branded as 'emotionally/behaviourally disordered'. When working with the 'sad', however, teachers move back into more covert regulations, as if the very realities of the lives of the 'sad' make us want to be/be seen to be more humane, more gentle, more understanding. Yet special educators are subjected by another powerful discourse that aims at the even more rigorous taming of these children so that they can be wanted by another family. The contradictions of implementing programs that make these children more desirable to those who might care for them, and our own feelings of anger and sadness at the types of services and support that are available to them, became part of our everyday work of the special school.

It is always the child who is purposefully branded, rather than, for example, the discourse through which the branding is done. Psychological discourses produce for teachers a split between emotions and rationality—separating them in such a way that being emotional, having strong feelings, is read as irrational. The dominant discursive practices in which we were immersed as special education teachers told us, and continue to tell special education teachers, that to get it right as teachers we must work with the 'sad' on their emotions in such a way that we teach them to control their emotions and their excesses. This separation of the rational and the emotional in the dominant discourses was made particularly clear to us when working with our 'sad' students. We had to be able to maintain our distance, through a pedagogy that denies the power relation with the child and that enabled us to keep a professional distance from children as their teachers. We responded to the call to maintain our 'emotional distance', not to be too enmeshed with the stories of their pain-full lives, but to fix their problematic behaviours.

The range of problematic behaviours of children living in state care is seen as wide and deep. The research tells us that being without a 'natural' family has a significant negative impact on children. Halfon, Mendonca and Berkowitz (1995) found that 84% of their foster care sample had developmental and emotional problems. They also found that

> younger children were more likely to have gross and fine motor problems. Language abnormalities were most frequently observed in children aged one to five. Cognitive problems affected approximately one third of the population under age five years and were detected in 52% of school-age children. Emotional, self-regulatory (coping and self-help), relational, and behavioural abnormalities were most prevalent in school-age children. (Halfon *et al.*, 1995, p. 389).

These children are also read as having impaired social skills, lacking self-esteem, and not having the skills of social conformity (Clarke, 1997a). They are seen as aggressive, depressed, withdrawn and impulsive, and are often over-represented in the population of those with a mild intellectual disability. They are also said to display an exaggerated dependency and "the tendency to compulsively, though unconsciously, evoke from the new environment a repetition of the original rejection" (Cashmore and Castell-McGregor, 1996, p. 367).

So it was with the little one in the previous story. He did not present as 'little orphan Annie', desperately, yet cutely, searching for another family. I read him as angry/sad with his *natural* family for hurting him, and angry/sad with those who took him away from his family/mother in spite of what was happening to him. While I read him as possibly knowing that he would not be allowed to go back home given the level of his mother's heroin addiction, it was where he had said he wanted to be most of all. Psychological discourses both contribute to and reflect dominant assumptions and debates about families. One of the dominant ideas about families is the reification of mothering—that this is the only type of love or care that is real, natural, 'normal'. The 'sad' take this up. Being back with their real mother is the place they want to be most of all. If this was not going to happen, the little one above told me later, he wanted to live somewhere that was relatively 'normal'. He was not happy with the foster family whom he had visited to see if he might live there—they were 'too tough'. Yet he said he would give them a go, as he wanted to get out of the group home. Like Annie. Unlike Annie, he did not show joy, and, most of all, he was not grateful that he was being rescued. Yet the literature referred to above sees him as having an "exaggerated dependency" (Steinhauer, 1991, p. 367) and evoking, even bringing on himself, rejection by a new family. The pain I feel him to be feeling is to be silenced—just as he is silent. The contradictory discourses around children in state care produced pain for me and for the school team. The stories of this pain "are held as painful secrets in the silence: a pain so bad that it can never be articulated is not an absence of pain, and can thus have an effect on others even though nothing is said" (Walkerdine, 1997, p. 43).

Walkerdine's (1997) work on the storyline of Annie and Daddy Warbucks has resonance with me. In Walkerdine's reading, *Annie* tells the story of "the poor little girl who has nothing who in fact has something very precious: her charm and capacity to induce love. Not only does this bring her the reward of a family, but it solves the problems of a nation" (1997, p. 104). In *Annie* the message for the working-class girl is that escape and finding a middle-class life/family is a solution that will take pain away.

She had failed again—the family didn't want her. They were sure that they were getting someone they could rescue. They weren't prepared for—were unable to see—that things couldn't just be fixed because someone gave her a 'normal' family. She hardly recognised any of us and just wanted to watch 'Annie'—which she did. No tears—just immersed in the movie.

Cath's Notes

Not only were some of the children at the school immersed in the fantasy of being Annie—being rescued and loved as she was seen to be, but also those who foster a child seem to be immersed in the storyline, and expect that the little girl they are rescuing will be cute and lovable—their own Annie.

THROUGH OBSERVATION

In the dominant discourses, to get it right as special education teachers we engage in trying to fix the problematic behaviours of children, firstly through close observation, on which we base intensive programs of intervention. We are required to observe students' behaviour to see how they start their work, how they ask for help, how they do their work. Not only is children's academic work the focus of our observations, but the way they relate to others must also be made 'normal'. In order to develop an appropriate intervention, we observe how students get on with others, meet and greet others, deal with praise, and deal with rejection. These are all closely observed and measured and the complexity of the individual is broken down into specific behaviours and responses. Through the observing, measuring and categorising, in the dominant discourse, it seems that we are required to engage in producing and reproducing "the object that is measured"—the 'emotionally/behaviourally disordered' child (Burman, 1994, p. 84). In order to do this, and to be read as effective teachers, we are almost required to make invisible the facts of these children's lives so that we can step into our interventions. By focussing on the objective, aberrant behaviour of the 'sad' we teach them to get it right as 'normal' students and help them to learn all the basic skills required. As competent teachers, we come to "rely on a psychological model of the child as learner which presupposes that knowledge is internalised activity" (Walkerdine, 1989, p. 143). For the 'sad', this internalised activity can be seen as lacking, interfered with by the sad realities that they do not have anyone to care for them and love them as a family would. So, as well as getting it right as students, we help to make them 'wantable'—to get it right as loving, lovable and 'normal' children able to live in a 'normal' family.

THROUGH A NORMALISING GAZE

In the dominant discourses, children with natural/normal parents are read as full of needs and as requiring attentive, indulging care from parents. Children who are in the care of the state, on whom the state "inscribes its learning schedules", are read as requiring regulation and training (Burman, 1994, p. 66). In helping children to get their behaviour right, I was informed by discourses constituting what is 'normal' and 'desirable' in a child—not desirable in the sexual sense but in the sense that they fulfill expectations as a child. They must learn to inhabit the category of child that someone would want to care for and look after. In this way I was compelled, to get it right as a teacher, to prepare children for the fiction of the 'normal' family. Looking reflexively at the dominant behaviourist psychological discourses that informed my practice, it was my job to analyse 'normal' behaviour and to "seek where it had deviated, what it was disturbed by, and how it could be brought back into normal working order" (Foucault, 1973, p. 35). I did this in the framework of the "reflexive and generalizing—and foundational—relationship that psychology establishes for itself" (Foucault, 1994, p. 258). This framework was foundational for our work with students at the school. To get special education practice right, teachers work to make students' development as learners 'normal' and fix up any learning problems they have. Teachers try to 'fix up' children's emotional development, and they place children's feelings and emotions, and how they deal with them, under scrutiny. Teachers instruct the 'sad' in how to make 'normal' and proper responses to rules and consequences; how to develop behaviours that make them desirable as children; and also how to eliminate behaviours that make them undesirable. All this was achieved through immersing our students, and ourselves, in psychological discourses that place these children under a normalising gaze that "dominates the entire field of possible knowledge" (Foucault, 1973, p. 167).

Through this normalising gaze, teaching practices are used to regulate and to help produce what it means to be a 'normal' child. Foucault saw that "education was given a positive value as enlightenment; to train was a way of bringing into the light" (1973, p. 64). This light encompasses the emotional development of the child, particularly where such development is thought to have been disrupted/damaged. In the regular school, teachers act as facilitators "to counter the effects of bad mothering" and engage in "the monitoring of normality and pathology" (Walkerdine, 1989, p. 78). This is partly achieved through regulating students' behaviour so that they become self-controlled, self-directed and obedient. Burman points out that "obedience is a covert [rather than an overt] outcome" (1994, p. 170) of child-centred practices, "since children are considered to be more willing to obey rules if these appear to arise out of their own deliberations and choices" (1994, p. 170). Not only must children obey rules, they must desire to be obedient. But more than this, to get it right in the dominant discourses, the 'sad' must come to know and use the behaviours, words, gestures of the 'normally' loved, and not the abused, child so that they can be loved and not abused. In this way abuse is normalised as how anyone would respond to an undesirable child. The normalising strategies of the 'normal', regular school are used in the special school in ways that focus on helping children to make the choice to be good and lovable so as to no longer invite abuse. The demonstration of such choice on the part of the child is most desired because it means that children are on the way to being cured, to being 'normal'. These strategies seem to be elongated in time and intensified in practice, almost to the extent that they become theatrical.

Peter is going into placement for a week as his mother feels she can't cope. He was going into placement this afternoon and didn't know yet—his mother not being able to find a way to tell him. I wanted him to know so that he could have time to think about it and get anything out before he went. It would be fatal for him if he mucked up. I also thought that it could be a lot longer than a week, but Community Services didn't want him to know that yet. I took him over to Sam's class to tell him, with Sam. Sam had similar experiences and I thought this might be helpful.

Cath:	*Sam, Peter's mum has been having a lot of trouble looking after him and he's going to live with another family for a week—have you ever gone to live somewhere else for a while?*
Sam:	*Yeah—give 'em heaps mate.*
Cath:	*Well that might be one way of dealing with it—I wonder what might happen if he gave them heaps?*
Peter:	*Where is it?*
Cath:	*It is close to here. I'm not sure who lives there. But, Sam, what was it like for you when you lived somewhere else?*
Sam:	*It was OK. Once I stayed in this place and it was really cool.*
Cath:	*Did you give them heaps?*
Sam:	*Nah. It was really strict but you did heaps of good stuff—like going out.*
Cath:	*Have you got any advice for Peter?*
Sam:	*If it's a good place you'll get to do good stuff, mate.*
Peter:	*How long will it be?*
Cath:	*It's probably just this week. You are supposed to go home on Friday night—how do you feel about it?*
Peter:	*I don't know.*
Cath:	*Do you think you and your mum will ever be able to live together in a way where you behave like she wants and she looks after you like you want?*
Peter:	*(teary) No.*
Sam:	*No mate that's not right. I used to hate my mum—she was a fucking bitch—but now—I love her.*
Cath:	*You know Sam—that's the first time I've ever heard you say that about your mum?*
Sam:	*Yeah.*
Cath:	*Peter, would you like to stay over here with Sam for a while and have a talk to him?*

Peter: *Yes!!*

I leave them to it—they don't talk any more about personal stuff and Sam teaches him how to play a game on the computer.

Cath's Notes

In this story I articulate those discursive practices that hold children and teachers in place. I am almost blaming of the mother that she is not able to get it right as a mother and at least tell him herself that she is sending him into care. I can see when I read this transcript as an object to be studied that I display little sympathy for what it would be like to tell your child this. As 'substitute' mother I am the one who 'needs' to tell him. In the discourses around children in state care there is heavy responsibility placed on women professionals to meet all the needs of children. It seems like, and feels like, "women, as teachers, mothers, carers and caring professionals, are absolutely necessary—and responsible—for the moral order" (Walkerdine, 1989, p. 76). I tell Peter when I do because I am immersed in the psychological discourse that tells me that he might need time to 'get things out'. This psychological and gendered discourse tells me of the possible dangers involved if boys do not get things out and, instead, have them eat away inside them. Not only is getting things out seen to avoid potential damage but also, once they are out, this should be sufficient to dissipate the problem—there should be no more need to 'carry on'. Such limits placed on emotions also relate to time, in that there seems to be a limited length of time for which emotions can be displayed. And there are limits on the intensity of emotions that can be 'normally' displayed. I also 'know' that if Peter is to be cared about, looked after by the state in this time of respite, then he has to get it right at being good. Not to show gratitude through good behaviour can be 'fatal' in terms of how he might be viewed. Not getting it right in this foster placement means that he may be viewed as problematic and find himself embarking on a care pathway that has him positioned as forever problematic. In involving another child I make explicit the idea that children in care come to distrust adults and to rely on other children for the 'real' facts.

Sam gives a different view to mine—if you have to live somewhere else, show your anger, "give them heaps"; though, when I suggest he consider another answer he rapidly corrects his initial suggestion. Some young people see foster care as too restrictive, others say they already have a family and do not wish to have another. The most common response by young people when asked what living situation they would choose is living by themselves with or without a worker (Gosbeli and Jenkins, 1999). The child's voice of experience with state care differs from my voice and, while not overtly silencing it, I use rational argument that silences it covertly. Once silenced, Sam demonstrates the sympathy and encouragement appropriate to an adult, telling Peter all the good things about being in care. I knew that it was possible that he would not be going home in a week and that he could be in state care for a lot longer. I read that by immediately asking Peter about the future for him and his mother, I possibly positioned the mother as not getting it right in her caring and the son not getting it right in his behaviour. I articulated the blaming practices of the dominant discourses. Peter saw 'reason' and acknowledged that living at home will probably not work and so he blamed his mother. It is Sam who may have moved away from blaming to being a 'good' son again, and he displays this by telling Peter of the possibility of loving his mother again. I left them together, confident that Peter was calm and that he would behave appropriately, obediently, while being in state care. I read this as all of us getting our performances right in the dominant discourses. This theatre of the naturalised role play becomes starkly real for me in an analysis in which I read the 'I' as performing the caring, yet controlling professional, Peter as performing the frightened then brave child in care, and Sam as performing the angry then caring ward with a 'heart of gold'.

THROUGH INDIVIDUALISING

To be too overt in making the 'sad' students come to desire obedience might be read, even in the dominant discourse that informs teachers that they must do this, as not being sufficiently compassionate about all that the 'sad' have been through. As competent and caring teachers we gain an understanding of the individual backgrounds of the students. This knowledge will be understood in the psychological context of the damage done, development impaired, psyche disturbed and behaviour not learned. We come to know the students as individuals, but with the overall goal of having their individual desires and actions normalised. Foucault thought that psychology could never "dissociate itself from a certain normative program" (1994, p. 255), and, being immersed in the psychological discourse, neither can special education teachers.

"Discourses of childhood are central to the ways we structure our own and others' sense of place and position" (Burman, 1994, p. 48). The discourses of childhood that surround us are to do with it being the 'happiest time of our lives' and, at the same time, a time of wildness being tamed, of instincts curbed and of becoming humanised. Ideas around the totalising aspects of children's intellectual, emotional and moral development have been specified by educational psychology and children's individual performance placed on a normative continuum. Through a focus on children's acquisition of finely detailed skills "the indeterminate, ambiguous and non-instrumental features" (Burman, 1994, p. 33) of childhood behaviours are suppressed and "normative descriptions" of behaviour become "naturalised prescriptions" for action (Burman, 1994, p. 4). 'Normal' development for a child is that which produces "the rational, independent, autonomous child as a quasi-natural phenomenon who progresses through a universalized development sequence towards the possibility of rational argument" (Walkerdine, 1990, p. 29). Such 'normal' development might not be available for the 'sad' if they are too immersed in the sadness of their lives. For the non-abused, 'normal' child, teachers focus on their learning, and children's lives at home are generally not the domain of teachers. Ideas about meeting the needs of "the 'whole child' come to be played out only in relation to the 'damaged' or 'disadvantaged child'" (Burman, 1994, p. 172). The abused, 'sad' child is read as damaged in the dominant psychological discourses and teachers see themselves as having the right, even the responsibility, to be engaged in the home life of the child. Teachers focus on each 'sad' child's intellectual, emotional and social development so that a new family, or a fixed family, comes to want to provide a home for the 'sad'. For the 'sad' must have a family, particularly a mother, quickly, if they are ever to be read as developing 'normally'. 'Normal' development of the child is seen as "depending on the presence of the mother" (Walkerdine, 1990, p. 29). Without a family/mother, 'sad' children might always be read as other than normal in the dominant educational and psychological discourses.

THROUGH TREATING

Burman proposes that abuse and neglect of children "have tended to be collapsed together with the treatment of the child *as* the problem" (1994, p. 56) and this is reflected in the types of services available. In this sense children in state care are provided primarily with residential services. Bath (1998) sees that practice in state care for children is not guided by a particular theory about how to help children. This reluctance is attributed to the focus on 'care' rather than 'treatment'. Ainsworth (1999) also sees that current approaches with an emphasis on 'care' lack the necessary power, intensity and duration needed by young people with high support needs. Gosbeli and Jenkins (1999) found that care workers were unwilling to embrace a particular theoretical perspective. Care workers described program models in terms of providing a home, unconditional care, a safe and nurturing environment, and a model of behaviour management involving boundaries and consequences.

The 'treatment' for children in state care involves firm behaviour management and a regime that helps them to acquire social skills and find appropriate ways to deal with anger, sadness, abuse and abandonment. It generally does not involve forms of psychological therapy. For those living in a foster family any form of psychotherapy is most often seen as unnecessary. Rather, all that is considered sufficient and necessary is the provision of a residential placement in which carers are sensitive and knowledgeable, the child resilient, and the biological parents caring and eager to participate in their children's lives (Rosenfeld *et al.*, 1997). While some children in state care might be considered to need psychotherapy, many do not receive it as they are seen as *not ready*. For therapy to be of use, in the psychotherapeutic discourse, it is considered that a child's external world must be stable and safe, and caretakers must be predictable (Rosenfeld *et al.*, 1997). Further, if stability cannot be provided quickly for children in state care, psychotherapy is seen as *mistakenly* recommended as if it were a panacea (Rosenfeld *et al.*, 1997). Psychotherapy is seen as only being able to help disturbed and disturbing children take advantage of good situations (Bettelheim and Rosenfeld, 1993). It is children themselves who are seen as needing to take advantage of any therapy other than a behaviour management therapy. Whether or not therapy can be seen as fixing what is broken, I observe a contradiction for children in care. If the same levels of disruption—sexual, physical and emotional abuse—happened to a child with a family by someone outside the family, a treatment modality of crisis and ongoing therapy would be seen as necessary. It is almost as if by being abused in and by the family the child gets it so wrong that 'normal' treatments are seen as unworkable or even unnecessary. Rather, what is thought to be needed is a brand new, appropriately caring family, and any damage is thought to then repair itself.

THROUGH HOLDING THE CHILD RESPONSIBLE

In making/helping to make the child in state care more obedient and desirable to families, including their family of birth, teachers are informed increasingly by ideas and practices around 'resilience'. I am coming to see how psychology "contributes to and reflects dominant assumptions and debates about families, both structuring research agendas and informing practice" (Burman, 1994, p. 73). The idea of resilience places the ability to deal with disadvantage/abuse/pain within the individual child. In this framework special education teachers ask questions about what it takes, not only to survive abuse and be in state care, but also to make the most of it and be a better person for it. There is much research considered to support the idea of resilience and the risk factors that can increase/decrease the likelihood of resilience as a psychological 'truth'. For example, Werner and Smith (1992) conducted an ongoing, thirty two year study of five hundred and five infants born in 1955 on Kauai, Hawaii. They concluded that two thirds of the children studied were exposed to four risk factors by the age of two (risk defined as, for example, poverty, moderate to severe perinatal stress, mothers with little education, family discord or divorce, parental alcoholism, parental mental illness), with subsequent outcomes that included learning disabilities, behavioural problems, teenage pregnancy and/or mental illness. On average, children in state care are considered to have been exposed to more than fourteen risk factors (Thorpe and Swart, 1992). Egeland and Brunnquell (1979) concluded that abuse combined with severe poverty and parental mental illness or addiction puts children in care at significant risk of adverse psychological outcomes if their situation is not alleviated by protective factors.

The children in Werner and Smith's (1992) study who were considered 'resilient' displayed the following: (1) at least average intelligence and a disposition that elicited positive responses from family members and strangers; (2) emotional ties with parent substitutes that encouraged trust, autonomy and initiative; and (3) an external support system in church, youth groups, or school. In looking for factors around resilience, Vailliant (1993) found that the single best predictor of good long-term outcomes for children in state care was a child's ability to form one good relationship with someone, not necessarily a parent or relative. This principle is seen to lie at the heart of the concept of foster families (Rosenfeld *et al.*, 1997). Consequently, encouraging children to form or maintain a good, supportive relationship is seen to be the most positive force in these children's lives. The importance of a relationship with a significant other is seen to rescue these children from being branded throughout their lives. This was a challenge for us at the special school: to form positive relationships with children seen in the dominant discourses as lacking the capacity to form attachments and, at the same time, to ensure that we maintained an emotionally detached, professional distance.

In a filmy and unfocussed way the dominant psychological discourses position the 'sad' as almost responsible for their predicament. This is achieved through the fine detail gathered about them that leads them to be classified as being in need of protection, being at-risk, coming from disruptive/disturbed/disadvantaged backgrounds. A binary is constructed that positions the 'sad' as in need of care and as simultaneously responsible for choosing any aberrant behaviour (thus being in need of control). It is as if we come to mean 'control' when we talk about 'care'. Burman sees the rhetoric of children's needs as possibly dangerous when such needs are seen as "some kind of inviolable category that is treated as self-evident rather than informed by and reflecting the socio-political pre-occupations of particular cultures and times" (1994, p. 53). In this particular culture and time, Marks (1996) has resonance for me when she talks of case conferences for children with special educational needs during which mothers are positioned as "bearing responsibility for any difficulties identified in their offspring" and "children appear overwhelmingly needy or wilful", while "fathers remain outside the boundaries" (Marks, 1996, pp. 139-140). In the same way that the 'normal' child is seen as innocent (and yet in need of taming) in the dominant discourses, the 'sad' child, because of experiences of abuse and rejection, is no longer innocent and is possibly guilty. In the special education discourse the 'sad' come to be seen as guilty if they cannot control their behaviour and be accepted by a new family, or even as 'mad' if they display too much emotion or pain for too long. In getting the dominant discourses right, special education teachers slip between seeing the 'sad' as vulnerable and seeing them as 'bad' and in need of changing their deviant behaviour. In this way the 'sad' often come to be seen as, at the least, being in the wrong, and they are treated in the same way as the 'mad/bad'.

THROUGH SILENCING SEXUALITY

Psychology and education produce the 'natural child'. Yet this child who is produced is the male child "who is playful, creative, naughty, rule-breaking, rational" (Walkerdine, 1997, p. 169). The girl child "suggests an unnatural pathology: she works to the child's play, she follows rules to his breaking of them, she is good, well-behaved and irrational. Femininity becomes the Other of rational childhood" (Walkerdine, 1997, p. 169). In this context, it is not surprising that most of the students at the school were boys. To get it right as a boy involves breaking rules. The boys at the school, ironically, might have been read as getting it too right at being boys. Yet this 'too right' has marginalised them, as the dominant discourses place limits on creativity and rule-breaking. The girls who are rule-breaking and naughty are positioned in the dominant discourses as causing even more consternation as they fail in their natural position and become an Other who is puzzling and even frightening.

A new student—an attractive girl—not yet ten years old has arrived. She has turned the place upside down. It's as if for the first time these boys have an available, attractive and interested female. The boys in Steve's class are particularly interested—they are hanging around the door of the classroom she's in. They are about her age. The older boys have yet to show interest. I am really concerned—for the stability of the place, for teacher morale and for her safety. At our debriefing meeting we discuss this impact.

Cath:	*What are we going to do about Chrissie?*
Steve:	*It's not a problem—I'm not going to see it as a problem.*
Cath:	*OK—be in denial—but she is having an impact and unless we figure it out I think the impact will increase. It seems like this is the first time our boys have had an attractive, available girl who is willing to accept them as a 'boyfriend'—she's had at least five different boyfriends this morning.*
Beti:	*All of the boys in my class wanted to be in her classroom—they hardly got any work done today.*
Lee:	*This could be a big problem—for her, the boys and for us.*

Cath's Notes

The way girls are produced becomes even more problematic when girls are seen to get it so wrong by being rule-breakers, and sexualised rule-breakers in particular. Many of the girls at the school had been sexually abused. Warner proposes that there needs to be a focus on understanding the "identities produced and reproduced in the deployment of sexuality, particularly as they coalesce around sexual abuse" (1996, p. 50). I read this transcript as showing that our concerns about Chrissie were initially about her power to disrupt stability of the order of the things, and, consequently, teacher morale. In a twinkling, we dismissed this power and read it as unsafe for a girl to have this power, and that, as teachers, we had a responsibility to protect her from this power. I do not think that we were idiosyncratic as teachers in reading the attractiveness and sexuality of girls as problematic for the order of schools—it is a statement I hear often from teachers. This may be because teachers, especially female teachers, often see themselves as unable to control the extreme behaviour of boys. Ironically, it is the boys that we also saw as in need of protection from the 'natural' consequences of her behaviour.

Chrissie's 'sad/bad' performance is seen as getting it wrong as a girl and as a victim. In the dominant discourses girls are expected to control their anxiety while teachers are expected to contain the anxiety in boys and take it "upon themselves to alleviate it" (Walkerdine, 1989, p. 115). When girls act out their anxieties and anger in violent ways this seems extremely problematic for them and for teachers. Anxious and violent girls become "pathologised in practices which help to produce sexual division" (Walkerdine, 1989, p. 115). As teachers, in the dominant discourse, we are extremely challenged by the violent acting-out of girls and their use of power.

I can't say how relieved I am that Carlene has not returned. She has been placed with a new family and is going to the local school close by. Carlene has all the abilities to start a riot—attractive, fearless, angry, unforgiving, and a leader.

Cath's Notes

The characteristics articulated in my notes that indicate the ability to lead other children and to stand against the power of teachers are normally reserved for boys. That a girl possesses such characteristics I read as producing confusion and fear. In such fear and confusion, I speculated that Carlene could lead all the students to defy teachers and start a riot. In my notes there is no such reference to a boy possessing this potential. Perhaps this could be read as a reflection of our being accustomed to attempting to control boys' 'normally' bad behaviour. When girls are read as refusing to control their behaviour, order breaks down and the idea of a riot is entertained. We are challenged when a Chrissie or a Carlene seems to refuse to take up the positions of 'good schoolgirls', and thus control themselves in ways that demonstrate awareness of their own vulnerability.

THROUGH SILENCING SADNESS

As Burman states, "contrasting models frequently coexist and compete, rather than succeed each other in a harmonious fashion" (1994, p. 53). The 'sad' are positioned as vulnerable and requiring protection and care. At the same time, they are positioned as dangerous and in need of control. There are multiple and often contradictory practices around the 'sad'. Some writers are uncomfortable with the notion of 'treatment' and see the 'sad' as "damaged and not sick" (Gosbeli and Jenkins, 1999, p. 26), while others believe that the 'sad' should not be read as damaged or as victims once they are no longer in an abusive situation (O'Brien, 1997). The 'sad' are also seen as a source of disruption and in need of discipline.

Peter's new carer told me today that he thought Peter had been "let run wild" while he was in the care of the state facility. He thought that Peter was basically a good kid who needed "tough loving" and "firm discipline" so that he "could get back on track".

Cath's Notes

Power relations are central to dominant psychological discourses. Discourses produce varieties of subjectivities that inhabit the frameworks of meaning that they delineate in such a way "that one is not uniquely positioned within relationships but multiple positions are made available through varieties of discursive practices" (Burman, 1994, p. 140). In this way, the 'sad' are to be both cared for and controlled. Peter's new carer articulated this in saying that Peter was in need of "tough loving". The binary of care/control is merged so that it is not seen as contradictory. In the dominant educational and psychological discourses, children in state care are seen as vulnerable and, at the same time, yet as a threat to the order of families, even to the social order. The dominant discourses include feelings of sadness and pity towards children in state care and, at the same time, yet these feelings are to be suppressed and placed at a distance. Ideas that children in state care should not be seen as damaged, as needing treatment, or as victims, helps to distance sadness or even anger about their situations. Focussing on their living arrangements also helps to distance sadness and anger and allows children's behaviour, rather than their pain, to be placed under scrutiny. I am not saying this is how it should be—it requires some quite hard work, emotional and intellectual, to make these discourses visible and to see how they work on us and through us.

Observing myself and my colleagues at work, I begin to see that to get it right as competent teachers, our sympathy for the 'sad' must be covert while we work overtly to teach them the skills they are lacking, to learn to control their emotions and become rational, learning beings. To do this effectively, emotion, in both teachers and children, is suppressed. As teachers we also work to protect children from harm and emotional damage, but as Burman (1994, p. 55) points out, there is a possibility that such protection of children is a way of "rendering them passive, dependent and malleable". Our work is like a high wire act. In trying to become the best teachers we can be according to the dominant discourses, we work to teach students how to become rational beings, silencing emotions and making our caring as rational as possible.

In the last week of term Anne was put into time-out. She had been running around throwing things and hitting Bob. I went into the room. She was hitting the walls. I told her to scream as long and as hard as she liked as that might make her feel a bit better. It worked for me sometimes. She told me another of her mice had died. She thought the mother had attacked it—or the father.

Anne: *Why would it do that?*

Cath: *Don't know. It happens. Sometimes things or people just don't know how to look after little ones. Not always their fault. Just happens. Anne, did you see on television last night where this man had a great big dog that had had puppies? The man didn't want the puppies so he put them in a big paper bag and buried them right down in the ground while the mother dog was tied up and watching. The mother dog got so distressed that in the night, she got free and dug and dug and dug and guess what?*

Anne: *What?*

Cath: *The puppies were alive. Then she howled and a neighbour heard this and rushed her and the puppies to the vet. They lived.*

Anne: *What happened?*

I told her again. I thought to myself—not a particularly therapeutic story to be telling this kid, Cath. Her therapist will be really impressed.

Anne: *But why did the man do that?*

Cath: *I don't know—some people just don't know how to look after little things—not their fault, they just don't know—nobody's fault—just happens.*

Anne: *Like my last carers?*

Cath: *Yes, I think so. Wasn't your fault—wasn't their fault. It's OK to still care about them even though they left you. It happens.*

Anne: *I don't think I want to be in another family again unless—*

Cath: *Unless what? What would help?*

[Anne looks embarrassed—then looks straight at me.]

Anne: *Unless it's someone like you who understands kids. Do you have kids?*

Cath: *No I don't Anne. I have puppies. I don't think I'd have the energy to worry about all you kids here if I had kids to worry about at home. But you know there are lots of people like me out there Anne. There are people who understand kids and want them in their family. This could happen for you.*

Anne: *Yeah. Maybe.*

I walked with her back to her class.

Cath's Notes

In reflecting on this story, the binary of care/control that helped to hold me in the dominant discourses becomes more transparent. Anne was put into time-out to calm down and for her to get her behaviour in order.

I went in, as I see myself as responsible for her safety, including her emotional safety. As principal I ensured order—policed the boundaries. As a female professional, I am also responsible "for the moral order" (Walkerdine, 1989, p. 76). So I made sure that she was not too frightened, too upset, too angry. In encouraging her to get her anger out, I demonstrate my immersion in a psychological practice of restraint/confinement being therapeutic when it leads to a cathartic expression of emotion. I read Anne as knowing the discourses around being 'sad/bad' and giving me a reason for her 'bad' behaviour—the death of her mouse. I read this as Anne also demonstrating her knowledge of psychological discourses and what it might take to get her out of trouble. In case she was really upset about the loss of the mouse I distracted her with the story of the dog. In doing this, perhaps I demonstrated the idea that teachers must prevent students from displaying too much emotion. In the discourses around children and children in state care, children get it wrong if they display too much emotion for too long. They get it right when they perform as resilient and get over things quickly.

I told Anne a story from television the previous night—a story about animals saved, rescued. I read this as my telling a heroic story intended to encourage her and to distract her from the death of the mouse. Yet it is a story that has some similarities with her life of abandonment and the death of her pet, and I demonstrated concern about how Anne might respond to this story, especially as she asked for it to be repeated. To remind her, open up her wounds of abandonment, is outside the educational discourse and more the domain of the psychologist/therapist. Consequently, I was concerned that I might be viewed as getting it wrong. While the dominant discourses position teachers as caring and supportive, this care is to be performed in a teacherly, motherly way. Teachers are expected to work with students to 'control' their emotions. I was aware that this story of the dog involved extreme emotions and that I may have stepped out of my place as a teacher. I knew this because I cried when I saw the story on television. By telling Anne a story that had touched me, perhaps I believed that she would be touched. Another possible reading is that I attempted to distract her from her pain by encouraging her to be more understanding of the pain of others so that she might not hurt others and not be so concerned with her own problems. I read this now as a way of ensuring that her pain is silenced. It seems that I am immersed in the discourse that avoids dwelling on children's pain through making them see that others are always worse off than they are.

When Anne made a connection about her home for herself with what happened to the puppies, she seemed fascinated. She refused to take up the idea that others are worse off than her and, instead, related the story to her situation. Perhaps she connected with the heroic, Disney-like ending and the possibility for her to have such an ending and find a place where she can be loved and happy. But the story is not balanced. There is nothing that happens to the 'evil' man. I think that she asks about him because what I told her is not balanced. In Disney/schooltime stories there is usually a consequence for the evildoer. In this story, there was not and perhaps Anne was interested in knowing why not. In the discourse of care and protection of children there is often no consequence for the adult 'evildoer'—the consequences are often only for the child.

Another possible reading of this story is that I took the risk of stepping out of the teacher discourse. The story of the attachment of the mother dog to her puppies could only have had partial resonance with Anne. Her family/mother had not rescued her and neither had her recent carers. Perhaps Anne also read my choice of story as my taking a risk and demonstrated her appreciation of this through her 'gift' to me in saying that I understand kids. There are many possible readings of these stories.

I focus on the silencing of sadness as it is a practice in the dominant special education discourse that I find most difficult to do. Yet, in this story, I read myself as opening up spaces in which to discuss and acknowledge pain and, at the same time, closing those spaces, in order to get it right as a teacher. In being complicit in silencing Anne's pain, I also silenced my own—a teacherly attempt to maintain the 'professional/emotional distance' required of me. The rationale for this distance and objectivity seems to concern the 'truth' of teachers being unable to be appropriate helpers if we get too close or are immobilised by the sadness of the 'sad'.

THROUGH MAKING POVERTY AND CLASS VISIBLE/INVISIBLE

Walkerdine proposes "that child protection as the outlawing of perversion and the keeping of a safe space of innocent childhood, can also be viewed as class specific" (1997, p. 184). Yet there is a great deal of debate and ambiguity about how poverty, child abuse, and state care of children interrelate. Pilger (1989) contended that one in five Australian children face the prospect of long-term poverty, and that a higher proportion of Australian children live in poverty than their counterparts in Britain, Germany, Canada, Sweden, Norway or Switzerland. While the rhetoric says that abuse happens across all classes and cultures, Tomison (1996) says that it can be viewed as an issue that most often brands those from socially disadvantaged backgrounds. Child abuse is disproportionately reported among poor families and, particularly in the case of neglect, is concentrated among the poorest of the poor (Wolock and Horowitz, 1984). There is debate as to "whether this association results from poverty-related conditions that precipitate abuse or from greater scrutiny by public agencies that results in over-reporting" (National Research Council, 1993, p. 133). Gil (1970) considers socioeconomic problems to be a major cause of abuse and Daro (1988) contends that empirical evidence continues to grow for the unique role of poverty as a causal factor for child abuse and developmental delays.

Tomison (1996) sees it as unfortunate that the analysis of social factors has not revealed the processes through which poverty, family instability and high concentrations of impoverished families combine to produce high rates of child abuse. Despite what he sees as the intuitive strength of poverty as a causal factor in child maltreatment, Tomison stresses that the reality is that not all poor parents abuse their children. As with all single factor explanations of child abuse, Tomison does not see it as useful to focus solely on poverty to the exclusion of other environmental or intra-familial factors, such as family structure, class or homelessness. Issues around poverty and child abuse are often silenced because of the 'fear' that we might be blaming the poor for abusing their children. Of course being poor does not provide the cause for child abuse. It might, however, provide the grounds on which we brand, target and marginalise the poor. Through scrutinising the way the poor raise their children, the poor are better able to be "segmented, isolated, penetrated, organized, enclosed in a definite milieu" (Foucault, 1977, p. 277). In this way the poor are produced as pathologised subjects.

In the United States, Coulton, Korbin, Su and Chow (1995) noted that poverty, unemployment, racial segregation, abandoned housing, population loss (significant decreases in an area's population over a decade), and female-headed households were all associated with a higher incidence of child abuse. Using U.S. National Center for Health Statistics data for 1976, Bachrach (1983) investigated differences in the socioeconomic characteristics of biological, step and adopted children. She concluded that families headed by single mothers (those who were never married and those with absent spouses) were the most economically disadvantaged group. She reported that two thirds of mothers who were never married had incomes under the poverty line. In an investigation of the effects of community influences on child abuse, Coulton reported that family "structure did not emerge as a separate dimension…largely because of the extremely strong relation between an area's poverty status and its proportion of female-headed families" (Coulton *et al.*, 1995, p. 1273). Gelles' (1989) investigation of violence and family structure suggested that the high rate of physical abuse committed by single mothers appeared to be a function of the "poverty that characterizes mother-only families" (Gelles, 1989, p. 499). Gelles contended that poverty, and the stresses associated with it, clearly placed children at greater risk of physical violence from their single mothers.

The links between single parent families, especially those headed by a single mother, and poverty are seen to make it difficult to determine the separate contributions of sole parenthood and poverty to child maltreatment (Tomison, 1994; Coulton *et al.*, 1995). Yet it is poor, single mothers that the dominant discourses target for prevention programs so that they are better able to raise their children in 'normal', 'proper' ways. Legislation proposed by the NSW Minister for Community Services indicates that young children will be made more available for adoption if parents do not provide appropriate care for them (Association of Children's Welfare Agencies, 2000). This is a reminder to parents/mothers to look after babies properly or they will lose them forever. It is a threat that only works if parents/mothers are subjected properly, and sufficiently engaged with caring and nurturing that having their babies taken from them is undesired. Yet in order to place their children in the care of the state, they are positioned as not caring, and that lack of caring is a problem that the threat can remedy. It is a threat intended for poor mothers since the dominant discourses carve out for them a category of those who might not get their parenting right. This strategy is not accompanied by any attempt to redress the effects of poverty, or any strategies that acknowledge the pain of living in poverty. This pain is silenced and those whom we contain and pathologise through surveillance and branding come to see themselves as inadequate rather than oppressed.

In the same way, non-white populations are targeted. In America, although non-whites make up 19% of the general population, 60% of foster children are African-American, Native American, and Latino (Tatara, 1993). In Australia, we continue to pathologise children and young people from Aboriginal backgrounds. The number of Aboriginal children and young persons in out-of-home care in NSW increased by over 90% between 2002 and 2008. The proportion of Aboriginal children in out-of-home care also rose from just over 25% in 2002 to 31% in 2008 (Wood, 2008, p. 597). For every thousand Aboriginal children and young persons in NSW in 2006/2007, twenty two entered care compared with a rate of two per thousand for non-Aboriginal children and young persons entering care (Wood, 2008, p. 600). It is those on the margins who are taken into care—to protect them from themselves.

"Debates about the nature of the child have been central to the ways the State has interacted with, and regulated, its citizens" (Burman, 1994, p. 53). In the same way, debates about the care of children and who can/cannot remain with their families are regulated through practices around child protection/abuse. Psychological discourses are used not only to regulate mothering and care of children, but also to regulate and marginalise groups in our society. The current construction of the needs of children "confirms social privileges and pathologises those who are already socially disadvantaged" (Burman, 1994, p. 163). It seems that psychology "has always been intimately bound up with the regulation of the masses" (Walkerdine, 1997, p. 16) and implicated in "maintaining social control within and between social groups and nations" (Burman, 1994, p. 19). Psychology has provided the main tool for this pathologising and regulation.

CONCLUSION

Dominant discourses define nurturing and caring for children as critical for producing the possibility of the autonomous individual. "To take apart that fantasy and the fears upon which it rests is a powerful and subversive act" (Walkerdine, 1989, p. 209). The fantasy of providing living arrangements as close as possible to 'family nurturing' persists in spite of this being clearly ineffective for many children living in out-of-home care. Over the past thirty years a range of strategies has been developed to protect children from abuse and to provide care for those who cannot live at home. Yet the strategies have doubtful effectiveness for children. For example, if a young man is in the care of the state, he is almost thirteen times more likely to enter a juvenile justice centre than if he was not in state care. A young woman in state care is almost thirty five times more likely to enter a juvenile justice centre than if she was not in state care (NSW Community Services Commission, 1996). After leaving the care system, those who have been in out-of-home care have lower levels of educational attainment, and higher rates of unemployment, mobility, homelessness, financial difficulty and loneliness, as well as higher rates of physical and mental health problems, than those who have not been in out-of-home care (Cashmore and Paxman, 1996, 2006). Yet it seems that these systems claim credit for successes while blaming the child and parent/mother for not succeeding.

I will close this chapter with a provocative thought: perhaps the practices used by the state are not intended to be so very effective. Walkerdine proposes that the idea of a protected childhood "has always been an idea that has come from the bourgeoisie" and is "projected on to working-class children…to save them from exploitation but also to stop them rebelling" (1997, p. 188). Perhaps, as for the 'mad' and 'bad', the practices of care/control serve to brand and create the category in order to position some groups as 'other than normal' and in need of specialist intervention and management. Perhaps the strategies are critical for producing, in contrast, the normative subject. The actual intended product is not the child who is in need of help but the one who is not. We are engaged, without realising it, in "producing normal subjects, subjects who would accept the moral and political order" (Walkerdine, 1997, p. 29). Those who seem not to accept such moral and political order are marginalised. Perhaps the sadness experienced by the teachers at our school, and myself, helps to ensure the care for children and the special education practices help to ensure their control. This chapter could have been about the 'angry', but the discursive practices around those children in the care of the state work to ensure that they, and we, remain the 'sad'.

In the next chapter, Chapter 6, Counteracting dominant discourses: using poststructuralist theory to bring about change, I examine the ways that agency, in terms of reading discursive practices against the grain and of recognising the workings of subjectivities, contains possibilities of resistance and of taking up positions other than those made inevitable within dominant discourses. These possibilities are explored particularly in the context of students at sport and other activities. The binds and the possibilities of agency at the special school are also discussed.

REFERENCES

Australian Institute of Health and Welfare. (2009). *Australia's welfare*. Canberra: Author.

Ainsworth, F. (1999). Social injustice for at-risk adolescents and their families. *Children Australia*, *24*(1), 14-18.

Ainsworth, F., & Hansen, P. (2005). A dream come true—no more residential care. A corrective note. *International Journal of Social Welfare*, *14,* 195-199.

Achenbach, T. M. (1991). *Manual for the Child Behaviour Checklist/4-18 and 1991 profile*. Burlington, VT: University of Vermont, Department of Psychiatry.

American Psychiatric Association. (1994). *Diagnostic and statistical manual of mental disorders* (4th ed.). Washington, DC: Author.

Association of Children's Welfare Agencies. (2000). *Recent announcements by Minister—return to adoption.* Sydney: Author.

Bachrach, C. A. (1983). Children in families: characteristics of biological, step-, and adopted children. *Journal of Marriage and the Family*, *45,* 171-179.

Bath, R. (1998). *Missing the mark: Contemporary out-of-home care services for young people with intensive support needs.* Sydney: Association of Children's Welfare Agencies.

Bettelheim, B., & Rosenfeld, A. A. (1993). *The art of the obvious: Developing insight for psychotherapy and everyday life.* New York: Knopf.

Bowlby, J. (1951). *Maternal care and mental health.* Geneva: World Health Organization.

Burman, E. (1994). *Deconstructing developmental psychology.* New York: Routledge.

Carter, J. (2002). *Towards better foster care: Reducing the risks.* Melbourne: The Children's Foundation.

Cashmore, J., & Castell-McGregor, S. (1996). The child protection and welfare system. In K. Funder (Ed.), *Citizen child: Australian law and children's rights*. Canberra: Australian Institute of Family Studies.

Cashmore, J., & Paxman, M. (1996). *Wards leaving care: A longitudinal study*. Sydney: New South Wales Department of Community Services.

Cashmore, J., & Paxman, M. (2006). Predicting outcomes for young people after leaving care: the importance of 'felt' security. *Child and Family Social Work: Special Issue on Leaving Care, 11,* 232-241.

Clark, R. (1997a). *A review of intensive out-of-home care support services.* Melbourne: Deakin Human Services.

Clark, R. (1997b). *A framework for the development out-of-home care support services*. Melbourne: Deakin Human Services.

Coulton, C. J., Korbin, J. E., Su, M., & Chow, J. (1995). Community level factors and child maltreatment rates. *Child Development*, *66,* 1262-1276.

Daro, D. (1988). *Confronting child abuse: Research for effective program design.* New York: Free Press.

Delfabbro, P., & Barber, J. (2003). Before it's too late: enhancing the early detection and prevention of long-term placement disruption. *Children Australia*, *28*(2), 14-18.

Delfabbro, P., Osborn, A., & Barber, J. (2005). Beyond the continuum: new perspectives on the future of out-of-home care in Australia. *Children Australia*, *30*(2), 11-18.

Egeland, B., & Brunnquell, D. (1979). An at-risk approach to the study of child abuse: some preliminary findings. *Journal of the American Academy of Child Psychiatry*, *18,* 219-235.

Festinger, T. (1983). *No one ever asked us: A postscript to foster care.* New York: Columbia University Press.

Flax, J. (1993). *Disputed subjects. Essays on psychoanalysis, politics and philosophy.* New York: Routledge.

Foucault, M. (1973). *The birth of the clinic.* London: Tavistock Publications.

Foucault, M. (1977). *Discipline and punish.* London: Penguin.

Foucault, M. (1994). *Aesthetics, method and epistemology.* London: Penguin.

Game, A., & Pringle, R. (1983). The making of the Australian family. In A. Burns, G. Bottomley & P. Jools (Eds.), *The family in the modern world.* Sydney: Allen & Unwin.

Gelles, R. J. (1989). Child abuse and violence in single-parent families: parent absence and economic deprivation. *American Journal of Orthopsychiatry*, *59*(4), 492-501.

Gil, D. (1970). *Violence against children.* Cambridge, MA: Harvard University Press.

Gosbeli, D., & Jenkins, F. (1999). *A home without parents: Young people with high support needs in substitute care.* Sydney: Association of Children's Welfare Agencies.

Hacsi, T. (1995). From indenture to family foster care: a brief history of child placing. *Child Welfare, LXXIV,* 162-180.

Halfon, N. G., Mendonca, A., & Berkowitz, G. (1995). Health status of children in foster care: the experience of the center for the vulnerable child. *Archives of Pediatrics and Adolescent Medicine, 149,* 386-392.

Healey, J. (1999). Adoption. In J. Healey (Ed.), *Issues in Society 110.* Balmain: Spinney Press.

Kempe C. H., Silverman, F. N., & Steele, B. F. (1962). The battered child syndrome. *Journal of the American Medical Association, 181,* 17-24.

Law Reform Society. (1997). *Seen and heard: Priority for children in the legal process.* Sydney: Australian Government Printing Service.

Laws, C., & Davies, B. (2000). Poststructuralist theory in practice: working with "behaviourally disturbed" children. *International Journal of Qualitative Studies in Education, 13*(3), 205-221.

Marks, S. (1996). Gendered 'care' and the structuring of group relations: child–professional–parent–researcher. In E. Burman, P. Alldred, C. Bewley, B. Goldberg, C. Heenan, D. Marks, J. Marshall, K. Taylor, R. Ullah & S. Warner, *Challenging women: Psychology's exclusions, feminist possibilities.* Buckingham: Open University Press.

National Research Council. (1993). *Understanding child abuse and neglect.* Washington, DC: National Academy Press.

NSW Community Services Commission. (1996). *The drift of children in care into the juvenile justice system. Turning victims into criminals.* Sydney: Author.

NSW Community Services Commission. (2000). *Inquiry into the practice and provision of substitute care in NSW.* Sydney: Author.

NSW Council of Social Services (NCOSS). (1987). *A balancing act—foster care in NSW.* Sydney: Author.

NSW Department of Community Services. (1998). *Connecting kin.* Sydney: NSW Government.

NSW Standing Committee on Social Issues. (1989). *Accessing adoption information.* Sydney: Parliament of NSW.

O'Brien, A. (1997). Consumer participation for young people in care. *Family Matters, 46*(Autumn). Australian Institute of Family Studies.

Osborn, A., & Delfabbro, P. H. (2006). An analysis of the social background and placement history of children with multiple and complex needs in Australian out of home care. *Communities, Children and Families Australia Journal, 1,* 33-42.

Proch, K., & Taber, M. (1985). Placement disruption: a review of the research. *Children and Youth Services, 7*(4), 309-320.

Rosenfeld, A. A., Pilowsky, D. J., Fine, P., Thorpe, M., Fein, E., Saletsky, M. D. R., & Nickman, S. (1997). Foster care: an update. *Journal of the American Academy of Child and Adolescent Psychiatry, 36*(4), 448-458.

Rosenfeld, A. A., Altman, R., Alfaro, J., & Pilowsky, D. J. (1994). Foster care, child abuse and neglect, and termination of parental rights. *Child and Adolescent Psychiatry Clinic of North America, 3,* 877-893.

Rutter, M. (1974). *The qualities of mothering. Maternal deprivation reassessed.* New York: Jason Aronson.

Smyth, C., & Eardley, T. (2008, February). *Out of home care for children in Australia: A review of literature and policy. Final Report.* Sydney: Social Policy Research Centre, University of New South Wales.

Tatara, T. (1993). *Characteristics of children in substitute and adoptive care, fiscal year 1989.* Washington, DC: American Public Welfare Association.

Thorpe, M., & Swart, G. T. (1992). Risk and protective factors affecting children in foster care: a pilot study of the role of siblings. *Canadian Journal of Psychiatry, 37,* 616-622.

Tomison, A. M. (1994). *An Evaluation of child abuse decision making in the Barwon region: A report for the Victorian Health Promotion Foundation. Volumes 1 and 2.* Melbourne: Monash University, Department of Social Work and Human Services.

Tomison, A. M. (1996). *Child maltreatment and family structure.* Canberra: National Child Protection Council Clearing House.

Usher, C. L., Randolph, K. A., & Gogan, H. C. (1999). Placement patterns in foster care. *Social Service Review, 73*(1), 22-29.

Vailliant, G. (1993). *Wisdom of the ego.* Cambridge, MA: Harvard University Press.

Walkerdine, V., & The Girls and Mathematics Unit, Institute of Education. (1989). *Counting girls out.* London: Virago Press.

Walkerdine, V. (1990). *Schoolgirl fictions.* London: Verso.

Walkerdine, V. (1997). *Daddy's girl.* London: Macmillan.

Warner, S. (1996). Constructing femininity: models of child sexual abuse and the production of 'woman'. In E. Burman, P. Alldred, C. Bewley, B. Goldberg, C. Heenan, D. Marks, J. Marshall, K. Taylor, R. Ullah & S. Warner, *Challenging women: Psychology's exclusions, feminist possibilities.* Buckingham: Open University Press.

Werner, E. E., & Smith R. S. (1992). *Overcoming the odds: High risk children from birth to adulthood.* Ithaca, NY: Cornell University Press.

Wolock, I., & Horowitz, B. (1984). *Child maltreatment as a social problem: The neglect of neglect.* Ottawa: National Clearinghouse on Family Violence.

Wood, J. AO. QC. (2008). *Report of the special commission of inquiry into child protection services in NSW.* Sydney: NSW Office of the Premier and Cabinet.

CHAPTER 6

Counteracting Dominant Discourses: Using Poststructuralist Theory to Bring about Change

Abstract: As detailed in Chapter 1, *Researching special schools: a poststructuralist approach*, this work explores the capacity to apply poststructuralism, in theory and in practice, in a setting where other discourses are dominant. I focus on my own work as principal in the context of a special education school where I worked with students categorised as 'emotionally/behaviourally disordered'. I analyse the discourses that inform this kind of work, both from the position of one who inevitably took them up, even becoming expert in them, and from a Foucauldian position of critique which sets out to render these discourses less able to be taken up.

By working in a poststructuralist framework, this chapter explores how there might be moments when students and staff at the special school are able to recognise students and themselves as already subjected and as having the kind of power that comes from that subjection. I examine the ways agency derives both from reading discursive practices 'correctly' *and* against the grain. These strategies contain the possibilities of resistance and of taking up positions other than those made inevitable within dominant discourses. The possibilities are explored in the context of students' everyday lives, at the special school, playing sport and away on camps. Finally, I discuss both the binds and the possibilities of agency.

Keywords: education, disability, emotional and behavioural disorders, poverty, agency, power, Foucault, poststructuralist research, deconstruction.

This work explores the capacity to apply poststructuralism, in theory and in practice, in a setting where other discourses are dominant. From the positions of principal of the special school, researcher and ironic commentator, I analyse the discourses that inform the work of a special school for students categorised as 'emotionally/behaviourally disordered', both from the position of one who inevitably took them up, even becoming expert in them, and from a Foucauldian position of critique which sets out to render those discourses less able to be taken up. In the first chapter I discussed the special school setting and a poststructuralist approach to research (Chapter 1, *Researching special schools: a poststructuralist approach)*. I then teased out how students are constituted as different and disturbed the discourses operating on those students (Chapter 2, *Discourses at work: examining the dominant discourses in the special education of students positioned as emotionally/behaviourally disordered).* I looked in more detail discursive practices around students categorised as Mad, Bad and Sad in three separate chapters (Chapter 3, *The Mad: being positioned as 'mad' and counteracting that positioning;* Chapter 4, *The Bad: being positioned as 'bad' and counteracting that positioning;* and Chapter 5, *The Sad: being positioned as 'sad' and counteracting that positioning*). Chapter 6, in many respects, answers the 'impossible' problems raised in these earlier chapters wherein the ways in which we were all, at the special school, inevitably subjected by dominant discourses appeared inescapable. Yet such escape is possible.

As in earlier chapters, I point out to the reader that I write the stories of myself, the teachers and the students at the school in very ironic ways. I use irony to catch myself out when reiterating dominant discourses and to raise the possibility that what seems to be 'normal' and 'true' might be read differently. Through playing with irony and watching and using it at play, I believe I have been better able to still myself and examine the practices around me.

Robert (eleven years old) is on the roof—calling out that he hates all of us—that he's going to burn the school down—that we're all stuffed. He's screaming about some injustice that happened to Paul (a younger boy with whom he travels to school). Robert has not been to regular school for two years and I know that the police won't go around to his home without taking two cars. I wonder what I will do as I know that if he really goes off he could do some damage.

Cath Laws

> *Cath:* *Be careful up there, it can get slippery.*
>
> *Robert:* *Get fucked. You're all bastards.*

I have some choices about what to say next—to ask what happened—to enter negotiations, to talk about consequences and making good or bad choices about behaviour. Instead I tried to reflect on the discourse in which he is operating. To look at this rebel, wronged, positioned against the always right, in control teacher.

> *Cath:* *I didn't know this about you.*
>
> *Robert:* *Fucking what?*
>
> *Cath:* *I didn't know that you had such a strong sense of justice and will do just about anything if you think a friend has been wronged.*

Silence. He comes down from the roof, picks up his bag and goes to class. Later I went over to see what was happening and he was sitting down, just doing his work.

Cath's Notes

In the above story Robert the delinquent could be read as becoming Robert the protester who has a right to be heard. Poststructuralist ideas can enable us to see the processes through which we are subjected and we may then be better positioned to resist particular forms of subjectivity, rather than clinging to them through a mistaken belief that they are the 'truth' about working with, or being, students. As Robert climbed down from the roof, perhaps even he was able to see the storylines that positioned him as 'mad/bad/sad' and to take up the storyline of being in reasonable protest in an agentic way. It is possible that it could be read that I engaged in a shift that opened up a different space in which it was possible for both of us to see things differently. This different reading might have been that resistance to being a 'normal school student' is not necessarily 'mad/bad/sad', but something that might matter in a positive sense and that might make Robert recognisable, by a person in authority, as someone to be valued.

AGENCY

How might it happen that we are able to come to resist being caught up and "do more than reiterate the conditions of subordination" (Butler, 1997b, p. 30)? Davies says that to conceive of agency "is to think of speaking subjects aware of the different ways in which they are made subject, who take up the act of *authorship*, of speaking and writing in ways that are disruptive to the current discourses, that invert, invent and break old bonds, that create new subject positions" (Davies, 1991, p. 50). How might this have been achieved in our work at the special school?

I walked around the back and three boys were on the roof.

> *Cath:* *You guys have missed the start to class. You have to stay up there for ten minutes now.*
>
> *Andy:* *Fuck you! You can't make us stay up here.*
>
> *Cath:* *Yes I can!*

They all got down and went to class.

Cath's Notes

When comparing this story to the opening story about Robert, differences stand out. In both cases the student(s) complied with the rules of the school—they went to class. Robert went to class with the possibility of being read, and reading himself, as other than a 'mad/bad/sad' student. The boys in this story went to class as ones who had done 'bad' even better—they showed me that they did not have to do as I asked. The 'trickery' used in reversing the direction is just that—tricks of language, of expectations of doing something different to get what I wanted. I do not read this story as a time where the boys gained a sense of themselves as possibly ones "who can go beyond the given meanings in any one discourse, and forge something new, through a combination of previously unrelated discourses, through the invention of words and concepts which capture a shift in consciousness that is beginning to occur, or through imagining not what *is* but what *might be*" (Davies, 1991, p. 51). Rather, I read this as an example of students being manipulated into doing the 'right' thing.

Agency, as opposed to such manipulation, "is fragmented, transitory, a discursive position that can be occupied within one discourse simultaneously with its non-occupation in another" (Davies, 1991, p. 52). With Robert, the possibilities of him being other than 'mad/bad/sad' were opened up. Through deconstructing the storylines and practices through which we come to know who we are, it is possible that we can take up positions other than those in which we are so thoroughly embedded. We can possibly "find ways of speaking that allow us to articulate this very multiplicity of our experiencing selves, our subjectivities" (Davies, 1990, p. 504).

BEING SUBJECTED

How might agency even be possible inside the space of the special school? The ways that we are so thoroughly subjected might be seen to leave no room for being/experiencing ourselves as anything other than the individualised self produced within categories and positionings of 'mad/bad/sad' or teacher/principal. Foucault wrote about the processes of subjectification through categorisation in which the subject "is either divided inside himself or divided from others. This process objectivizes him. Examples are the mad and the sane, the sick and the healthy, the criminals and the "good boys"" (1982, p. 208). The students at our and other special schools were, and continue to be, objectivised as 'mad/bad/sad' and divided from others. They are also divided inside themselves, for example as mad/bad/sad in one moment/place, and a good friend and protector in another moment/place. Dividing practices for the students in the special school operate though the physical division of being at the special school and also inside themselves when positioned as, and taking on for themselves, the not-normal subject. How is it possible to break from these positions and to occupy positions that dismantle the apparent inevitability of these positionings?

Subjection "signifies the process of becoming subordinated by power as well as the process of becoming a subject" (Butler, 1997b, p. 2). As Butler observes in her analysis of Althusser's writing on the process by which one is subjected, the idea of the 'bad' or unformed subject is the starting point of subjection: each person has to constantly achieve themselves as 'not bad' in order to be recognised as an acceptably formed subject. To become a 'subject' is thus to have been presumed guilty, then tried and declared innocent. Because this declaration is not a single act but a status incessantly *reproduced*, to become a 'subject' is to be continuously in the process of acquitting oneself of the accusation of guilt. It is to have become an emblem of lawfulness, a citizen in good standing, but one for whom that status is tenuous, indeed one who has known—somehow, somewhere—what it is *not* to have that standing and hence to have been cast out as guilty. Yet because this guilt conditions the subject, it constitutes the prehistory of the subjection to the law by which the subject is produced. Here one might usefully conjecture that the reason there are so few references to 'bad subjects' in Althusser is that the term tends towards the oxymoronic. To be 'bad' is not yet to be a subject, not yet to have acquitted oneself of the allegation of guilt (Butler, 1997b, pp. 118-119).

If children begin their lives as 'guilty', uncivilised, natural and untamed then the process of maturing, growing up and becoming socialised is desired because it is a state that has privilege. It is a state where one has got it right and is no longer guilty—free of the 'original sin' of not being correctly subjected.

Steve was talking to Charlie who had just punched and hurt a younger student.

Steve: *How would you like it if someone had done that to you?*

[Charlie shrugs.]

Cath: *Empathy, Sir—that's a bit much to ask for!*

Steve: *I know but I keep trying.*

Cath's Notes

In special schools we look, sometimes hopefully, for signs that students are developing an appropriate morality and catch ourselves desiring in our students this 'normal development'. This idea of the 'norm' does not operate simply through external pressure. Butler sees that the "norm does not merely reinstate social power, it becomes formative and vulnerable in highly specific ways" (1997b, p. 21). The power of the norm can operate to ensure appropriate subjection. As I will discuss later, power also contains within it the seeds of its own vulnerability. For those students who are not sent to the special school, appropriate subjection involves getting appropriate learning and behaviour right. The students at the special school acted as if they were yet to be subjected: guilty in not getting it right and sent to a special place for training in getting it right. At the special school students can learn to be properly subjected and subordinated, and to possibly live their lives in that way. "The violence of social regulation is not to be found in its unilateral action, but in the circuitous route by which the psyche accuses itself of its own worthlessness" (Butler, 1997b, p. 184). The way in which Steve may have felt that he was not getting it right as a teacher by not making Charlie display empathy; the way Charlie took on that he was not getting it right as a developing child; even the way I pointed out to both that expecting empathy is too much from a 'disturbed' child—we all accused ourselves of getting it wrong. And we so much desire to get it right.

In the dominant humanist discourses, desire is used as an indicator of who we 'really' are, deep down, as signifying an essential self who is 'natural' and independent of social influences. To get it right as teachers in the dominant discourses, we look for the essential goodness and normalcy of ourselves and of our students as though it must be there. Like peeling an onion, we believe that the goodness, the wanting to get it right, is there deep down and we try to find ways to bring this core of goodness to the surface. Even if the original state is badness with goodness written on to it, we look for the signs that goodness can overcome the badness so that we can help to construct/rediscover the good person: make them want to be good, be motivated to care about themselves and others, as 'normal' people do. Davies argues that "desire is spoken into existence, it is shaped through discursive and interactive practices, through the symbolic and the semiotic. Desires are constituted through the narratives and storylines, the metaphors, the very language and patterns of existence through which we are "interpellated" into the social world (see Althusser, 1971)" (2000, p. 37). We come to desire our subjection, our getting it right, and being read as getting it right.

Ian is really worried about going to high school next year. While he has spent some time in regular primary school it hasn't been all that successful. We were talking about how he would manage today.

Cath: *So what are you most worried about?*

Ian: *You know—I'm weird.*

Cath: *I know you do stuff that people find surprising. But you are really smart and people sometimes see that as…*

Ian: *(laughing) Fucked.*

Cath: *Well that's one way of looking at it! (laughing) I was thinking more eccentric, you know, lots of smart people are a bit quirky.*

Ian: *Like Einstein.*

Cath: *Like lots of people who say lots of things that are really funny and others might just see as a bit eccentric.*

Ian: *Like when I went off my brain and told you I was in hell and then you said it was only purgatory. That was funny.*

Cath: *Hmm. Ian, we're all a bit eccentric. Work on eccentric—I think it would be OK.*

Ian:	*The nutty professor.*

Cath's Notes

In this story I read Ian as desiring to get it right at school. He saw himself as weird and saw that others would see him as weird and that this would cause problems for him. It may be that, in coming to be subjected as other than 'normal', he had participated around that, even desired to be seen as different than the 'normal'. Foucault saw the word 'subject' to have two meanings: "subject to someone else by control and dependence, and tied to his own identity by a conscience or self-knowledge. Both meanings suggest a form of power that subjugates and makes subject to" (1982, p. 212). In this way it makes sense to me that Ian had come to tie his own identity to being different, to knowing himself as other than the 'normal', the mundane. In this subjection, he had no control over the fine line between 'different' and 'abnormal', and recognised himself as 'not normal'. I heard him as wanting to be other than 'abnormal'. Yet the possibilities open to him are few given that he has been so thoroughly subjected as 'abnormal'. I read my suggestion of 'eccentric' as having offered another reading of weird—one that would enable him to be seen as different, yet 'normal'. I read him as understanding this and seeing the possibilities of not being seen as 'mad'. With eccentricity comes the possibility of being seen as amusing which will possibly elicit acceptance from others rather than the ridicule that Ian had come to expect. He also reflected that my behaviour could be read as a bit eccentric. The 'normal' response from the principal to students saying that they were in hell was not to confirm that things could get worse. He remembered this interaction as amusing and possibly took it as an indication that eccentric could work for some people. I heard him as seeing that being read as other than weird might have possibilities that he could work at and that he might not always be in a negative category formed by others. I heard him as connecting what I said with a recognisable subject position—the eccentric/nutty professor. As Flax observes, the subject is inevitably an unfinished, but ongoing, contradictory set of processes:

> The subject *is* a shifting and always changing intersection of complex, contradictory, and unfinished processes. Total access to or control over these processes *is* an illusion, for (among other reasons) the outer world will not provide the resources for us to discover all of them or the space to express them. (1993, p. 108)

Perhaps the category of eccentric gave Ian a way of seeing possibilities for action that would not position him as confined, completed and subjected in the category of 'mad' forever.

AGENCY IN SUBJECTION

In the dominant humanist discourses, power emerges as something that we see as belonging to our self—or to other selves. Individuals are read as powerful/powerless. This is done in such a way that the operation of power in subjection is made almost invisible.

Peter's regular school teacher is really worried about his 'obsessive compulsive' behaviour—tidying and putting things away all the time. He was out in the playground. This was rare, as he usually hated to be out there with the bullies.

Cath:	*Nice to see you out here—you're usually in the classroom.*
Peter:	*Miss said I had to come and get some fresh air.*
Cath:	*How's it going at regular school?*
Peter:	*It's all right.*
Cath:	*People are a bit worried about the tidying stuff.*
Peter:	*I like to do it.*
Cath:	*I know. So do I. But is class time the time to do it?*

[Silence.]

I was wondering if there was another way you could do the tidying stuff?

Peter: *Like how?*

Cath: *I don't know—like maybe do it in a way that people see as OK—I love it when you clean up my office. Maybe you could do that stuff at school—helping at lunch or something.*

Peter: *Like a monitor?*

Cath: *Yes! Does your class have them?*

Peter: *Yeah—I don't do it.*

Cath: *What do you think would happen if I asked your teacher to make you a monitor? Would it work?*

Peter: *Don't know. Probably.*

I asked his teacher to make him a monitor. She was worried at first that it might be 'feeding' his disturbance but she did it—said she'd listen to the 'expert'. I had no idea but I knew that making a huge issue of it wasn't going to work—he would only feel weirder. A month later it was working.

Cath's Notes

It could be read that Peter's interest in keeping things tidy was something that could be valued. Yet he was read by his teacher as going beyond being the 'normal' tidy person, possibly because the behaviour was performed too often. In this sense, he began to be read as having a psychological disturbance—as obsessive-compulsive—as 'mad'. The way he refused to stop this behaviour, in spite of the support of those around him, positioned him as continuing it deliberately and, therefore, 'bad'. In this 'mad/bad' category he was seen to have a kind of power that produced fear in others—fear of his diagnosis, his behaviour and the way he that he would not change. In spite of the fact that his behaviour was relatively benign—tidying things—he was read as 'mad/bad' and treated with caution. The idea of allowing Peter to tidy things in a way that could be read as acceptable was treated by his teacher with caution. The dominant psychological discourses around madness include ideas about 'normalising' the 'mad'. To allow Peter to engage in tidying is read as 'feeding the madness'. Madness must be starved so it will die off. The rational, 'normal' self is achieved at the cost of eliminating personal idiosyncrasies. To be 'cured' means that the personal likes/dislikes and idiosyncrasies of people must be 'treated/managed' until they get it right as 'normal'. In the dominant discourses, Peter needed be treated/managed until he gave up tidying.

All of the players in this story, including me, believed we had some power that was our own. Peter's power was to do something he liked to do, my power lay in being read as the expert who knew what was best, and the class teacher had the power to accept or reject Peter in her class. We come to think that we have power that is our own—power as students and power as teachers. At the same time, all of us are powerless: Peter was seen as 'not normal'; I was powerless in making Peter get it right at school and making the teacher accept him; and the teacher was powerless in trying to ensure that Peter got it right as a regular school student. Powerlessness, in this sense, worked to make invisible the possibility of interrupting the dominant psychological discourse that lodged the 'tidying problem' *inside* Peter.

Rather than being continually caught up in the binary of power/powerless, power can be read differently. There is the possibility that "agency exceeds the power by which it is enabled" (Butler, 1997b, p. 15). There is the possibility, within the 'normal' world of school routine, of someone like Peter being seen as idiosyncratic and for this not to be seen as 'mad'. In this story I read Peter as considering the idea of him being a monitor as a something that might allow his desire for order to be read as normal. The reluctance of the teacher to try such a strategy might have indicated the difficulty in refusing a discourse that has idiosyncratic behaviour read as normal. Yet the class teacher chose to recognise the power in my discursive category of 'expert'. In this way it was possible to shift an otherwise intractable situation.

Butler proposes that "the power that initiates the subject fails to remain continuous with the power that is the subject's agency" (1997b, p. 12). The power that forms the subject may, in that very formation, be transformed—be different from the power that is/can be exercised by the subject. Power contains the seeds of its own vulnerability as "power assumed may at once retain and resist that subordination" (Butler, 1997b, p. 13) and exceed "the power by which it is enabled" (Butler, 1997b, p. 15). The process of subordination may in itself provide the very possibility of agency.

Lee told me about her conversation with Glen today. He is fourteen years old and she had asked him to help Matthew, who is six, to make a cake.

Glen: *I've never made a fucking cake in my life, Miss.*

Lee: *No, but Matthew doesn't know that. He just wants to work with you.*

Glen: *But what if I do it wrong?*

Lee: *Who would know if you got it wrong?*

Glen: *Yeah—it's just a cake—the instructions are on the pack, right?*

Lee: *Right!*

He helped Matthew to make the cake.

Cath's Notes

Subjection involves a "fundamental dependency on a discourse we never chose but that, paradoxically, initiates and sustains our agency" (Butler, 1997b, p. 2). In this story, Glen read himself as someone who did not know how to make a cake. Yet, if he was read by others as having this knowledge, then it was possible for him to take up the position of having it. I use this as an illustration of the possible complexities of agency. Glen did not become 'other than subjected' through seeing himself differently. Subjectivities cannot be escaped or be risen above. Rather, we can come to recognise and re-cognise the categories in which we are positioned and find the possibilities of being located otherwise. Lee used irony to point out to Glen that no one knew the particular position he held. I see this as ironic in that they both knew that he did not know how to make a cake. Perhaps through the use of irony in this particular situation, Glen began to know what has to be done to be read differently. I see this as different to being the subject-as-usual, in that multiple ways of being are made more possible. Perhaps Glen began to read himself as someone who could take up multiple, contradictory positions at the same time; he could become someone who knew he couldn't make a cake and at the same time someone who could advise a six year old on how to make a cake. Butler suggests that "the subject emerges both as the *effect* of a prior power and as a *condition of possibility* for a radically conditioned form of agency" (1997b, pp. 14-15). Glen was subjected as one who is powerless, yet in that very subjection are the possibilities for him to use the kind of power that comes from that subjection to explore the possibilities of recognising and re-cognising himself differently.

DESIRE TO EXIST AND BE 'NORMAL'

While there may be the possibility of agency in the very act of subjection, how is it that we desire subjection? How is it that we do not resist subjection more than we do? Butler maintains that "the attachment to subjection is produced through the workings of power" (1997b, p. 6). The desire "to be" is seen by Butler as a "pervasively exploitable desire" (1997b, p. 7); if there were an option of being or not being, then overwhelmingly the desire would be to survive. Existing, even in subordination, is considered by most as preferable to not existing at all. Consequently, we come to desire being 'normal' even if the consequence is subjection and regulation. "Where social categories guarantee a recognizable and enduring social existence, the embrace of such categories, even as they work in the service of subjection, is often preferred to no social existence at all" (Butler, 1997b, p. 20).

I went into Mark's class today—I feel he is really losing it inside and I think about him injuring himself.

Even though he is only seven, suicide is always a possibility and when you think about it a lot it becomes the only possibility. I went over to his desk with Robbie, the stuffed dog.

Cath:	*Mark, have you met Robbie?*
Mark:	*Yes, it's a stuffed toy.*
Cath:	*(talking to the dog) No, don't worry Robbie—he doesn't know about you—he didn't mean to insult you, he really is a great kid. Yes, I know he has lots of stuffed toys at home—but it really is Mark that I want you to play with.*
Mark:	*But it's just a stuffed toy.*
Cath:	*Mary, you used to take Robbie home, remember?*
Mary:	*Yes, she's great.*
Mark:	*It's just a stuffed toy.*
Cath:	*Mary, remember, when you were feeling unhappy you took Robbie home to talk to? Did she help?*
Mary:	*Yes, she was great to talk to. Take her home Mark.*
Cath:	*Do you want to take her home on the weekend, Mark?*

Mark nodded—with a nervous mouth movement. I sat Robbie on his desk and left. Mark had Robbie with him all day Friday—even in assembly. Clutching him to his chest.

Cath's Notes

This story has resonance with me in showing how the desire for continued existence is a most important desire. In my fear that Mark's sadness could have resulted in him taking his own life, I moved into a therapeutic discourse. I offered him a connection with us at the school—someone to talk with in his times of darkness. I found myself talking to the dog as though it was alive, silent but alive. Mark continued to point out to me that it was just a stuffed toy—his realism in stark contrast to my fanciful behaviour. I enlisted the assistance of Mary and made the point through her. Through Mary I told him that there were times when people are really sad and talking to someone helps, even if it is a stuffed toy. Mary joined with me in opening up this possibility. Perhaps she read my insistence that Mark engage with Robbie, the dog, as important. She joined with me in convincing Mark to take the dog home. I have no idea if she read my concerns for his safety, his life. She usually had great difficulties in sharing, and her usual response would have been to accept Mark's initial decline of the offer and ask to take Robbie home herself. She did not do this but affirmed Robbie's usefulness. Mark accepted and used the animal in the way that I had intended—something to hold on to. In my concern for his safety I offered Mark a position in a therapeutic discourse. He took up the position as one who needed comforting, as one who was helpless and in need of gentle direction: he cuddled the dog in assembly, in front of all the tough boys.

I desired some type of normalising for Mark, one that would keep him safe and the gaze of the therapeutic did it for me: "within subjection the price of existence is subordination" (Butler, 1997b, p. 20). Butler asks:

> How is survival to be maintained if the terms by which existence is guaranteed are precisely those that demand and institute subordination? On this understanding, subjection is the paradoxical effect of a regime of power in which the very "conditions of existence", the possibility of continuing as a recognizable social being, requires the formation and maintenance of the subject in subordination. (1997b, p. 27).

Subjection enables our very existence. Certainly, for many of our students, their existence as 'normal students' is annihilated by stepping out of the norm. For Mark, taking up a therapeutic practice may have helped to continue his existence.

POSSIBILITIES

Butler asks: "What would it mean for the subject to desire something other than its continued 'social existence'?" (1997b, p. 28). If continued social existence is rejected, this rejection most often results in being positioned in undesirable categories including the anti-social, the unsocialised and even the 'mad/bad/sad'. Is it possible to reject 'normal' without being positioned in undesirable categories? Usually not. If we fail to get 'normal' right then we are subjected to sanctions and further undesirable and painful positionings. Yet Butler also asks, "without a repetition that risks life—in its current organization—how might we begin to imagine the contingency of that organization, and performatively reconfigure the contours of the conditions of life?" (1997b, p. 29).

Chrissie's first day. After recess she was up a tree. Three boys were up there with her. Bees to the honey pot.

Cath:	*C'mon guys—it's class time.*
Chrissie:	*You don't have to do what she says.*
Cath:	*Guys—class.*
	[They come down and go to class. Chrissie looks at me.]
Cath:	*I know you're not really happy about being here—but I am glad you are.*
Chrissie:	*Yeah, right!*
Cath:	*No, I am. We don't often have kids here who are so strong—and stand up for themselves. I really admire it.*

She came down and went to class. She probably didn't believe me; but I really did admire her strength.

Cath's Notes

Chrissie was new to the school, attractive to the boys and powerful in the ways that she performed being 'bad'. Her attractiveness to the boys was both in a bodily sense and in a sense that she displayed 'power' in a courageous way—flaunting the request of the principal. Power was often attributed to our students on the assumption that they did know the right thing to do and that they were capable of choosing to ignore what is right, 'normal'. They were believed to deliberately choose 'bad' over 'good', 'abnormal' over 'normal', and were assumed to have been formed as others have been formed and to be illegitimately seizing a strategy that "eclipses power with power" (Butler, 1997b, p. 14). Chrissie would have been read in the 'normal' school discourse as deliberately eclipsing my power with her power, telling the boys to take her side. My response could also be read as responding to her power and demonstrating my power over the boys. This story encapsulates the usually unspoken conflict and power that surrounds the adult/child, teacher/student relationship. In this case it is spoken—"you do not have to do as she says". I could not read Chrissie's mind at that moment, only my own. I felt sympathy for her as I had demonstrated my power and the boys did as I asked. The experience of students, particularly girls, as generally powerless in an overt way affected me then and continues to affect me. I know that girls can be powerful in other ways but I was concerned that I had participated in so effectively stripping Chrissie of her power over the boys. Butler asks "is there a way to affirm complicity as the basis of political agency, yet insist that political agency may do more than reiterate the conditions of subordination?" (1997b, pp. 29-30). Is there a way that we can do more than acknowledge subordination, and come to understand the power that forms us and use that understanding to do something differently both within and outside the confines of that formative power? I do not read Chrissie as having agency in this story. I do, however, see that there were possibilities opened up for her that she had not usually had. In naming her acts of 'badness' as standing up for herself, and as being admired by someone in authority for being strong, I spoke something different than she normally heard, and perhaps opened up a space where agency was a possibility.

MAKING DISCOURSES VISIBLE

Using poststructuralist theorising, the discursive practices at work are made visible and revisable. Making discourses visible has been the first step for me in making them revisable. Davies suggests that "individuals who understand the processes through which they are made subject are better positioned to resist particular forms of subjectivity rather than cling to them through a mistaken belief that they are their own—that they signal who they are" (1992, p. 56). In the following story, I show how teachers and students can powerfully use the discourses that shape us (Laws and Davies, 2000).

Bob is twelve and always 'off' when the bigger kids—particularly George—come into the room. I went over today and he was running around being a real pain—but not really out of control.

Cath:	*Bob, why do you do this stuff when George and others are here?*
Bob:	*Don't know but it's not why you think it is.*
	[I'm surprised that he thought I had a clue!]
Cath:	*What do you think I think the reason is?*
Bob:	*You think that I'm scared when the others are here so I do this so I won't get hurt.*
Cath:	*And it's not that?*
Bob:	*No.*
Cath:	*OK. Would you like to come and send some faxes for me?*
Bob:	*OK.*

Cath's Notes

A possible reading of this moment is that the relationships between teacher/student and adult/child were maintained, reiterating power relationships. At first we talked of the 'why' informed by ideas that it was possible to pour into a child the rationality that will change behaviour and that Bob was denying the 'real' truth of his behaviour. Another reading is that Bob and I possibly challenged the position of the 'helping professional'. From a poststructuralist perspective, I now read Bob as both using and rejecting a particular psychological discourse. He rejected an explanation that produced him as weak, as flawed in the take-up of himself as 'boy'. The positioning of Bob as one who had the power to reject the constitutive force of demeaning discourses may have made him recognisable as a legitimate student. I do not understand this as a change in the 'essential Bob' but as a shift in positioning which may or may not be taken up by Bob on future occasions. The moments of making discourses visible cannot be considered as the difference that makes the ultimate difference. Such thinking would be taking up the psychological discourse of discovering the 'cure' for Bob. Rather, it is a moment when other possibilities are made available.

It is risky to refuse the normative forms of subjection made available to us. As Butler says, "if one fails to reinstate the norm "in the right way", one becomes subject to further sanction, one feels the prevailing conditions of existence threatened" (1997b, pp. 28-29). This story could be read, in the dominant special education discourse, as my getting it absolutely wrong as a principal in letting myself be manipulated by Bob. In dominant psychological discourses that position Bob as one who seeks to control adults and bend them to untamed wishes, Bob was successful and I was unsuccessful. He managed to get out of the classroom and do things other than those he had been asked to do by his teacher. If I had been totally immersed in that way of thinking I would have positioned him as seeking control, seeking power to which, as a child, he had no right.

This term Bob has settled pretty well with a new teacher. In Week 3 he picked up this large sandstone rock and threw it at the door of his classroom after he walked out. I was really busy and walking past him on the way to my office.

Cath:	*Bob, I'm really busy at the moment. You know how when this happens, I take you to time-out, you put three holes in the wall, and then you cry and then I get you to do some things for me? Well I'm really flat out at the moment and need your help—I promise we'll get to do the kicking the wall stuff later—but can you give it a miss*

right now and come and help me?

Bob: *(laughing) OK—but you take all the fun out of it Miss!*

[He comes and helps me. Of course we don't do the other stuff later.]

Cath's Notes

In this story, Bob was doing/being 'bad/mad'. The usual patterns of the behaviourist psychological discourse to which students and teachers are subjected in the special school are made visible. I set out before him the usual pattern of control of his body and control of his behaviour, including the reconciliation at the end—crying and then forgiveness through doing things to help out. There is irony in this in that it was usually other teachers who went through the first phases with him and, once he settled, he spent time with me. Both of us 'fixing' it. It is possible that Bob saw the process of the management of the 'bad' encapsulated before him and he found it amusing. The reality is painful, but the patterns, when seen, can seem silly, even amusing. Perhaps the 'bad' behaviour was just put on hold. I collaborated with Bob to achieve a moment of resistance to the patterns in which we were both caught up. Perhaps I positioned Bob as one who had the right to speak, and myself as one who could hear.

WORKING TOWARD RESISTANCE

Resistance to the "dominant at the level of the individual subject is the first stage in the production of alternative forms of knowledge or where such alternatives already exist, of winning individuals over to these discourses and gradually increasing their social power" (Weedon, 1987, p. 111). Resisting the dominant discourses that hold us in place can be empowering. This is not a possession of power by the individual but the ability to see the dominant discourses and either refuse or work with them. Such recognition or resignification "requires opening new contexts, speaking in ways that have never yet been legitimated, and hence producing legitimation in new and future forms" (Butler, 1997a, p. 41).

Just before lunch, Steve came in with Brad who was unhappy about not getting an award at assembly. They sat in my office.

Cath: *What awards are we talking about?*

Brad: *Any awards—Daniel got one.*

Steve: *And you got one too.*

Brad: *Yes, but Andy didn't and I...*

Cath: *Not the awards that you get an ice cream for.*

Brad: *No not them. There are other kids that have been better.*

[I think that he is talking about the fact that he didn't get an award that included an ice cream but he doesn't want to seem greedy.]

Cath: *You think things have been better for you this week than Shaun, than Anne, than Sam?*

Brad: *No, but that's not the point. I have really tried and so have others—but they don't ever get them.*

Cath: *You think the wrong kids get awards?*

Brad: *No—not all of them. But some kids have really deserved them. It's not about me.*

[He's getting very angry now.]

Cath: *Brad, one of the really great things about you is your sense of fairness. I'd like to formalise that—to have you speak out about what's fair and what's not. Do you want to help me next week to work out the awards?*

[Brad seems to think about it.]

Brad: *OK.*

Cath's Notes

In this story Brad approached me with concerns about the awards that were given at assembly. I made the assumption that he had come to complain that he did not get an award that carried with it an edible reinforcer—an ice cream. When he pointed out to me that other kids had been much better, I assumed that he was talking about himself. I positioned him as being concerned for himself and that he had come to 'negotiate' an ice cream award for himself. This is how rewards/awards work. They individualise, place one student as getting it more right than another, and point to what it is to get it not right enough. Perhaps the paraphernalia associated with behaviour management forms part of the mirror that is held up to children so that they can come to see the self they ought to be, desire it and be subjected as at least moving towards being an appropriate student. Lacan (1977) spoke of a mirror phase where the self is split into the 'I' who is watching and the 'I' who is watched. Butler proposes that "this mirroring transforms a lived sense of disunity and loss of control into an ideal of integrity and control" (1993, p. 75). The operations of schooling seem to work in such ways that, for students in the special school, the 'I' who is watched is always less than sufficient, less 'normal'. Our students had mirrored back to them deficiency, disturbance, being other than 'normal'. So when Brad raised the issue of the award I did not resist mirroring for him that he was making demands for himself. That I made sense of his behaviour in the context of 'mirroring' reflects one of the battery of strategies made available to me in educational and psychological discourses that I drew on as a special education teacher. In teasing this out, I tried to make the workings of these strategies visible and opened up the possibility of not falling into particular forms of narrow-mindedness and their apparent self-congratulatory inevitabilities. Students often helped me to achieve this. Brad resisted taking up a psychological version of himself. He told me that I had got it wrong, that he was not the problem.

'Resistance' can be made sense of in many ways. It can be read as refusal to take up the right way of being and thinking. In this sense our students were experts at resistance. Resistance can be read as standing against the dominant discourses—in this sense their behaviour could be read as resisting the dominant normalising discourses. Yet their very act of resistance is not resistance in that sense of challenging discourses. Their actions placed them in a discourse in which they are read as disturbed. It is possible that if the students resisted the discourse of the other than normal. the 'mad/bad/sad', they may also have been able to resist dominant, normalising discourses. I read Brad as resisting the practices around the 'mad/bad/sad' discourse—we did not give the right kids the awards. I finally believed that it was not about him—and so resisted the practices that see teachers as right and children as selfish, egocentric. I moved to read that he was raising issues around fairness. I resisted holding a mirror to him that told him that this was about him; resisted trying to convince him that he was wrong, only a student. I read him as having resisted the position of a greedy student, an uninformed student and a 'mad/bad' student. I listened to what he was saying and took it at what I believed was face value—that I was being unfair. I do not read that I was manipulating him, conning him, in saying that I acknowledged his fairness and inviting him to take up the position of helping us become more fair. I also do not read that either of us engaged in a resistance that would right wrongs. I do read that it is possible that we both engaged in a resistance that could lead to imagining selves different to 'mad/bad/sad' or all-powerful teacher. It may have also been a resistance that could have gradually increased our social power, perhaps even our power to do further resistance.

Sporting Selves

One of the sites for our students to take up a position as recognisably 'normal' students was through sport. Sport was the domain of boys, and of most girls, at our school. Sport is a site where students perform themselves as strong, competitive, able to absorb pain and able to be recognised by others as getting it right. Sport was, then, an important focus of teachers' work with students.

We decided to play a game of soccer with another school. The boys had been asking for this—they enjoyed soccer at recess and wanted so much to do 'normal', competitive sport. Adam and Steve, teachers, were fantastic at getting the boys ready—getting them ready to play a friendly game—apparently a sporting term for when people don't kick the shit out of each other too much. Adam succeeded because he had the respect of the kids as a 'professional' soccer player and Steve because of his enthusiasm. Watching them play with the boys at recess was a real joy sometimes. Both Adam and Steve were 'getting it' that the soccer was not really about sport—but about using sport for the kids to learn how to deal with all sorts of things.

Cath's Notes

The boys had experienced themselves as competent at sport in the special school with Adam and Steve and wanted to try it out in the 'normal' setting. Perhaps they had come to desire to do what is required of students in the 'normal' setting—they wanted to 'play the game' in the real world. This would be considered an improvement within the dominant special education discourse, since it is in the sporting arena that they could show that they could get it right as 'normal' boys. Yet, as teachers, we were aware of the risk of their failure at doing/being 'normal'. In spite of the desire and commitment that the students often displayed in doing/being 'normal', the position of 'mad/bad/sad' was waiting to catch them. Too much enthusiasm can be read as rebellion and as a sign that they were failing to get it right as 'normal' students. To experience being read as 'abnormal' in an activity where the boys saw themselves as mostly 'normal', we believed, could be catastrophic. So we structured the experience—wrote the beginning of the script to be played out. The soccer match, therefore, was not to be read as competitive but as 'friendly'. It was not to be played with same aged students but with students at least two years older than our students. In this way any loss in the game could be put down to ideas about age rather than ideas about them being 'losers'. In my notes, I state that this was about 'using sport' for the students to learn all sorts of things. This reflects a learning discourse where students are seen as deficient and needing to acquire particular skills in order to be better functioning humans. This is the special education discourse in which I was trained. Yet I read in this story slivers of the possibility of being able to work with and within discourses in ways that might give teachers, and students, the possibility of agency.

Adam really picked up on how important it was for the boys to have a story about themselves that was respectful to them. A story where they came out of this encounter feeling respect for themselves, respect for each other and respect for the fact that they could play normal—better than normal—for a time. Paul was our captain and responded really well to the leadership opportunities offered on the soccer field—the rest of the kids ebbed and flowed about who would be able to keep it together most. Adam organised the props—shirts with the school name, proper soccer gloves. We lost but we knew—and the kids knew—that losing the game didn't matter.

Cath's Notes

As the stories of the soccer matches continued, these possibilities of agency became more apparent to me. I talked of students having stories about themselves other than the 'mad/bad/sad', other than stories of incompetence. These different stories are ones that speak of competence and being recognised as getting it right as students.

We have decided to have another soccer match this year and the kids have been working very hard—trying to work as a team. I went down there at recess. Andy came and sat beside me.

Cath: *Are you looking forward to the match?*

Andy: *Yeah.*

Cath: *Who is captain?*

Andy: *Dunno—I've had my go—I don't think it's fair that I do it again.*

Cath: *So who do you think is ready for it?*

Andy: *I reckon Susan should be it. She's our next best player.*

Cath: *But she's so young—and little—and we're playing a high school.*

Andy:	*But she's fearless Miss—she doesn't take shit from anyone—and all the kids listen to her.*
Cath:	*OK—I'll take your advice.*

Susan, half the size of the other players, fearlessly put in the winning goal at the game. Andy knew better than I did.

Cath's Notes

In this story Andy demonstrated that he was getting it right as a student—one who shared positions of power with other students and was not 'too greedy'. He shared. He did not see it as fair that he have more than one go at being captain of the soccer team. I read him as performing the mature, sharing, considerate student appropriately. He also knew that the position of captain required 'readiness'. The captain has to perform as someone who is ready to lead others—someone who is capable in the skills of the game and who is respected by the other students. I read Andy as being able to accurately read the discourse of being a captain of a soccer team. I read him as knowing this better than I did. I was doubtful of his recommendation. Maturity and size through age were signs to me that people in sport could perform themselves as leaders. Yet Andy was able to read the discourse of sport much better than I read it. Andy knew that it required courage—a courage that gained respect. In this way, I demonstrated that I could be so immersed in the developmental discourse of schooling that I had not even entertained that Susan could be the captain. I pointed out to Andy that he was getting it wrong. He pointed out to me that I was getting it wrong. At this point it would have been so easy for me to take up the position as the principal/teacher, as one who knew better than the student. In resisting this I was able to see myself as one who is able to take advice—even from a student. I read Andy as also being able to see himself differently in the dominant discourses of 'normal student'. He challenged what I said. The 'proper' student would have had few options other than to say that the principal was right, or at the least stay silent. I read him as also stepping out of the 'mad/bad/sad', 'special' student position. While he swore, it was for emphasis. He signalled the appropriate power deference by calling me 'Miss'. He had a view that he argued coherently and calmly. He was given the respect due to a person who has a convincing point of view. In him giving me advice and in my taking his advice, I read that we both found a sliver of space and time where we could be other than that as which we have been subjected. As it turned out, taking Andy's advice gave me one of the most joyous times in my teaching/learning experience. The score at the big game had been even when Susan, the captain of the team, fearlessly scored the winning goal. The boys gave her the respect and admiration that was her due.

Crafting Selves

The complexity of gender was also played out at the special school in ways where girls came to experience themselves differently. Just as sport is a site that can be done differently, so is the work that was done specifically with girls. Very few girls were referred to our school. This is mostly because the type of 'mad/bad/sad' done by girls is usually turned in on themselves. Such self-destruction is not read, in the dominant education discourse, as disturbing to schools as is the destruction of order. The girls who came to the school were exceptional in that they performed 'bad' in a regular school to such an extent that they were banished. As a feminist, it was not within my thinking that I would have adopted discursive practices to tame the girls, make them more amenable. Rather, I encouraged them to explore and use their power.

This term I made Xena costumes with the five girls. It took all term. During one costume-making session a couple of boys got cranky that the girls were getting special time. Today Simon and a couple of boys came into the room.

Chrissie:	*Get out—this is girls' only.*
Simon:	*This is my fucking room as well.*
Cath:	*The girls are trying stuff on Simon, you'll need to go out.*
Simon:	*When are we going to get to do stuff?*

Cath:	*Oh you mean like computer games and soccer games?*
Anne:	*Yeah. You boys have got heaps of stuff. This is our stuff.*
Chrissie:	*(moving towards him, her fist held up) Get out!!!*
Simon:	*All right I'm fucking going! Miss, when are you going to make something with the boys?*
Cath:	*If you want to make costumes I'll set something up—but really this is just for the girls.*
	[He leaves.]

We made the costumes and the girls dressed up in them. We took pictures with the cardboard cut-out of Xena—it looked fantastic.

A postscript to this story was a 'complaint' by one of the carers of one of the girls. She was concerned that Xena was too exciting for her—they didn't let her watch it at home as it made her too excited.

Cath's Notes

Foucault proposes that we might "investigate forms of resistance" (1982, p. 211) so that we can get a better idea of the workings of power. It is possible that this story allowed me to do this. In helping the girls to make costumes so they could play at Xena, I was encouraging them to take up powerful positions. Unlike the way they admired Susan at soccer, the boys seemed resentful of this. They invaded and wanted to take back 'their' space. Even though the time spent on this project was thirty minutes each day, the boys wanted that space and that time as well. The boys allowed, even encouraged, Susan to lead them in soccer. I read that the girls making costumes so they could dress up and perform as powerful Xenas was not acceptable to the boys and that they wanted to put a stop to it. The girls stood their ground; they were powerful in demanding their space. It was not my pointing out to them the facts about them dominating the space, time and activities of the school that resulted in the exit of the boys from the room. It was the unreasoning and aggressive stance of Chrissie that ensured that the girls had their space. The usual practice of girls getting it right as girls and giving over their space to the boys is not present in this story. The 'normal' practices that involve the girls reading themselves as not deserving of their own space/time is rejected and a different space is made possible. In this different space, they demonstrate strength. In an attempt at being fair I offered the boys a similar sort of space but at the same time I caught myself bending to what I saw as unreasonable demands, and then reiterated that the space/place/time was really just for the girls.

The challenge in this story for me is teasing out issues of agency and issues of strength and violence. It is the very strength that Chrissie displayed that resulted in her being at the special school in the first place. It was her powerful/aggressive way of demanding the space that was read as 'mad/bad/sad' in the regular school. I am informed by a gender equity discourse that tells me to open up spaces where girls are not positioned as 'other'. I see that being stuck in a position as only being the good girl involves the loss of the self and so I tried to open up spaces where girls could be strong and not weak, where they could have a voice and not be silenced. In order to get it right as a teacher I was aware that I must struggle to question the ways girls are positioned and fight for them to have their individual voices. The ideas of 'equity' informed me that I must stand against anything that privileges one sex over another, or that favours the rights of individual students to be/do something different from the rest of the group. The feedback from the carers was that they had some concern about the opening up of spaces for the girls to be anything other than placid and calm. Foucault pointed to this binary when he spoke of struggles that "assert the right to be different and underline everything which makes individuals truly individual. On the other hand, they attack everything that separates the individual, breaks his[/her] links with others, splits up community life, forces the individual back on himself[/herself] and ties him[/her] to his[/her] own identity in a constraining way" (1982, pp. 211-212). In opening up the space for girls to be other than compliant, I may have been also opening them up to being seen as not getting right as girls. Yet the struggles against the "government of 'individualization'" (Foucault, 1982, p. 212) are important as they enable a radical disruption of the taken-for-granted readings of practices, and open up moments in which it is possible to go beyond the conditions of our subjection.

Selves in the Wild

At the special school we had programs where we took students on camps. As special education teachers we knew the ideas about wilderness camps and their aims to bring about attitudinal, perceptual and behavioural changes by giving students challenging experiences where disequilibrium and dissonance occur (Handley, 1994). Facing a challenge and overcoming it at all odds involves a particular thinking that, in some cathartic way, extreme experience will bring a person out the other side—cured. I read this approach as honouring individualism in a very disturbing way.

At camp, they all left to walk up to the 'haunted house' in the dark. There was a major fight and all the kids came back—high as kites. I finally ordered them all to bed—most went. Three teachers were sitting on the steps of the house, talking about what had happened—what had gone wrong. Charlie was playing with a ball—listening. He had not gone to bed. Then he spoke up.

Charlie:	*Well, I'm not surprised they didn't want to go—they're all frightened by the stories.*
Cath:	*What do you mean?*
Charlie:	*Well, all the stories have made us scared.*
Cath:	*Do you mean all the stories before the camp?*
Charlie:	*Yes.*
Cath:	*Do you think it's safe up there?*
Charlie:	*I don't know.*
Cath:	*Well, I'll rely on you tomorrow night to make the call—to let me know when to come back if you think that it's not safe. It's time to go to bed now. Goodnight Charlie.*
	[He goes to the tent.]

Cath's Notes

In the preparation for the camp, teachers had talked with students about the dangers of the bush—the snakes, the spiders, the waterhole. Students needed to be aware of these things for their own safety. There was an old house close by that had been talked about as the 'ghost house', the 'scary house'. On the way to the house several students engaged in fights and they did not make it to the ghost house. In talking about what had gone wrong as a team, we had canvassed many possibilities—students were overtired, individual students were being difficult and 'winding up' others, teacher were tired. Charlie's idea had not occurred to me. I had been so immersed in the ideas about facing challenge and overcoming odds that I had not opened up a space for thinking about fear and the way it can be played out. When Charlie opened up a space for this idea, I knew exactly what he meant. I continue to be surprised at the readings children give situations, and the difficulty that we have as teachers in finding a space to hear what children are saying. What I find of interest about this story is that I did not ask Charlie if he thought the students were scared of going to the haunted house. I believe that if I had asked Charlie directly if he was scared he might have said that he was not really—but that the others were. He certainly would not have said he was scared if the other boys had been there. By listening to the teachers talk, he could advise us. Then by asking him to let us know the next day if it was 'safe', a potential space was opened up where he could give his opinion without admitting to fear in front of the other boys.

On reflection, I think that I handed Charlie the idea of safety because I understood what it took for him to say that the others were 'frightened'. Yet I was concerned, once the challenge had been put to them of going to the scary house, that if they did not go, then they would see themselves as failures. Not only are students in the special school seen as 'mad/bad/sad' but they often seem to fail in the very things that position them that way—taking risks and aggression. To let them see themselves as failing at this task is something that I was not able to entertain. Yet I believe that this very competitiveness, this practice of having winners and losers, is something that children are confronted with every day of their school lives. I believed that it was important that we visit the scary house. In handing to Charlie the decision about what was safe and what was too unsafe, it is possible that I positioned him as one who could be heard, not dismissed, not seen as lacking in courage. Rather, I read him as one who had enormous courage in even speaking out. The students did visit the house the next night. They came back with various stories of it not being scary at all and, at the same time, of seeing the ghost.

The idea of challenge was evident in our work with students at the special school. Rather than challenges that involved the individual achieving against great odds, we explored the possibilities of different forms of subjectivity "through the refusal of this kind of individuality which has been imposed on us for several centuries" (Foucault, 1982, p. 216). It seems that the branding of students as 'mad/bad/sad' and their subjection at the margins ensures that their decisions are almost always read as irrational, as manipulative and as doing something other than what is said.

The camps really help make a difference. For a few weeks after the ropes course we talked about 'making it to the top'. We had decided that making it to the end wouldn't be our target—just getting up the ladder would be enough. The kids had added in making it to the end but went with us that the important thing was making it to the top. Those that made it to the end of the ropes course were really proud of it. I was sitting with Chris at recess, watching the kids climb a tree.

Chris: *Check out Paul, Miss. He really goes up that tree.*

Cath: *Pretty high up.*

Chris: *He made it to the end at camp.*

Cath: *Did he?*

Chris: *Yeah, him, Peter, Adam, Andy and me.*

Cath: *You all did really well.*

Chris: *You know Miss, maybe I am ready to try regular school full-time.*

Cath: *What, because you made it to the end?*

Chris: *No, not just that. I think I can make it now.*

Cath: *Why now?*

Chris: *Dunno—it's not as hard as I thought it was going to be and I'm doing OK at work—I'd just like to give it a go.*

Cath: *OK, I'll see what I can do.*

[He runs off to join the others climbing the tree.]

Cath's Notes

The camp had had an effect on the students. As a school team, we had resisted positioning students as only being winners if they had made it to the end of the ropes course. We had been excited if they had made it to the top of the ladder. The students, however, may have had a different reading. They knew who had made it to the end. The effects of power are visible to me. The students saw competence and achievement relative to each other as important. In spite of our efforts to encourage them to read it differently, they had attached meaning to the achievement in making it to the end of the ropes course that privileged those who made it over those who did not. Chris saw the achievement of making it to the end of the ropes course as important. I was surprised that he made a connection to achievements in other areas. I should not have been surprised; that is the very goal of such wilderness programs in the dominant discourses. I read myself as wary because I see such individualistic goal achievement as short-lived. I see it as a manipulation—power operating in a way that ensures subjection. Foucault saw power applying "itself to immediate everyday life which categorizes the individual, marks him by his own individuality, attaches him to his own identity, imposes a law of truth on him which he must recognize and which others have to recognize in him. It is a form of power which makes individuals subjects" (1982, p. 212).

I read Chris applying his experience of achievement on the ropes course as him reiterating the conditions of his subjection. In this reading, I placed myself in a double bind. The students at our school were positioned as other than 'normal', as 'mad/bad/sad' and as getting it wrong at being properly subjected students. When students performed themselves as properly subjected I should have been excited. Chris believed that he could be successful at regular school, that he could perform the position of 'normal' student successfully. This had to be more desirable than the dominant position that had branded him, confined him, and in which he saw himself as somehow deformed. Yet I had desired that he acquired a sense of agency rather than simply getting it right at doing/being 'normal'. Consequently, I questioned what he was saying, challenged him. Is it sufficient that he had found a way to resist the 'abnormal' positionings and give the 'normal' a go? Was I stuck in the humanist, rescuing discourse that wanted him to fight against subjection as 'normal' and come to know multiple positions? I told him that I would try to get him more time at his regular school. I knew that getting him more time would be a struggle. While he had decided to try 'normal' I doubted very much that his regular school would even entertain the possibility. Perhaps helping Chris to see himself as something other than 'mad/bad/sad' was a sufficient achievement. The struggle to help him to take up doing/being a 'normal' student in the regular school, and to be read by others as 'normal', might have been something neither of us could have achieved.

THE BINDS OF AGENCY

The question could be asked why our students, unlike others, had not gotten it right and were unable to perform as sane/compliant/happy students. Certainly the processes of schooling are relentless in their individualising, surveilling, disciplining and punishing. Perhaps our students were so consistently read as not having gotten it right that it became increasingly difficult for them to achieve a reading of themselves as anything other than 'mad/bad/sad' subjects. Butler sees that the

> power of discourse to materialize its effects is thus consonant with the power of discourse to circumscribe the domain of intelligibility. Hence, the reading of "performativity" as willful and arbitrary choice misses the point that the historicity of discourse and, in particular, the historicity of norms (the "chains" of iteration invoked and dissimulated in the imperative utterance) constitute the power of discourse to enact what it names. (1993, p. 187).

The power of the discourse to produce what it names is evident as the students in the special school go about their lives as 'mad/bad/sad' and are constantly read in those ways. In this chapter and in Chapter 5, *The Sad: Being positioned as 'sad' and counteracting that positioning*, I discuss aspects of the story of Chrissie, a girl new to the school who had an impact on the boys. The story below discusses Chrissie further.

Cath: *I'm wondering if we think it is her problem? What about the boys—can't she do her stuff without having them all over her?*

Allison: *If she stayed inside the classroom mostly.*

Cath: *Here is this powerful girl—if she was eighteen and walked into a dance club and had every guy falling over themselves we would say "Yes! go for it" and admire that power she had over them.*

[Nodding agreement from teachers.]

I guess we need to ask ourselves: what are the possible positions for a girl to take up in a place like this? Anywhere in fact! What would we want for her?

Beti: *(laughing at herself) I would like her to be a nun!*

Steve: *(laughing) I'd like her to be a businesswoman—to come to school in a suit with a little briefcase!*

Cath: *I'm wondering how we can acknowledge the power she has—it's what has got her through a tough life so far—without her being forced to take up the usual positions available to girls?*

Lee: *My fear is that if it keeps going the way it is, a possible end will be that some boys will get angry with her and attack her, so we have to do something.*

Cath's Notes

One reading of this story is that we were all concerned about, and for, Chrissie. But when we talked of the impact that she could have on the school we caught ourselves making her 'the problem'. Chrissie was at continual risk of being that which she was named: 'bad' in her behaviour, 'doubly bad' in getting it wrong as a girl, 'triply bad' in using her sex to have power over the boys. I say 'caught ourselves' because I read the teachers as seeing other possibilities than seeing her as that which she had been named. We discussed how, in another guise, we would have been admiring of the power we attached to her. We saw that her actual behaviour was not 'bad' but rather that the way the boys were reading her was problematic. The dominant discourses position girls as other, as sexual, and even as playthings for the boys. In asking ourselves what the other possibilities were for her in a place with boys positioned as 'mad/bad/sad', we gave versions of the possibilities usually available. These included girls as pure and virginal (nun) and girls as academic—concerned only with the business of school. These position the girls as 'sexless'. I read these now as ironic —knowing the limited positions that were available to girls. I also read this discussion now as a moment when the teachers, in taking up a way of thinking made possible by poststructuralism, enabled a radical disruption of the taken-for-granted readings of educational practices—a moment in which we could go beyond the conditions of our subjection. Butler proposes that the "power of the discourse to materialize its effects" (1993, p. 187) is not stable. I read in this story that we were able to exploit the instability of the discourses that held us, 'normally', and thus resist positioning Chrissie as getting it wrong. As Butler proposes, this possible resistance "is not to be thought of as (a) a resistance that is *really* a recuperation of power or (b) a recuperation that is *really* a resistance. It is both at once, and this ambivalence forms the bind of agency" (1997b, p. 13).

The power of the discourse to establish what qualifies as getting 'normal' right seems to work, not only through performing 'normal' again and again, but also through excluding performances that get it wrong. Butler proposes that "those exclusions haunt signification as its abject borders or as that which is strictly foreclosed: the unlivable, the nonnarrativizable, the traumatic" (Butler, 1993, p. 188). Further "identity always requires precisely that which it cannot abide" (Butler, 1993, p. 188). The space of 'mad/bad/sad' for our students was often unlivable and traumatic. The excessive deprivation of a sense of their own power could serve as a partial explanation of the emotional excesses that they sometimes engaged in—anger, violence, sadness. In 'emotional excesses' I also include an excess of rationalism and a lack of perceived emotion. Perhaps, at least, there is some power in being read as beyond the control of others. Perhaps the category of 'abnormal' is less boring, sometimes powerful, and even sometimes safer. Perhaps our students desired some aspects of 'abnormal' and at the same time desired 'normal'. Perhaps they took up and were subjected as 'mad/bad/sad' and *at the same time* they required normalcy.

Chrissie was ready to go back to regular school full-time. We were waiting in the office area and an adult from the school came to talk to her. She talked to Chrissie in the open space, with other kids able to hear some very personal details. I expected Chrissie to stand up and, at the least, hit her but she didn't. She just sat there, answering yes and no appropriately. Afterward, we were walking out to the car.

Cath: *You were really good with that woman—that could have been embarrassing but you handled it really well.*

Chrissie: *Oh, her! She's fucked, Miss. But a girl's gotta do what a girl's gotta do.*

Cath: *Yep.*

Cath's Notes

I read Chrissie as wanting the normalcy of attending the regular school. I read her as knowing that to continue being read, and reading herself, as 'mad/bad/sad' was no longer livable to her. So she did what she had to do—she demonstrated appropriate subjection. I also read her as reading this subjection, and the behaviour of some adults around her, as also unlivable, fucked. It would be reading too much into the situation to suggest that she had agency in the sense that she could articulate the multiple and contradictory ways in which she positions herself and is positioned in the various discourses she encounters (Davies, 1989). Yet I do read her as reading the behaviour of the adult towards her, in spite of its normalcy, as not appropriate and as an invasion of her privacy. I believe that she knew that, and was silent. Her silence in the office allowed her to be read as 'normal'; her comment to me allowed her to be read as seeing at least some of the discourses which held her in place, and taking action so as not to be read as 'mad/bad/sad'. Flax observes that if the person's notion of subjectivity is of a unitary self, and not one of multiple selves, then "it can only sustain its unity by splitting off or repressing other parts of its own and others' subjectivity" (1993. p. 93). It is Flax's view that the sense of multiplicity is necessary for rebellion to take place: "only multiple subjects can invent ways to struggle against domination that will not merely recreate it" (1993, p. 93). I read Chrissie as having moved towards acquiring a sense of multiple selves. Yet for Chrissie to be read as 'normal', she had to silence the rebellious self. Rebellious voices, particularly if they are voices from the margins of our society, are almost always silenced.

SUMMING UP

> To sum up, the main objective of these struggles is to attack not so much "such or such" an institution of power, or group, or elite, or class, but rather a technique, a form of power. (Foucault, 1982, p. 212).

I have discussed above the possibilities of students positioned as 'mad/bad/sad' at the special school doing something different, not only in the sense of getting it right as students, but in resisting the discourses that hold them so firmly and consistently in place. In looking at the possibilities of doing something other than reiterating the conditions of subjection, I see myself as having been in a struggle against the forms of power that subject the students, continuously and inevitability, as other than 'normal'. I have discussed moments when the students at the special school took up a kind of agency, moments of deconstructing discursive practices, of recognising the workings of subjectivities and 'experimenting' with the possibilities of taking up positions other than those made inevitable within dominant discourses. It seems that the more unstructured moments at school, such as camping and excursions, provided the space for teachers and students to do/be something different.

In reflecting on the possibility of agency, it may be that those who are read as 'normal' seem to have more opportunities to take up multiple/different positions. The 'normal' are given the benefit of the doubt and allowed more fluid movement in and between categories. In the category of the 'mad/bad/sad' it seems that there are few moments when students can take up other positions, including 'normal'. They seem to be inevitably confined and returned to doing/being 'mad/bad/sad'. Yet my (poststructuralist) work challenges that inevitability, and it is important to tease out the implications of such challenging.

IMPLICATIONS FOR GENERAL AND SPECIAL EDUCATION

The world of special education is constructed as a world for those children who are positioned as other than 'normal'. The dominant discourses in special education are similar to those operating in regular education. The dominant educational discourses are rational, humanist, and functionalist in the sense that general education is mostly about preparing young people for the world of work. The dominant educational discourses operate to subject children as rational students who work to get it right at their learning and take up appropriate behaviour. Such subjection is achieved in ways that are almost invisible and results in the great majority of students not only participating effectively in schools, but *desiring* to participate effectively. The practices that achieve effective teachers and teaching and effective students and learning are structured so that in schools we all come to desire getting it right—as students, as teachers, as autonomous and caring individuals. The dominant discourses work in ways that individualise and subject, and work through binarisms that are rarely seen as contradictory but often make sense to those in schools in apparently coherent and seamless ways.

Yet, in this operation of power-knowledge, in the ways we take up our positionings, in the ways we are subjected and desire the subjection as powerful, autonomous and humane individuals, there are cracks. Perhaps in the very way power works, as Butler (1997b) proposes, we are never fully subjected. If we were, I could not be writing this, and perhaps Foucault might not have been able to imagine his ideas. Desiring subjection and taking up positions of getting it right as appropriate/good teachers and students is made possible by the workings of power-knowledge. This is both a desire to get it right and a desire not to be positioned as 'other' than getting it right.

Regular schools, in the dominant educational and psychological discourses, work in ways that brand and label those who are not getting it right, those who are other than 'normal'. Skrtic argues that the "existence of special education distorts the anomaly of school failure by objectifying it as a student disability, thus eliminating it as an occasion for educators to question their conventional practice" (1995, pp. 69-70). The outcome for those students positioned as 'special' is that they are placed at the margins and subjected to educational practices different from the 'normal'. Yet I do not see that educators in regular schools consciously refuse to include all students or refuse to change their practices so that they can be more inclusive. It is my experience that most educators in regular schools review their conventional practice and try to get their teaching and students' learning right. For the great majority of students this seems to work. Rather, I see teachers as implicated, in that they are subjected as teachers and play out their positioning as teachers. I use 'implicated' not in the sense of 'blaming' teachers for teaching-as-usual practices that might be read as marginalising some students, or in the sense that teachers 'blame' students for failing to get it right at performing as 'normal', but in the sense that they are implicated in, and through, the dominant educational discourses. While there are places in this work and this chapter where the words of teachers make me cringe, and arouse anger and pain, I see them as doing no more, and no less, than performing the dominant educational and psychological discourses through which they are subjected. In the modern rationalist discourse, educational practices work to produce individuals who are productive members of society. These educational practices include many seemingly opposing ideas, such as a whole language approach to reading and a decoding approach to reading. While these approaches may seem contradictory, they are both based on rationalist thought, individual development and educational psychological practices. The contradictory approaches to teaching and learning bounce teachers back and forth between the prominent practices of the day. Yet teachers are able to work with, and in, these contradictions to produce classroom practice as though it is coherent. Teachers work with categories, such as whole language/decoding, deductive/inductive, male/female, and normal/abnormal in such ways that they themselves are categorised as traditional/innovative, good/bad, regular/special. The binaries that work on and through teachers are deeper than competing theoretical approaches. Binaries work to categorise and position in ways that distribute power-knowledge so that individual teachers come to desire getting it right in the dominant rationalist educational discourses.

The very idea of special education works to establish a category of *other* than 'normal'. It works as a binary other to regular so that regular is produced. Special education practices are a more finely elaborated and sequenced version of regular education practices. Special education practices include the regular practices around the curriculum, finely detailed and analysed so that special students can also learn what all students are designated as needing to know in the dominant educational discourses. This curriculum is extended and elaborated over time so that special students acquire the knowledge, skills and understandings at a different rate than regular students as prescribed by the developmental psychological discourses. As for many special education students, the curriculum for the students at the special school in this work was extended to focus more on the personal and social development of the child than on academic development. Such a focus elaborates how students are to view and feel about themselves through implementing programs designed to increase self-esteem and train students in social skills so that they can relate to each other appropriately. While these strategies are similar for students in regular education, they are applied in a more elaborated and intense way to students positioned as other than 'normal'. The special/abnormal students are subjected in ways that name them as special individuals, highlighting deficits, placing them under close observation and surveillance so that they come to take up 'normal' behaviour. In this sense, the special education tactic of normalisation has come to have multiple and different meanings to me.

I now think about the possibilities of what it might mean for students and teachers engaged in special education to be positioned as 'other' than 'normal' and the ways that the position of 'other' serves to target/label/categorise those students who do not fit or might be too difficult to teach/learn in the usual way, and to move them out of regular education. At the same time the 'normal' who remain in regular schools come to see what it might be like to be marginalised as 'other' and come to desire, even more, to get it right at doing 'normal'. Special education and regular education are "constituted by the same grid of social regularities" (Scheurich, 1997, p. 99) that constitute education in a western democracy.

IMPLICATIONS FOR 'EMOTIONALLY/BEHAVIOURALLY DISORDERED' STUDENTS

In examining the details of the practices around the categories of 'mad', 'bad' and 'sad' students I have made more visible the workings of these categories and how students come to take up doing/being 'disturbed'. There are similarities and differences in the workings of these categories. Foucault's work provides a conceptual framework through which to focus on the practices at the special school and make more visible the ways some children come to be read as/perform as predominantly 'mad'. The systematic management of behaviour through close surveillance and observation, rewards and punishment, ordering of students' lives, and medication, all work to form and maintain the category of 'mad', and the madness of the individual student in that category. While these same practices are used with those adults who are read as/perform as 'mad', there is a doubling back on children. As the dominant discourses around childhood involve reading it as a time of innocence, children who are read as/perform as 'mad' are not named as 'mad'. Notwithstanding the silencing of any open talk of 'madness' around children, they are subject to the same practices as adults who are named as 'mad'. These practices are even more intensely performed so that these students might get 'normal' right before they become, possibly, 'mad' adults. In teasing out the complexity around children at the special school who were read as 'mad', the workings of the dominant discourses can be seen to marginalise those children and it becomes important, for the smoother functioning of rationalist discourses, to maintain them at the margins.

The practices around students who are read as/perform as predominantly 'bad' are perhaps even more complex. While many, if not all, students in schools perform some 'bad' behaviours, this is read, in the dominant discourses, as an aspect of being a student. The students at a special school come to be read as 'abnormally bad'. Performing as 'abnormally bad' is read in the dominant discourses as a deliberate 'choice' to not get it right as a student. The practices of discipline in schools work through constructing an individual who desires to perform/get it right as a student. Punishment works to demonstrate what can happen when students do not get it right and, simultaneously, to construct the considerate, autonomous individual who acts in the right way because it is the morally right thing to do/be. Many students who do not take up the performance of good student do remain in the regular school setting, possibly because their performance of 'bad' does not generally involve violence that is read as unpredictable and unreasonable. Also, these students perform appropriate contrition and demonstrate the appropriate humanist conscience at the right times. In this way some 'bad' students are able to remain in the regular school setting and make connections with teachers. They also serve as a marker to good students by demonstrating the pain of what it might be like to be positioned as 'other than good'. I propose that what is read, in the dominant educational and psychological discourses, as 'unpredictable' and 'unreasonable' violence, is that violence which is performed against teachers and more helpless students, and which is read as being performed with deliberate intent and with little contrition for the act or demonstration of conscience. Students who perform violence in this way are read as/take up the position of the 'abnormally bad' and are sent to the special school where the dominant special education discourse ensures that the 'abnormally bad' are subject to the principles of correction, classification, modulation of consequences, education and supervision. Yet in getting 'abnormally bad' right these students can do little else than perform as deliberately tough. Perhaps they believe that displaying contrition or an excess of emotion might signal that they are on the way to 'healing'. Such a 'healing' might put them at risk in their worlds since being 'bad' gives them a way of surviving that they would not otherwise have.

Some students are read/perform as predominantly 'sad' because they are no longer living with their families. They are taken into the care of the state because they have been subjected to abuse/neglect and then subjected to a doubling back in the dominant psychological discourses. In the dominant discourses it seems that these students are permitted to be read as 'sad' because of the pain they have suffered. Yet this reading of sadness is to be momentary as these children are expected to 'get over' any loss, including the loss of a family, quickly. Teachers of the 'sad' need to teach them how to get it right as appropriate students and as appropriately lovable children. To achieve this, the same correction, classification, modulation of consequences, education and supervision are used as with those positioned as 'mad' and/or 'bad'. In addition, the 'sad' are subjected to an intense regime of getting it right as a child who might be desirable enough to be taken in by another family.

The dominant special educational practices around 'mad', 'bad' or 'sad' students seem to have some differences. 'Madness' is not to be spoken but children are covertly read as having little choice except in the types of 'mad' behaviour produced—'madness' is of the body, an illness. 'Badness' is read as a deliberate refusal to get it right—'badness' is of the mind, rational, calculated and conscious. 'Sadness' is read, at first, not as the fault of the child, but then the child must make a choice to get over abuse/separation and do/get better. 'Sadness' is of the body and of the mind, pain of the body that must be overcome by the rationality of the mind.

The similarities for children who are read/perform as 'mad/bad/sad' include the strategies used to control/change their aberrant behaviours. These include behaviourist strategies designed to eliminate undesired behaviours and to reward desired behaviours, as well as cognitive psychological strategies designed to have the 'mad/bad/sad' set and achieve goals, identify their needs, and reflect on how helpful their behaviour is in helping them to reach their goals. Of course, the desired behaviours are those that are identified in the dominant educational discourses as those required to get it right as good students in schools.

The most significant similarity for me is the categories themselves. While the dominant psychological discourses categorise the mostly 'mad' as different from the mostly 'bad' and from the mostly 'sad', the students move in, between and through these categories. When they are performing as 'mad', they can also be performing as 'bad' and 'sad' at the same time. They perform as 'mad/bad/sad' from moment to moment, from day to day. While the categories serve to name who they are, and often their performances match a particular category, this is only for a particular moment. They also perform as rational, autonomous individuals getting it right as students from moment to moment and from day to day.

In performing as 'mad/bad/sad' students are positioned at the margins of society. Their social situation also positions them in this way. I do not see it as accidental that the 'mad/bad/sad' students in the special school came from the poorest and most marginalised groups in our society. Overall, I see the categorising of the 'mad/bad/sad' as part of the workings of power-knowledge that are utilised as strategies to supervise and contain the poor. I do not see this as slipping into a binary of rich/poor, middle-class/working-class. Such categories as normal/abnormal and 'mad/bad/sad' have not been established so that the power of the richer can be better wielded against the power of the poorer. Rather, as Foucault stated, individuals "are the vehicles of power, not its points of application" (1980, p. 98). For Foucault the techniques of power have come to "reveal their political usefulness and to lend themselves to economic profit" (1980, p. 101):

> It is only if we grasp these techniques of power and demonstrate the economic advantages or political utility that derives from them in a given context for specific reasons, that we can understand how these mechanisms come to be effectively incorporated into the social whole. (Foucault, 1980, p. 101)

Marginalising the poor and confining students who are read as 'mad/bad/sad' works in the interests of those who are financially and politically more advantaged, and more 'normal'.

IMPLICATIONS OF POSTSTRUCTURALIST THEORY

In this work, I followed Foucault in examining issues relating to power-knowledge, desire, agency and being subjected as other than 'normal'. I followed his advice when he said "one should try to locate power at the extreme points of its exercise" (Foucault, 1980, p. 97). I have examined ideas of madness and delinquency—the dark side of how dominant discourses marginalise those who fail to get 'normal' behaviour right.

In examining power-knowledge as it is exercised for the 'mad/bad/sad', I have come to see how "[i]t is not possible for power to be exercised without knowledge, it is impossible for knowledge not to engender power" (Foucault, 1980, p. 52). Power-knowledge works through "the very grain of individuals, touches their bodies and inserts itself into their actions and attitudes, their discourses, learning processes and everyday lives" (Foucault, 1980, p. 39). The dominant educational and psychological discourses worked through the very grain of the students in our special school and positioned them as other than 'normal'. The technologies of discipline and punishment worked so that the students came to know themselves as other than 'normal'. In analysing those processes of individualising and humanising as they played on our students in the special school it is possible to see glimpses of the workings of a world other than 'normal'. Poststructuralism has enabled me

> to entertain the claims to attention of local, discontinuous, disqualified, illegitimate knowledges against the claims of a unitary body of theory which would filter, hierarchise and order them in the name of some true knowledge and some arbitrary idea of what constitutes a science and its objects. (Foucault, 1980, p. 83).

The knowledges of teachers and students at the special school should not be disqualified. Rather, they can be the focus. The "illegitimate" knowledges of how the students read themselves and each other and how the discourse of 'abnormal' works on and through them need to be, as much as I am able to make them so, legitimised.

Sam: *This place sucks. I hate it here. Everyone is really weird.*

Peter: *Who's the one in the special school, dickhead?*

Cath's Notes

The exchange between the two students encapsulates for me the play of normal, abnormal, special and regular, and how the conversations of students can be used to comment legitimately on their positionings.

There are also possibilities of students, who are positioned/performing as 'mad/bad/sad', doing something different. This difference is not only in the sense of performing as 'good' students, but of resisting the discourses that position them at the margins. The 'normal' seem to have more opportunities to take up multiple/different positions while the 'mad/bad/sad' have few moments when they can take up other positions, including 'normal'. They seem to be inevitably confined and returned to performing as 'mad/bad/sad'. It is important to challenge that inevitability.

Developing a sense of agency has been the focus of my work with students, teachers and myself. I think of agency as our coming to understand the discourses that shape us and shape our world and, at the same time, developing strategies to undo marginal positionings. In recognising that existence is only possible through subjection, I do not see agency in the sense of humanist empowerment where one breaks free of subjection. Rather, I understand the moments of agency as the possibilities of using the kind of power that comes from that subjection to explore the possibilities of being read as other than 'mad/bad/sad' or teacher/carer/controller, thus recognising and re-cognising themselves/ourselves differently. I have presented moments where students and teachers articulated the discourses that subjected them. I have presented moments when students and teachers performed in ways that could be read as resistance to those discourses. For students, these were times when they recognised the discourse of 'mad/bad/sad' student and, concurrently, the 'good' student discourses. These were times when students acted to undo their marginal positioning as 'mad/bad/sad' and saw the good student discourse, not as the morally right way, but as something that might be taken to be, at times, in their own interest—"a girl's gotta do what a girl's gotta do". There were times when teachers saw the 'good teacher' discourse and acted with agency, within either that discourse or another discourse.

The strategies that I used to trouble discourses and make them visible include the following.

- Reading/naming particular discursive practices both with students and with teachers, for example making more visible the doubling-back on the 'sad' so that they come to get it right as 'Annie'.
- Naming a behaviour as outside a particular discourse and inside another, for example naming a behaviour as involving a sense of justice rather than 'badness'.
- Using humour and irony to defuse descriptions by deforming them so that descriptions of categories begin to disintegrate, for example using 'mad/bad/sad' or asking Shane if all the voices in his head "had taken a vote".

These moments are not intended to indicate an escape from discourse. They are intended to be simply, and complexly, possibilities of playing with and deconstructing the discourses that shape us. I am troubled by the idea that I might be read as tricking students and teachers into doing something different, simply being 'manipulating' while being 'truly' engaged in humanism. Perhaps there are moments when this happened, for I cannot ever fully escape the humanist discourses that constitute me. Agency can only be within a particular subjectivity and without subjectivity there can be no existence. Yet there were moments when I believe that students and teachers at the special school recognised the discursive practices that constitute them and acted to resist and subvert those discourses.

POSTSTRUCTURALIST RESEARCH

My work involved developing the capacity to apply poststructuralist theory in a place where other discourses are dominant. This approach has significant implications for possibilities of using the ideas of poststructuralist theory in the everyday life of work. I do not pretend that my work is new in doing this—many have gone before me. What I see as different in this work are the possibilities offered by poststructuralist theory to be both the researcher and the subject of the research. In this work I have explored the possibilities of opening a space requiring "that the differences between the subjectivity of the researcher and the practices of the research be erased" (Scheurich, 1997, p. 171). In empirical research this would not have been a possibility. To write as the principal of the special school, to move in and through the practices that subjected me, to write of 'me' in this process, could only have been possible through poststructuralist theory. I say possible, but perhaps poststructuralist writing can be no less than that.

In collecting the data/notes, in forming and re-forming ideas in the discussion of my ideas with both students and teachers, there was movement, questioning, doubting, and moments of clarity, together. The writing and the ideas in the writing were also shared and bounced between each other. Subjecting myself to scrutiny facilitated the development of a piece of work different from anything I imagined. Yet this was not an easy task. The questioning of everything that I, and those working with me, had come to believe about our practices and performances was not without some pain and, at times, deep confusion. There is difficulty in keeping the day-to-day life of a school humming—implementing new curricula, new policy, new practices, maintaining the old, and managing a budget. It was challenging to do all of this while being taken up with the possible meanings of a word, a phrase, a glimpse that I heard/saw/made in passing.

The guidance offered by bodies of writing on poststructuralist theory, the ideas of subjectivity, resistance, problematising, deconstruction, discourse, desire and agency can be worked with in any context and at any site. I was immersed in considering the difficulties of the very complexity of the special school, the ethical issues of working with students and teachers in different ways, the complexity of choices in examining a particular word/phrase/story from the thousands that are seen/heard/felt in a day at work, and the tight hold of other discourses on all of us at the school. Yet perhaps all of these difficulties became more apparent and clearer in looking through poststructuralist eyes.

FOR THE STUDENTS

My work at the special school might be read as simply using a different language to disguise the humanist imperative to change others and rescue them from their troubled lives. If my work is read in this way, then I am not unduly troubled, for it is in the humanist discourse that I must perform to get it right as an educator. I am more troubled by the possibility of the students experiencing similar shock/immobility to that which I did in my journey with poststructuralist theory. To recognise the implications of being positioned/performing as 'mad/bad/sad' or even as 'good' student can be immobilising. But possibly no more immobilising than being positioned/performing in the category of other than 'normal'. To say that the students at the school already troubled the good student discourse would be an understatement. I believe that I behaved in an ethical way by working with them to trouble the category of 'mad/bad/sad'. At the risk of stepping into a humanist discourse, I hope that the students were better positioned, as a result of this work, to recognise their subjectivity and better able to act with agency and be read and read themselves as other than 'mad/bad/sad'. Or not. For the point is, for me, that it is in seeing the possibilities that one has agency to act in multiple ways at different times. Possibly, this work led to change in their lives—a change that was positive and empowering. For, like Davies, "I am not willing to forgo the possibility of conceptualising and bringing about change" (2000, p. 134). I believe that this work, and know that working in this way, brought about change in the lives of our students.

FOR THE SCHOOL TEAM

If I had been less experienced as a teacher and as a principal and less of an 'expert' in the field of 'emotional/behavioural disorders', I might not have been able to engender the confidence in others that enabled them to take the risk of joining the journey. While there were significant guides and bodies of writing along the way, poststructuralist theory is new to the field of special education. There were moments when I was troubled by the ethics of working with teachers in such a way that we got the special education discourse 'wrong', since they might have been viewed as not getting it right as competent special education teachers. During my time at the special school all permanent teachers were engaged in postgraduate work in special education. Almost all of the teachers' aides/support personnel were also studying part-time to become teachers. I know that such an immersion in academic study is rare for a school team. Teachers are usually immersed in the practical and not the academic. There were moments when we all acted as a support group for each other, exchanging ideas, references, planning assignments, working together on a particular reading or a mathematics program that might be due as an assignment for one person or another. I could possibly be read as a principal of excellence in that I established a school where such a culture of learning was lived. Instead, I read it as lucky that such a school team came together at that moment in time. I also feel some relief that the teachers were trained as experts in the field of special education. When they examined a discursive practice they did so from a position of knowing well a particular practice, its origins, its intent and its effects. In knowing this I am less troubled. I read the teachers as committed, ethical and talented. I loved to watch them at their work and loved to work with them. For them, I see that, as a result of this constant questioning and re-thinking in which we were engaged, they are better able to see the discourses that hold them in place and act within a discourse knowingly, or within a different discourse, or not. Again, we were all engaged in a process of bringing about change and I would not want to have forgone this possibility.

FOR MYSELF

As a principal of a government school, there were moments when I was concerned that I might be causing/looking for trouble. After all, the educational and special educational discursive practices, in which I was required to engage, were laid out before me to use. Moreover, as an 'author' of many of those practices, my professionalism, commitment and even sanity could be questioned—how is it that I was engaged in examining such widely used, research-based and proven practices so critically? I troubled this issue with a great deal of caution but without regret. I am aware that poststructuralist theory is often read by many as nihilistic and anti-ethical. This has not been my experience. As one who continues to be consulted by educational and social welfare policy writers on the development of new materials, I find my responses differ greatly from those I would have given five years or even one year ago. I now look at the subtext, the discourse in which the writing is immersed, the positionings of those for whom the policy is intended and the implications of the policy on those positionings. I have yet to see the impact of these comments. Perhaps I will never see them. It is sufficient for me that those with whom I directly engage begin to see the practices of dominant discourses that are not normally visible to them, and the possibilities of an agency that is more than just struggling to get it right within the terms of the dominant discourse. This writing of the special school is over, but my working and playing in education continues as I "play endlessly with the discursive possibilities that have been made observable through poststructuralist analysis" (Davies, 2000, p. 137).

CONCLUDING AND BEGINNING

Foucault (1980, p. 79) wrote of his works:

> *They are, in the final analysis, just fragments, and it is up to you or me to see what we can make of them. For my part, it has struck me that I might have seemed a bit like a whale that leaps to the surface of the water disturbing it momentarily with a tiny jet of spray and lets it be believed, or pretends to believe, or wants to believe, or himself does in fact indeed believe, that down in the depths where no one sees him any more, where he is no longer witnessed nor controlled by anyone, he follows a more profound, coherent and reasoned trajectory. Well, anyway, that was more or less how I at least conceived the situation; it could be that you perceived it differently.*

How do I more or less conceive the situation? I smile at Foucault's image of the whale, spurting itself to the surface. But this is too 'boy' for me. Yet what he says has deep resonance. My mind also goes to water—to that of Monet's water garden. The waterlilies challenge me to make sense of Deleuze and Guattari's (1987) idea of multiple, diverse, connections rather than the possibility of one central truth like a tree with branches. What goes on beneath the water in that beautiful garden? For me, through the journey of this work, it seems like I have engaged in the examination of the details of the life of our work at school and the children's lives and their work at school. Looking below the surface at the details I might be seen to believe, even catch myself believing, that I had been following a coherent and profound trajectory. Yet, these moments read by me as coherence and deep profundity are only moments, glimpses not of a truth, but of something startling, even frightening, and at the same time, joyous. If I imagine myself beneath that water I know that I really had no idea of the direction in which I was heading. I was simply and complexly looking at the details. At times, I found myself heading into dangerous parts, knotted by root systems, impossible to get over, under or through. I am not one who performs surrender and I was able to work, slowly and methodically through obstructions...and then go on again, lost in the exploration, and get excited about seeing something new and different below the surface. Well, anyway, that was more or less how it seemed to me; it could be that you read it differently.

Cath's Notes

REFERENCES

Althusser, L. (1971). *Lenin and philosophy and other essays.* London: New Left Books.

Butler, J. (1993). *Bodies that matter.* New York: Routledge.

Butler, J. (1997a). *Excitable speech. A politics of the performative.* New York: Routledge.

Butler, J. (1997b). *The psychic life of power.* Stanford, CA: Stanford University Press.

Davies, B. (1989). The discursive production of the male/female dualism in school settings. *Oxford Review of Education, 15*(3), 229-241.

Davies, B. (1990). The problem of desire. *Social Problems, 37*(4), 501-516.

Davies, B. (1991). The concept of agency: a feminist poststructuralist analysis. *Social Analysis, 30,* 42-53.

Davies, B. (1992). Women's subjectivity and feminist stories. In C. Ellis & M. Flaherty (Eds.), *Investigating subjectivity: Research on lived experience* (pp. 53-76). Newbury Park, CA: Sage.

Davies, B. (2000). *A body of writing 1989-1999.* Walnut Creek, CA: AltaMira Press.

Deleuze, G., & Guattari, F. (1987). *A thousand plateaus: Capitalism and schizophrenia.* Minneapolis, MN: University of Minnesota Press.

Flax, J. (1993). *Disputed subjects. Essays on psychoanalysis, politics and philosophy.* New York: Routledge.

Foucault, M. (1980). *Power/Knowledge: Selected interviews and other writings 1972-77.* Brighton: Harvester Press.

Foucault, M. (1982). Afterword. The subject and power. In H. Dreyfus & P. Rabinow (Eds.), *Michel Foucault: Beyond structuralism and hermeneutics.* Chicago: University of Chicago Press.

Handley, R. (1994). Out of the bush—into the wilderness: tension and change. In M. Tainsh & J. Izard (Eds.), *Widening horizons: New challenges, directions and achievements.* Camberwell: Australian Council for Educational Research.

Lacan, J. (1977). *The four fundamental concepts of psychoanalysis.* London: Hogarth Press.

Laws, C., & Davies, B. (2000). Poststructuralist theory in practice: working with "behaviourally disturbed" children. *International Journal of Qualitative Studies in Education*, *13*(3), 205-221.

Scheurich, J. J. (1997). *Research methods in the postmodern.* London: Falmer Press.

Skrtic, T. M. (1995). *Disability and democracy: Reconstructing (special) education for postmodernity.* New York: Teachers College Press.

Steinhauer, P. D. (1991). *The least detrimental alternative: A systematic guide to case planning and decision making for children in care*. Toronto: University of Toronto Press.

Weedon, C. (1987). *Feminist practice and poststructuralist theory.* Oxford: Blackwell.

Index

A

B

C

D

E

Cath Laws

F

G

H

I

L

M

O

P

www.ingramcontent.com/pod-product-compliance
Lightning Source LLC
LaVergne TN
LVHW070953210926
848482LV00002B/200